NORTH ATLANTIC CROSSROADS

NORTH ATLANTIC CROSSROADS

The Royal Air Force Ferry Command Gander Unit, 1940–1946

Darrell Hillier

Atlantic Crossroads Press
aviationcrossroads@gmail.com
https://crossroadsoftheworld.ca/

Hillier, Darrell, 1966–
North Atlantic Crossroads: The Royal Air Force Ferry Command Gander Unit, 1940–1946 / Darrell Hillier
Includes bibliographical references and index.
ISBN: 978-1-9990000-2-8

Cover design: Corey D. Majeau. https://majeaudesigns.com/

DEDICATED TO THE MEMORY OF JOHN JOSEPH "JOE" GILMORE AND SQUADRON LEADER FRANK L. RATCLIFFE, AND TO MY FATHER, RAYMOND HILLIER, WHO INSPIRED MY APPRECIATION FOR HISTORY

United States Army Air Forces

Courtesy Gander Heritage Trails

Royal Canadian
Air Force

Canadian Army

Royal Air Force
Ferry Command

CONTENTS

PREFACE AND ACKNOWLEDGMENTS

Ferry Command delivered thousands of aircraft across the North Atlantic during the Second World War, aided in no small part by the men and women of Gander. What began as an odds-against experiment with seven aircraft in November 1940 quickly evolved into something extraordinary. Indeed, in addition to delivering much-needed bombers to Britain, Ferry Command opened the transatlantic skyways and accelerated the growth enjoyed by commercial carriers in the immediate postwar years. The ferry organization and its aircrews were trailblazers, pioneers in the truest form, and Gander was in the middle of it – an Atlantic crossroads as it were.

Those on the ground in support roles at the Ferry Command Gander unit came from Great Britain and Canada, and more still from tiny coastal communities scattered throughout Newfoundland and Labrador, or larger centres like St. John's. It was an unusual arrangement, to say the least: a blending of civilian staff and Royal Air Force (RAF) service personnel. However, the majority were civilian, and most retained their civilian status while working under a military umbrella. A small number of them, mainly those holding supervisory positions, received special RAF commissions. Many stayed at Gander for the duration of the war and beyond, working in some capacity within the burgeoning postwar commercial aviation industry. Several of Gander's Newfoundland-born wireless staff even joined the Ferry Command.

Canadian and American forces arrived early in the war, making Gander a very busy place. Their stories deserve telling, but that is outside the scope of this work. Nor is this a history of Ferry Command per se, except where it becomes necessary for context. For that, I recommend Carl A. Christie's prodigious *Ocean Bridge: The History of RAF Ferry Command*. In light of Gander's significance in this great endeavour, Christie gives the airfield its due credit. What follows here might better qualify as a microhistory, presented chronologically and specific to the activities at Gander's Ferry Command unit, and more especially the work of its aircraft maintenance department, headed by the incomparable John Joseph "Joe" Gilmore. The year 1942 was particularly busy for Gilmore's men. In the interests of better narrative organization, their efforts for that year only are described in a separate chapter.

Many people deserve recognition for making this book possible. First, I wish to thank those who were there and lived the Ferry Command experience. The late John Murphy, confidential secretary to each successive unit commanding officer, graciously and without fail answered a plethora of emails and questions. It was a privilege to continue our conversations in person when he made regular pilgrimages from Arizona to his birthplace, St. John's, Newfoundland. Reverend James Reid kindly shared his stories of the maintenance section, and Eileen Elms and Dr. Peter Blackie recounted theirs as children growing up on a busy, multi-national air base. Sean Gilmore reviewed my manuscript and shared many reflections on his father, Joe Gilmore, and some boyhood stories of his own. Thanks as well to his late brother Pat, who provided details on his father's career and set me on my way some years back.

Robert Pelley, Gander historian and administrator of *Bob's Gander History* website, gave unfailingly of his help, often going to great lengths to flush out answers to my questions. He did not stop there and kindly agreed to read my manuscript, and afterwards offered many constructive suggestions. Aviation researcher, blogger, and Quebecer, Diana Trafford, went "above and beyond," so to speak, giving freely of her time to review and copy documents at the national archives in Ottawa, and then to read and reread my manuscript and provide invaluable editorial expertise. Her uncle, Bruce Watt, was among the pioneers of Ferry Command, serving with them from October 1940 until May 1945. Doctor Sean Nicklin at the University of Ottawa made available a wealth of research material specific to his dissertation on North Atlantic civil aviation. Rob Teteruck shared photographs and information on his grandfather, Ferry Command pilot Vladimir Kabin. Verne Scouten shared biographical details on family member and ferry pilot A.F.J. "Bud" Scouten. I am grateful to the family of Flight Lieutenant John Narburgh, in particular, Beverley Narburgh, who thoughtfully provided a copy of his delightful unpublished autobiography. One fateful day in December 1944, Flight Lieutenant Narburgh force-landed in the snowy wilds of Newfoundland. In an unusual twist, his wife was among the passengers. Her short story of their "Three Nights in the Snow" was equally intriguing and likewise appreciated. Such firsthand accounts of the Ferry Command Gander unit are rare gems. Narburgh's radio operator that day was Newfoundlander Flight Lieutenant Maxwell Hutchings, and to his daughter, Phyllise Stickel, a nine-year-old awaiting her father's return home that Christmas, I extend my thanks for her contribution.

My appreciation to the staff at Library and Archives Canada, the British Airways Museum, The Rooms Provincial Archives of Newfoundland and Labrador, the Thomas Fisher Rare Book Library at the University of Toronto, and the Royal Air Force Museum, Hendon. Also to Jack Pinsent with the Gander Airport Historical Society, Gander Heritage Trails office coordinator Paddy Penney, Linda White at Archives and Special Collections, Memorial University of Newfoundland, and Nicola Hellmann-McFarland, Special Collections, University of Miami. Major Mathias Joost, Nicholas Muggeridge, and Nicolas Lamothe at the Department of National Defence, Directorate of History and Heritage in Ottawa, and Sandra Seaward, executive director of the North Atlantic Aviation Museum, provided vital assistance. Editor Joan Sullivan carefully read my manuscript and made numerous helpful suggestions and stylistic recommendations. I likewise thank the following: Bob Banting,

Dennis Burke, Dr. Lisa Daly, Dr. Michael Deal, Richard Goodlet, Hugh Halliday, David Hanson, David Hebbard, Gary Hebbard, Glenn Keough, Walter Longley, Jock Manson, Errol Martyn, David Moore, Marilyn Pasternak, Douglas Pelley, Gary Rideout, the late Robert Schamper and Nelson Sherren, Heather Stemp, Robert Stitt, Frank Tibbo, and Guy Warner. Lastly, heartfelt thanks to my family and friends for all their help and support during the many years of my research, with special recognition to my sister, Denise Hillier Blundon, for taking time from her busy schedule to read and improve upon my manuscript. My apologies in advance to anyone I have inadvertently overlooked or subjected to endless prodding with questions and inquiries over the years.

The writer has made every attempt to ensure accuracy; however, any errors are of his own doing. Finally, the ferry service began and ended under different designations, but for clarity and consistency, it is hereafter identified mostly using its more commonly remembered name, Ferry Command.

ACRONYMS AND ABBREVIATIONS

AAFBU	Army Air Forces Base Unit
a/c	aircraft
A/C	Air Commodore
A/C/M	Air Chief Marshal
AEA	American Export Airlines
AFB	Air Force Base
AFHRA	Air Force Historical Research Agency (United States)
AIR	Air Ministry (United Kingdom)
AOA	American Overseas Airlines
AOC	air officer commanding
ATFERO	Atlantic Ferry Organization
AVIA	Air Ministry, Civil Aviation Files (United Kingdom)
A/V/M	Air Vice-Marshal
BCATP	British Commonwealth Air Training Plan
BOAC	British Overseas Airways Corporation
BW	Bluie West (as in BW-1 airfield in Greenland)
CBC	Canadian Broadcasting Corporation
CC	Civilian Component
CO	commanding officer
coll	collection
Cpl	Corporal
CPR	Canadian Pacific Railway
Cst	Constable
DFC	Distinguished Flying Cross
DH	de Havilland
DHH	Department of National Defence, Directorate of History and Heritage, Ottawa
DND	Department of National Defence (Canadian)
Dr.	Doctor
ET	*Evening Telegram*
ETA	estimated time of arrival
F/L	Flight Lieutenant

F/O	Flying Officer
FSgt	Flight Sergeant
ft	feet
gals	gallons
G/C	Group Captain
GCA	Ground Control Approach
GMT	Greenwich Mean Time
GN	Government of Newfoundland and Labrador
HMCS	His Majesty's Canadian Ship
HMS	His Majesty's Ship
hrs	hours
IRA	Irish Republican Army
KLM	Koninklijke Luchtvaart Maatschappij (Royal Dutch Airlines)
LAC	Library and Archives Canada
Lt	Lieutenant
Lt-Col	Lieutenant Colonel
MAP	Ministry of Aircraft Production (UK)
MBE	Member of the Most Excellent Order of the British Empire
MG	Manuscript Group
mph	miles per hour
NL	Newfoundland and Labrador
no.	number
ORB	Operations Record Book
PAA	Pan American Airways
P/O	Pilot Officer
PU	Public Utilities (Newfoundland Commission of Government)
PW	Public Works (Newfoundland Commission of Government)
QDM	course to steer
QRT	stop sending
QTE	bearing
RAAF	Royal Australian Air Force
RAF	Royal Air Force

RAFFC	Royal Air Force Ferry Command
RAFTC	Royal Air Force Transport Command
RAFVR	Royal Air Force Volunteer Reserve
RCAF	Royal Canadian Air Force
RCMP	Royal Canadian Mounted Police
RCN	Royal Canadian Navy
RG	Record Group
rpm	revolutions per minute
SAS	Scandinavian Airlines System
SASO	senior air staff officer
SFCO	senior flying control officer
SFTS	Service Flying Training School
Sgt	Sergeant
SILA	Swedish Intercontinental Airlines
S/L	Squadron Leader
SSDA	Secretary of State for Dominion Affairs (United Kingdom)
TCA	Trans-Canada Air Lines
TNA	The National Archives (of the United Kingdom and Northern Ireland)
TWA	Transcontinental and Western Airlines
UK	United Kingdom
US	United States
USAAF	United States Army Air Forces
USATC	United States Air Transport Command
USO	United Service Organizations
USS	United States Ship
VIP	very important person
V-J	Victory over Japan
WAAF	Women's Auxiliary Air Force
W/C	Wing Commander
W/T	wireless telegraphy

Captain John Joseph Gilmore and de Havilland DH.83 Fox Moth at Gander. Courtesy Gander Airport Historical Society.

CHAPTER 1 | GANDER: GENESIS

Former federal and provincial politician and wartime radio broadcaster Don Jamieson remarked, "In some respects, Newfoundland's greatest contribution to the war effort lay simply in being there."[1] Notwithstanding the contributions by its men and women civilian and uniformed service personnel, Jamieson may not be far off the mark.

Politically, Newfoundland at the outbreak of war in September 1939 was a constitutionally suspended British dominion, having witnessed in 1934 the dissolution of seventy-nine years of responsible government. With the dominion saddled with debt from railway construction and the Great War, and amid allegations of political corruption in the early 1920s and again during the harsh Depression era, the people of Newfoundland had lost faith in their government. In 1932, thousands of members of the electorate marched in protest to the Colonial Building in St. John's, the seat of government and the home of the House of Assembly. The demonstration soon turned into a riot, with Liberal Prime Minister Sir Richard A. Squires and other government members barely escaping injury. The affray effectively brought down the Squires government. In the election that followed, St. John's businessman Frederick C. Alderdice campaigned on a promise to examine the feasibility of having the country administered by a commission of government for a period of years until conditions improved. Alderdice's United Newfoundland Party won an overwhelming victory. In office, the new prime minister considered a partial default on Newfoundland's debt. This troubled the British secretary of state for Dominion Affairs, who feared a financial crisis in Newfoundland and a tarnished reputation for the Commonwealth. Canada, in turn, feared for both its banks and its dollar (in Newfoundland, the dollar replaced the pound as currency in 1865). The British and Canadian governments intervened and provided a joint loan on the condition that Newfoundland accept the appointment of a commission to investigate its political and economic affairs. The Alderdice administration did not object.[2]

The British government appointed Sir William W. Mackenzie, first Baron Amulree, to chair the royal commission, with a mandate to "examine into the future of Newfoundland and, in particular, to report on the financial situation and prospects therein." The commission set to work in March 1933, travelling across Newfoundland interviewing people and collecting evidence and then meeting members of the Canadian government in Ottawa. After consultation with the British government, Lord Amulree's exhaustive report was published late in 1933. In it, the commission recommended that "the county should be given a rest from party politics for a period of years" by suspending the existing form of government. In its place, "a special Commission of Government would be created which would be presided over by His Excellency the Governor … [and] composed of six members, exclusive of the Governor, three of whom would be drawn from Newfoundland and three from the United Kingdom."[3] The Newfoundland legislature debated the report and thereafter requested that the Crown suspend the constitution and implement Amulree's recommendations. In February 1934, the Commission of Government was sworn in and responsible government ended.[4] Newfoundland reverted to the status of a Crown Colony and remained a dominion in name only, but continued to report to the Dominions Office in London. This political arrangement lasted throughout the war years, which saw Newfoundland and Labrador, and Gander in particular, develop as a geographically strategic location for military transatlantic aviation.

The new Commission had not long taken office when the business of aviation entered the agenda. Advancements in aircraft technology had brought commercial transatlantic flying closer to reality, and interest among other European nations soon compelled "the British Commonwealth to decide what part they were to take, and to make definite plans for the future."[5] That future would include Newfoundland as a site for a transatlantic terminal base, by virtue of its location on the proposed air route. The matter came under broader discussion at the 1935 Ottawa Conference, where the United Kingdom (UK), Canada, the Irish Free State, and Newfoundland, represented by Thomas Lodge, Commissioner for Public Utilities, sat during November and December for intensive deliberations aimed at introducing transatlantic air services for the carriage of mail, and eventually passengers and freight. The attending nation governments agreed to cooperate in a "programme of development" involving surveys, experimental flights, and ultimately the establishment of a regular service.[6] Preliminary work had been ongoing for several years. At the Imperial Economic Conference in Ottawa in 1932, the same attending nations had formed the Air Communication Committee, "pledging to work together in developing a transatlantic air service over the direct or non-stop route."[7] This route via Newfoundland, as opposed to the southern route through Bermuda and the Azores, was the most attractive and practical, despite the challenges presented by weather conditions. Attendees saw the 1935 conference as a natural sequence to the work of this committee and subsequent conferences held in Newfoundland and Canada.

The day after reaching agreement in December 1935, representatives from Canada, the UK, and the Irish Free State departed Ottawa for Washington to meet with American officials and Juan Trippe, president of Pan American Airways (PAA). Lodge had been summoned to London and did not attend. Pan American was also anxious to start experimental transatlantic services, and the Washington discussions produced an understanding on reciprocal landing rights for PAA and the British carrier Imperial Airways.[8]

Aerial Surveys and Groundwork

At that time, flying boats offered the most practical means of introducing a scheduled transatlantic service. Besides possessing the necessary flight range, flying boats required no expensive land-based runways, just a relatively calm body of water. So to get things moving, a seaplane base was needed. Nevertheless, the progenitors of the conference agreement, eyeing the future, also proposed to experiment with long-range land-based aircraft, more specifically the de Havilland DH.91 Albatross, then under development in the UK. In Newfoundland's case at least, flying boats could operate only after the bays and harbours were clear of winter ice. Land planes, on the other hand, could operate year-round, "despite the psychological disadvantages of the use of this type of machine over long sea crossings," recognized British Air Ministry officials.[9] Of course, this method of transatlantic travel required building an airfield, and it happened that preparatory surveys to fulfill such requirements had begun several months before the 1935 conference. That August, Ivor McClure, operational advisor with the British Directorate of Civil Aviation, and his technical assistant, Maurice Banks, arrived at St. John's by ship with instructions to select suitable sites for a flying boat base and land aerodrome. During their two-week stay, the pair met with Newfoundland governor Sir David Murray Anderson and other government officials, and obtained access to four reports on air terminal facilities in Newfoundland, produced from 1932 to 1934 by Air Communication Committee member and non-member countries. The Royal Canadian Air Force (RCAF) had prepared two reports for the Canadian government on an experimental ship-to-shore airmail service, with aircraft collecting mailbags from passing steamers for delivery in stages to Canada via Red Bay, Labrador. Under the guidance of pioneer Newfoundland aviator Douglas Fraser, owner-operator of Fraser Airways, aviator/surveyor Robert A. Logan wrote a report for PAA in 1932, and Imperial Airways publicity manager Charles F. Snowden Gamble prepared another in 1934.

The locations proposed by the RCAF turned out to be inadequate for the type of aircraft required for a transatlantic service, while the other reports omitted details on land aerodromes, but as pilot Fraser explained, "he had never had in mind requirements such as" those identified by McClure and Banks. The reports nevertheless saved time and included an able summary by Logan of Newfoundland's weather lore.[10] The Snowden Gamble document proved of some value, having identified possible seaplane sites near St. John's, Argentia, Botwood, Deer Lake, Stephenville, and Port aux Basques, and on the north side of Gander Lake near Glenwood. Anything above north latitude 49.30, added the writer, held little potential, "for the whole ground is impenetrable marsh and bog land." The only location with suitable facilities and recommended by Snowden Gamble was on the north bank of the Exploits River near the seaport town of Botwood, where Australian Sidney Cotton operated an aerial seal-spotting service in the early 1920s.[11]

So, with Fraser as their pilot, McClure, Banks, and T.A. Hall, consulting engineer to the Newfoundland Commission of Government, flew "up country" for five days to carry out their own aerial survey.[12] Fraser had by this time sold his airways company to the Newfoundland government, which in turn leased the operation to Imperial Airways, who then hired Fraser as one of its pilots.[13] McClure and Banks set their sights a short distance from the area on the Exploits identified by Snowden Gamble and recommended Botwood itself as a principal seaplane terminal. The weather there, insisted Fraser, was "better than anywhere else on the east coast." The harbour was of adequate size and depth for alighting aircraft, unaffected by ocean swell, and generally ice-free from June until November. Furthermore, the town was accessible by a railway branch line and coastal steamers owned by the pulp and paper industry's Anglo-Newfoundland Development Company. McClure and Banks also recommended nearby Gander Lake as an emergency alternate to Botwood. The deep, freshwater lake with its large landing area lay close to the rail line and enjoyed similar weather and ice-free conditions.

North of Gander Lake and adjacent to the railway, the aerial survey identified a large plateau four hundred feet high. Speaking with Newfoundland railway chief engineer John Powell, the men learned that the plateau had few ponds or extensive bogs and that "the soil was gravel covered with small boulders." A five-mile cut made between two ponds in the area some years previous, added Powell, showed the ground to be level. Construction profiles of the railway suggested much the same. Powell also praised the weather as the best of any place along the railway on the east side of the island. Still, determining the suitability of the terrain for an airfield required closer inspection, so Hall instructed engineer Allan Vatcher, "the most experienced bushman surveyor in the island," to carry out a detailed ground inspection. If the site proved unsatisfactory, Vatcher would focus his attention on a patch of land south of Terra Nova at railway milepost 161.[14]

Having secured from the Newfoundland government a two-hundred-dollar advance and a railway ticket, and with specifications in hand outlining the desired characteristics for an airfield, Vatcher explored between mileposts 213 (Hattie's Camp) and 216 (Cobbs Camp), the latter a flag stop on the Newfoundland Railway. The area around Hattie's Camp offered the best possibilities, Vatcher concluded, being relatively flat and mostly bare of dense growth due to a fire some forty years earlier. The land "sloped slightly but uniformly" from west to east and north to south, which aided in drainage. "The topographical features of the site," he observed, "made possible the location of the runways to conform with the specifications both as to their direction and relative positions."[15] In addition to its convenient location adjacent to the railway, the site, like Botwood, boasted relatively good, fog-free weather, and most importantly, lay on the great circle route, the shortest geographic air route from eastern North America to Europe.[16]

To maintain Newfoundland's interest in the project, and bearing in mind its financial limitations, the UK proposed to assume five-sixths of the capital costs (excluding the cost of radio and meteorological equipment) and to allow Newfoundland to construct, own, and maintain the airfield.[17] The suggested arrangement did not sit well with Commissioner Lodge, the man responsible for airport matters in Newfoundland. The opinionated Lodge, who gave Sir Harry Batterbee of the Dominions Office a dreadfully despondent view of predicted living conditions at Botwood and Hattie's Camp, saw the endeavour as utterly wasteful, unnecessary, and extravagant, and even at one-sixth of the cost, beyond Newfoundland's financial wherewithal. Besides, he argued to Batterbee, commercial aircraft would come to Newfoundland only because they had to, not because they wanted to, and eventually they might bypass the island altogether. "Therefore," the commissioner rationalized, "for the time being an independent Newfoundland has something to give, not something it ought to be expected to pay for."[18] Batterbee decided to give Lodge's views no further circulation in government circles and deferred to visiting British Treasury official Edward Hale to make the commissioner "take up a more sensible attitude."[19] In the end, Lodge's viewpoints held little sway and the Commission of Government accepted the proposal and joint arrangement in October 1936, by which time groundwork at Hattie's Camp was underway. The men working the site, reported Lodge, were troubled mostly by bears "which raid the stores from time to time."[20] The Newfoundland government engaged Hall and Vatcher as chief and assistant engineers, respectively (despite their having no experience in airport projects), and by year's end, workers had cleared, grubbed, and burned hundreds of acres of land. Buildings at the rapidly developing site included a construction headquarters, workshops, cookhouses, living quarters, and dining huts. Several miles east of the airport, another group of employees was busily engaged at the former Benton Quarry, now renamed Hall's Quarry to honour the project's chief engineer. From the quarry's new large crushing plant, railway ballast dump cars brought the stone to a siding at the airport to be re-crushed to the desired grade for surfacing the runways. The airport and quarry combined employed 310 men.[21]

Experimental Crossings

Things were progressing at Botwood too, with plans taking shape for the first experimental transatlantic flights. The agreed arrangement would see two flying boats, one each from Imperial Airways and PAA, flying simultaneously, one eastward and the other westward. The man on the ground in charge at Botwood and making preparations to receive the visiting aircraft was Squadron Leader Harold A.L. Pattison, soon to become a key figure at the developing Hattie's Camp site.[22] The British Air Ministry had sent the experienced signals officer to Newfoundland in 1936 to supervise the erection and installation of the Marconi wireless station at Botwood and to act for the initial period as civil aviation liaison officer. These liaison duties authorized Pattison to act as local representative of the Air Ministry and as the channel of communication between the ministry and the Newfoundland Department of Public Utilities.[23] During June 1937, Pattison directed dredging operations and efforts to equip the seaport with concrete moorings, temporary buoys (locally made from petrol drums), motor launches, petrol, and accommodations for ground engineers and crews. The alternate landing site at Gleneagles on Gander Lake, near the town of Glenwood, was similarly equipped with moorings, buoys, a flare path, and a wharf, slipway, and boathouse for a motor launch for conveying passengers.[24] Permanent staff at the shore base included a motor launch crew, one meteorological observer, and operators for the auxiliary wireless transmitter signal station. For accommodations, the Newfoundland government approached Robin Reid of the Reid Newfoundland Railway family, who operated the Gleneagles Hotel, a tourist lodge located at the selected site. When Reid could not guarantee the required lodging for twelve, the government erected its own staff house. The building provided accommodations only and Reid's hotel looked after the meals.[25]

Whether Gleneagles or Botwood offered better facilities for flying boats was still up for debate. Consequently, when Air Ministry officials met late in 1936, the suggested approach was to make the decision based on the experience gained during the upcoming experimental stage and until such time, keep expenditures on permanent works at a minimum.[26]

On the evening of 5 July 1937, Imperial's Short Empire flying boat *Caledonia* lifted off from Foynes, Ireland, maintaining an average cruising speed of 133 miles per hour (mph) and keeping "a remarkably straight course in the face of a moderate wind blowing at an average of 27 miles per hour." Captain Arthur S. Wilcockson landed the *Caledonia* at Botwood the following morning after a fifteen-hour crossing. Winging its way eastward from Botwood that same night was a PAA Sikorsky S-42B flying boat named *Clipper III*, piloted by Captain Harold Gray. The clipper maintained an average cruising speed of 157 mph and landed at Foynes after a flight duration of twelve and a half hours. The return flights ten days later proved equally successful, with both aircraft maintaining a parallel course forty miles apart.[27] More experimental round-trip flights followed that summer and fall and for the next couple of years, marking "the beginning of a new stage in intercontinental aviation."[28]

The Airfield Takes Shape

Work on the aerodrome, now named Newfoundland Airport, began in earnest in 1937, with upwards of eight hundred workers employed during peak periods. "Generally speaking the artizan [sic] class is good," reported H.A. Lewis-Dale, the Air Ministry's deputy director of works and buildings, sent out to establish project cost estimates and advise the government on the layout and construction of the airport. Nevertheless, assistant engineer T.B. Woodyatt, having replaced an ailing Vatcher, expressed concerns about some of the unskilled labourers that poor-relief (welfare) officers with the Department of Public Health and Welfare were sending his way. Many were physically unfit and some even malnourished, which led to low productivity and several minor accidents. In one instance, eight new hires went immediately to the medical hut for treatment. Woodyatt was sympathetic and even willing to "nurse" these men for a week or two, "and in many cases they make good," he told Lewis-Dale. Even so, with the work "being carried out under rush conditions and with a minimum of money in the Estimate," Lewis-Dale asked that the government send only those men who could handle a pick, shovel, and axe.[29]

Cutting, grubbing, burning, draining, and ditching at the runway sites continued during the first half of 1937. Bulldozers and Athey wagons were in constant motion, levelling the ground and removing earth. At Hall's Quarry, sixty thousand tons of rock were crushed and delivered to the airport. Construction began on a powerhouse, administration building, and hangar, and workers cleared land for the erection of wireless transmitting and receiving buildings. Eventually, communication cables linked the administration building with each wireless station. During the second half of 1937, the cable ship *Leapin' Lena* laid cable across Gander Lake for Lorenz blind-landing navigation equipment, and railway tank cars delivered asphalt from a plant in Clarenville for paving the runways.[30] The Lorenz system was purchased through British agents of the Telefunken Company of Berlin and installed by British engineers. This fuelled rumours, prevalent during wartime, that the Germans had constructed the airfield.[31]

The year 1938 opened with Douglas Fraser and his engineer, George Lace, making the first landing at the airport. The runways were not yet finished, so Fraser set down on the snow, piloting the Newfoundland government's ski-equipped de Havilland DH.83 Fox Moth VO-ADE, which would become a stalwart rescue craft during the coming war.[32] Some managerial reorganization early that year saw F.C. Jewett arrive on loan from the Montréal Harbour Works to replace resigning chief engineer T.A. Hall. Jewett brought with him Robert A. Bradley as assistant engineer and certain of Hall's St. John's staff, their office equipment, supplies, and records.[33] With the airfield taking shape, Newfoundland desired to appoint Botwood's Squadron Leader Pattison as airport manager. The British obliged and granted his release from the RAF to become the Newfoundland Airport's aerodrome control officer.[34] That fall, an electrician from Westinghouse finished installing field and runway centre lighting. All four runways were paved with a minimum width of three hundred feet, and by September, the airport was considered operational and "ready for use by modern aircraft under day conditions."[35] With the season's work winding down and projects nearing completion, the camp population of 730 workers remained "stationary or slightly on the wane as the occasional employee who wearies for the fleshpots and passes on is in most cases not replaced," reported Jewett. That fall, civilian visitors Alfred and Constance Wolf of Philadelphia landed their float-equipped Fairchild aircraft on Gander Lake and spent several days touring the airfield. They returned home via the Strait of Belle Isle and the Labrador coast, but not before taking airport staff aloft to view their handiwork from above, "something that we all had long wished for but had never achieved," said Jewett.[36]

As agreed at the Ottawa Conference, Canada established a meteorological office at Botwood but moved it to Gander late in 1938. The British Air Ministry operated the wireless radio receiving and transmitting stations northwest and south of the airfield, respectively. They were set apart about four miles to minimize interference from the different medium- and short-wave services and to negate any flying hazard presented by the high radio masts.[37] Among the radio supervisory staff was Englishman Cecil M. Brant. For a while, his wife represented Gander's one and only female. When the Brants first moved to Gander before the Second World War, roads were few and radio staff either skied to work or took the "Prairie Schooner," a small, tractor-pulled house on skids containing food supplies and a coal stove. The chances of becoming lost in a snowstorm were good, so a compass was vital. One time, the pair skied to the railway station, a mere shack, for food supplies and was snowbound for four days: a lesson learned "that sufficient food supplies must be kept."[38]

An Uncertain Future

By spring 1939, Newfoundland Airport (hereafter identified as Gander) boasted four hard-surfaced runways, all in excess of four thousand feet, one large hangar, an administration building complete with control tower and rotating beacon, quarters for married officials, a staff house with fifty single bedrooms, and thousands of gallons of gasoline.[39] The completion of the project that year was cause for celebration, and "the entire personnel turned out in one huge spontaneous parade with trucks, brooms and shovels over shoulder, graders, pavers and every piece of moving equipment."[40] Soon, the nucleus of a small town began to evolve. The female population increased to twenty, and Gander's first child was born to a Newfoundland member of the radio staff. There were parties and dances at the administration building, where the dining room doubled as a cinema and for twenty-five cents many Newfoundlanders saw their first movie.

The outbreak of war in September 1939 brought on uncertainty with transatlantic commercial operations, but the civil staff was retained, although no one knew what the future held for the new airport.[41] The aircraft landing register shows that the primary activity in 1939 was upper-air meteorological observation and data collection. Each day, weather permitting, pilots Douglas Fraser, Clifford Kent, and Donald McGregor took aloft the Newfoundland government's Fox Moth or its Fairchild 71C (VO-AFG),[42] measuring atmospheric properties with a meteorograph and strut psychrometer. These observations, reported the *Evening Telegram*, "gave the only information available on the structure of the 'fronts' moving out over the Atlantic, [and] the associated icing conditions and cloud systems."[43] The work of Fraser, Kent, and McGregor marked "the first time we knew anything about what went on" from ten to twenty-five thousand feet above Newfoundland, remarked Dr. Patrick D. McTaggart-Cowan, then head of Gander's meteorological section.[44]

By year's end, the airfield had yet to receive an aircraft on the transatlantic service as the landplanes were not ready, and their construction was now halted due to the war, reported the Dominions Office.[45] Nor had the airfield received many visitors, save twenty-five-year-old Swedish-American Charles Backman, piloting the first aircraft to arrive from abroad, and some curious American tourists from Delaware. The ill-prepared Backman, delivering Monocoupe 90A SE-AGM to his native Sweden, arrived with little more than a railway map. Pattison's wife prepared and wrapped some sandwiches for the trip across, securing them from a string above the pilot's head. It was a moment for the history books, as Backman's fuel-laden aircraft became the first to depart the airfield on a transatlantic flight. He was never heard from again.[46]

The aerial vacationers from Delaware arrived in August in a Waco EQC-6, an enclosed-cockpit biplane with United States (US) registration NC500, owned and operated by Henry B. duPont, member of the duPont chemical family and recent founder of an aircraft sales and distributorship business for the Waco Aircraft Company. DuPont stayed for a few days and took Pattison and some of the engineering and radio staff on short local flights, including the airfield's first night flying.[47]

Other aerial activity in 1939 saw two British Handley Page Harrow tanker aircraft conduct mid-air-refuelling trials in conjunction with Imperial Airways' transatlantic flying boat service at Botwood, but even that service shut down in October. "To fly the North Atlantic later than that," explains historian Carl Christie, "was considered too hazardous." Indeed, "At the outbreak of war," he adds, "transatlantic flying attracted no military interest."[48] Nor did Gander, suggests McTaggart-Cowan, having "received instructions from Ottawa to close down the meteorological section, because it wouldn't be used." Likewise, he claims, Ottawa sent instructions to mine the runways, lest they fall into German hands,[49] putting enemy aircraft within striking distance of the Maritimes and shipping through the Strait of Belle Isle and Cabot Strait.[50] "We dragged our feet" on the matter, admitted McTaggart-Cowan, and deliberately submitted "incomplete interim reports and refused to carry out orders."[51]

As it then stood, Gander was less an asset than a liability, but by mid-1940 that thinking had changed. The implications of enemy control of the airfield, railway, and Botwood seaplane base now had Newfoundland Governor Sir Humphrey Walwyn raising alarms over "the defenceless condition of this country."[52] Newfoundland could expect little help from Britain, then focussed on its own survival, but it allowed Canada to send to Gander a detachment of Douglas Digby patrol bombers from No. 10 (Bomber Reconnaissance) Squadron for general reconnaissance and local air defence. More RCAF antisubmarine squadrons followed as the war progressed, but for the time being at least, the airport remained under the management of aerodrome control officer Pattison.

Atlantic Air Bridge

Gander's potential for other future uses soon came up for discussion. Significantly, the air officer commanding at Eastern Air Command, RCAF, in Halifax foretold in a secret communiqué to the Canadian Department of National Defence in May 1940, the airfield could "be of paramount importance to the Allied War Effort as the main aerodrome on this side of the Atlantic from which to dispatch" aircraft for delivery by air to England.[53] Early in the war, American-made aircraft purchased by the British Ministry of Aircraft Production (MAP) were dismantled, shipped by sea, and reassembled in the UK. This method of transportation created considerable delays and was impractical for the larger four-engine bombers. Additionally, there were losses caused by marauding German U-boats. To circumvent these obstacles, Minister of Aircraft Production Lord Beaverbrook, Canadian-born William Maxwell Aitken, spearheaded a scheme to fly the aircraft overseas instead. Gander airport's easternmost location in North America made it the logical departure point.

The first point of order was to find an organization to deliver the aircraft. Beaverbrook set that process in motion by appointing Morris W. Wilson, president of the Royal Bank of Canada, as his MAP representative in Canada and the US. Wilson contacted Sir Edward Beatty, president of the Canadian Pacific Railway (CPR) Company in Montréal, "exploring the company's willingness to inaugurate a service."[54] Beatty was receptive, and by August 1940 a contract was in place. The man chosen to set up the organization, to be called the CPR Air Service Department, was former Imperial

Airways managing director George Woods Humphrey. The contract established the initial managerial hierarchy of the air service with Beatty as chairman, Humphrey as vice-chairman, and Lieutenant-Colonel H. Burchall as general manager, assisted by Captain Arthur S. Wilcockson, previously in charge of Imperial Airways' Atlantic division and the man who piloted the *Caledonia* into Botwood in 1937. From the British Overseas Airways Corporation (BOAC), created in 1939 following the merger of British Airways Ltd. and Imperial Airways, came Australian Captain D.C.T. "Don" Bennett as flying superintendent, and Captains Humphrey Page and I.G. "Ian" Ross as assistants. The new air service would handle all technical aspects of the scheme, including aircrew recruitment and training, and aircraft maintenance ten miles east of downtown Montréal at Saint-Hubert aerodrome, which would receive the aircraft direct from the Lockheed Aircraft Corporation in Burbank, California. The contract also covered ground preparations at the main ocean terminals at Gander and Aldergrove, near Belfast in Northern Ireland. What the future held for the organization was unknown, as the first series of flights were experimental and meant only to determine the feasibility of an Atlantic air ferry service.[55]

Hudson bombers soon began to trickle in at Saint-Hubert, but not direct from the factory as planned. American customs and neutrality regulations made it necessary to fly the aircraft to Pembina, North Dakota, and have horses tow them across the border into Manitoba. The first two Hudsons to arrive became trainers for use by instructors Page and Ross. Meanwhile, Wilcockson had been busily engaged in interviewing potential pilots. Those selected came from varied backgrounds and included barnstormers, crop-dusters, flying instructors, Canadian bush pilots, and "throw-outs from the American airlines," recalled Bennett.[56] The Canadian Department of Transport loaned experienced radio operators and BOAC more of its captains. Qualified navigators were scarce, so the plan moving forward would see the first delivery flight dispatched in loose formation with only the lead aircraft carrying a navigator.[57] At Saint-Hubert, ground engineers began preparing the first Hudsons earmarked for delivery. For new aircraft, they had their share of problems, and the resident expert tasked with addressing them was John Joseph Gilmore. He quickly discovered that some Hudsons arrived with cracked cowlings, fractured air shutters, and metal particles in their oil tank filters. Oil cooler failures happened with regularity. Gilmore and his team removed engines and carburetors, repositioned compasses, modified oxygen supply systems, and installed locally made hot-air shutters.[58] The men worked tirelessly. Gilmore, praised Bennett, "turned out to be such a pillar of strength on the engineering side in the first year of the Atlantic Ferry."[59] Lockheed technicians had also fitted each Hudson with overload fuel tanks for the long overseas flight. The upshot of this was greatly increased endurance, but it also turned each aircraft into "a flying gas tank."[60]

Former British transatlantic pilot Squadron Leader Griffith "Taffy" Powell headed preparations at Gander. He arrived early in October 1940 to find accommodations minimal, and certainly "no means of housing the sort of aircrew flow that we had in mind." Powell therefore arranged to have the Newfoundland Railway bring two narrow-gauge sleeping cars and a restaurant car to a siding near the hangar. One of the sleeping car cabins became Powell's headquarters. He soon became acquainted with some of Gander's "resident stars," Squadron Leader Pattison and "his two highly professional assistants," airport operations officer Tom McGrath and wireless supervisor Frank L. Ratcliffe.[61] McGrath, one of the original Newfoundland Airport staff, first arrived in November 1937 as clerk-secretary to the chief engineer of the Marconi Wireless Telegraph Company of England, which was erecting the airport's wireless apparatus. Still, what the young Newfoundlander really wanted was a career in aviation, and when the opportunity arose, he later said, "I applied for and won the job of Junior Operations Officer" at Botwood under Pattison.[62] Joined by his wife, Ruth, he soon returned to Gander as operations officer and assistant to Pattison, performing "his work with great zeal and ability."[63] Even in government circles, McGrath was making a name for himself. Following an on-site appraisal of staff and facilities, an impressed Raymond Manning, Newfoundland secretary for Public Utilities, suggested that the government send him to a large, well-organized airport to gain experience so that he might one day take charge at Gander.[64] In any event, the airport's "brightest star," insisted Powell, was meteorologist McTaggart-Cowan. Using reports from US and Canadian sources, he drew his own synoptic charts "and developed the art of Atlantic weather forecasting to an extraordinary degree." Countless aircrew came to value and trust McTaggart-Cowan as the weather authority at Gander and later at Dorval, a new airfield west of Montréal where he and the forecasting centre relocated in 1942. His extensive knowledge of North Atlantic meteorology even earned him an affectionate nickname – "McFog."[65]

By the end of October, Powell had completed arrangements at Gander and had at his disposal a tiny contingent consisting of three labourers and two ground engineers. With the Hudsons anticipated any day, Powell pressed to have the runways constantly cleared of snow.[66] The first arrived from Saint-Hubert on 29 October, with "slush, snow and water" blanketing the cockpit "in what seemed like a solid mass" as the Hudson settled on the runway, recalled radio officer C.M. "Curly" Tripp. He thought for "sure we would nose over," but Captain Ralph E. Adams "gunned her and we stayed all down." The slush caused considerable damage to the flaps and elevators, "but otherwise all was well." Personnel of the RCAF's resident bomber reconnaissance detachment helped with repairs and aided the crews in preparation for their overseas flight. On the positive side, said Tripp, the first in got to pick out "for ourselves the best bunks in the sleeping car we were to use." Two more Hudsons arrived before month's end and another on 2 November. A pair came in on the sixth and the last and seventh aircraft of the flight formation, Hudson T9422, landed on the afternoon of 9 November at the hands of Don Bennett. The six aircraft that preceded him to Gander each carried a captain, second pilot, and radio operator. Anticipating a heavy workload, Bennett's Hudson carried an extra or relief radio man, for a total of twenty-two men.[67]

En route, Bennett had signalled Gander to have all the aircraft prepared for immediate departure, but it was not to be. On arrival, he found all the Hudsons coated "with half an inch of clear steel-like ice." The men began chipping away using any tool they could find. After an hour or so, it became clear to Bennett that they would not get away that evening, so he postponed the departure for twenty-four hours. Bennett spent the next day with McTaggart-Cowan, studying weather maps and forecasts and preparing flight plans for each aircraft.[68] In the early evening, he gathered the crews in the administration building control tower for a briefing. Bennett was a perfectionist, and "so thoroughly had he covered every phase of this first flight," said Tripp, that no questions were asked. An hour later, they were ready to go.[69] Recognizing the significance of the date, 10 November, Pattison's wife presented each crewman with an Armistice Day poppy. To allow the aircraft to take off in quick succession, ground crew "positioned the aircraft in line abreast on the main wide runway ... We warmed up all the engines just before dark [and] topped up the tanks," said Powell. When the big moment came, "all aircraft started without trouble as the starter trolley moved down the line." Powell was especially relieved "after endless difficulties with flat batteries, changing spark plugs and the continual cold wind." A military band from The Queen's Own Rifles of Canada, assigned on airport defence duty, turned out to play them off. However, the band members could not read their sheet music in the darkness, so they played a hymn they all knew from memory. To the tune of "Nearer, My God, to Thee," hardly a morale lifter for the occasion, but a kind gesture nonetheless, all seven Hudsons departed over a ten-minute span, "the purple flames from the exhausts leaping from the silhouette of each of them upon the runway against the airport lights."[70]

Bennett as navigator led the way. He first circled the airport "in a gentle turn so that each could pick up his position in the formation." As soon as they "had settled on the climb," he handed over to the second pilot, Emmett F. Clausewitz, and moved to the navigator's table. Bennett shouldered considerable responsibility. Never before had anyone attempted the Atlantic this time of year. North Atlantic weather was notoriously unpredictable, and "with practically no radio aids available, my sextant and myself were rather vital to the proceedings." While studying his charts, Bennett happened to glance towards the cockpit, "to note with considerable surprise" that his second pilot "was wearing Texas cowboy boots with fancy leather-work and high heels! For luck, I believe!" Bennett was indeed among a cosmopolitan group of airmen.[71]

Not everything ran smoothly. "For the first hour," said Tripp in a wartime publication, "there seemed to be planes all around us." The problem was identifying the leader, Bennett. Then Captain Ralph Adams turned the aircraft, Hudson T9458, over to second pilot Dana Gentry and went aft to examine the ship using a torchlight. Adams discovered that the starboard oil tank had ruptured and was leaking badly. He signalled Bennett but eventually determined that the leak was diminishing and decided to carry on. Next, Tripp's radio shorted out. Adams yelled at him to shut it off, but "I had beat him to the gun," said Tripp. "With that load of gas it isn't pleasant to have fire skipping around the cockpit," he added, "and the corona from that transmitter was really something." A little over the halfway mark, with the bomb-bay tank running dry, both motors started cutting out. "I was not expecting it," admitted Tripp, "and even if Ralph and Dana were, the way they went for that hand pump and gas valve made me think they didn't like it any better than I did." The two Wright engines "hit their stride again" and settled "down to a steady drone." Things suddenly got worse as Tripp was taking a bearing on Bennett. The indicator on the radio compass broke "and I really felt up the creek without a paddle. No transmitter or compass and out over the Atlantic Ocean." He decided not to tell Adams. The crew chugged onwards, sucking oxygen from a rubber tube at higher altitudes.[72]

Three-quarters of the way along, the group encountered a weather front later than forecast and higher than expected. The icing was severe and Bennett could not climb above it. He soon found himself enveloped in dense cloud and as a precaution signalled to separate. Bennett took comfort knowing that the group was on track and nearing its destination. Daylight broke as he approached the coast of Ireland. "We descended through a fairly low cloud base with beautiful clear visibility below," he wrote, "and steamed round the north coast of Ireland at low level and on into Aldergrove. Another Hudson had joined the circuit just ahead of us."[73] Tripp's aircraft was in rain cloud on and off as they neared the coast. At 0800 Greenwich Mean Time (GMT), Captain Adams began his descent. At five thousand feet the crew sighted land, quickly identified as Catlin Island. They had just crossed over Lough Neagh when suddenly Adams shouted, "There's Aldergrove right over there," and "with that he shoved the throttles forward and the way that Hudson jumped was like a horse coming down the home stretch. After one circuit we were down." Now on the ground, an anxious Bennett, observed Tripp, "would not leave the window of the mess" until "that seventh ship rolled to a stop." They had done it, completing the first mid-winter flight, and at a one hundred percent success rate.

The next difficult task was to convince the receptionist and staff at the Belfast hotel that the twenty-two unshaven men standing before them had just arrived from England, not North America. "It was a necessary security measure," explained Tripp, "but the ten-gallon hats, the high-heeled Texas boots, and Canadian hooded parkas, led by Bennett's inevitable black homberg hat and brief case, caused many penetrating looks."[74] The crews flew to Blackpool the next day, with hopes of exploring wartime England, and for some, "a chance of at least having one or two bombs dropped on their heads." It came as a great disappointment that they had to immediately board a ship sailing from Liverpool to Canada. Bennett went on to London, reporting to Beaverbrook, who "was smiles from ear to ear."[75]

The successful crossing of 10/11 November 1940 was followed by three more formation flights of Hudsons to Aldergrove before year's end, for a total of twenty-five aircraft delivered (two landed at Prestwick and one at Liverpool). The second group of Hudsons arrived at Gander in mid-November, and by the time they got the green light later that month, winter had fully set in with regularly occurring snowfalls. Heavy snowdrifts around the aircraft and ice deposits on the wings required constant attention. On two occasions, said Powell, with exceptionally good flying weather forecast, "we had to postpone owing to the ground conditions and problems with cold engine oil." The second group eventually got over safely, led by Captain Humphrey Page in Hudson T9427, as did Captain Gordon Store's third group on 17 December.[76] All had been nighttime departures, timed for a daylight arrival in the UK. The operation had unquestionably exceeded expectations as British officials were prepared to "give the plan up [only] if fewer than three of the seven aircraft arrived safely."[77] The only mishap at Gander during the flight experiment of 1940 was nonetheless near fatal.

Gander's First Crash

The fourth and last of the group departure flights, again led by Captain Bennett, prepared to lift off from runway No. 1 at Gander the night of 28 December. All boundary lights were in operation and a row of thirty-eight paraffin flares evenly spaced the entire length of the runway's centerline. "The runway was in good condition," reported Pattison, "with an average of one inch of frozen snow over the surface." American V. Edward Smith, among the pilots to make the historic flight of 10/11 November, would tonight deliver Hudson T9446. First officer Arthur Bruce Watt was first to board the aircraft. This would be his inaugural transatlantic flight. He completed a cockpit check, after which ground crew towed T9446 from the hangar. Watt started both engines, which showed satisfactory oil pressure and temperatures, and then gave way his seat to the captain, who also did a cockpit check. The Hudson was still on the hangar ramp when Alton M. Loughridge entered and took his position in the radio operator's compartment, just as he had done for Smith on the night of 10 November. Smith taxied to the southeast end of runway No. 1 and took up aircraft position number six on Captain Bennett's starboard side, as was the sequence in November. The engines on T9446 continued to warm as Smith made his take-off check – airscrews (propellers) in low pitch, carburetor heat hot, tail wheel unlocked, autopilot off, trim tabs at zero, and so on. The first five Hudson bombers lifted off in succession without incident. Smith was next. He made a final cockpit check and looked at Watt, who was slowly operating the fuel hand pump with one hand while the other was on the tail wheel lever.[78] Watt described the take-off run:

> After about fifty feet Smith called tail wheel locked. I pulled the tail lever down into the locked position and called tail wheel locked. Smith concentrated on the take-off while I slowly operated the fuel pump. The take-off was normal for the Hudson loaded to that weight and when we were about halfway down the runway it slowly left the ground.
>
> After a second or two the aircraft slowly began to bank to the left, gently at first but increasing. Looking over at Captain Smith I saw he was fighting for control and as the bank was still increasing he quickly reached around the pedestal (as I learned later) to check the automatic pilot which had been in the off position at the start of the take-off.
>
> I did not interfere, continued pumping and looking out the windshield, and I watched the bank become more steep and as the nose of the aircraft dropped below the level of the lights on buildings in front of us, I switched off the main ignition switch — then CRASH.
>
> On recovering from the shock I observed Captain Smith assisting Radio Operator Loughridge out through the side port window. Flames outside in front and on both sides. I tried to open the emergency hatch above me, but using all my strength I could not make it operate. The side starboard window being partly broken I broke the remaining glass in it and made my exit while Captain Smith was going through the port side window.[79]

Smith, suffering from shock and minor cuts and abrasions, later described his initial take-off run as "perfectly normal." Passing the control tower, he noticed a slight aileron flutter, but then "the ship had approximate flying speed and came unstuck and settled back. At that point the automatic pilot took over control," evidently having crept forward from the "off" position. The Hudson yawed sharply, the left wing dropping as Smith fought for control.[80] It continued swerving to the left as the wing tip scraped the runway for three hundred feet, at which point the propeller cut into another twenty-two feet of tarmac. The stricken ship continued to the edge of the runway, flattening a boundary cone light before coming to rest in flames in an open ditch.[81] The airport crash tender shortly arrived on scene near the west end of runway No. 1

and pulled to within three feet of the port wing. The fire crew dispersed CO_2 gas upon the burning fuselage. The effort was in vain, for just as quickly as they extinguished the flames, so did gasoline flow back and reignite. On being told that the crew had escaped, and with the blaze "completely beyond control," reported fireman R.N. Wells, "we stood by until it sufficiently cooled down when our 2-gallon Suds Extinguishers were used to save what was possible of the starboard engine and to extinguish small burning parts."[82] A detachment of The Royal Rifles of Canada, having recently assumed responsibility for Gander's ground defence and security, afterwards guarded the wreckage.

Pattison, unsure how best to proceed with a MAP-owned aircraft, cabled general manager Burchall in Montréal. Burchall's response left the matter in Pattison's hands. Assisted by RCAF pilot Flight Lieutenant Dennis, operations officer McGrath, and Gander CPR air service staff members Lloyd Sampson and chief aircraft maintenance engineer Jerome Coulombe, Pattison carried out a daylight examination of the wreckage. The Hudson had come to rest nearly parallel to the ditch with the wings on opposite sides. The starboard engine remained in position, unlike the port engine, which rested six feet from the port wing tip. The intense heat had rendered the front cockpit unrecognizable. The tail wheel showed as locked and the starboard wing flaps were in the up position. The men could find no component or control of the automatic pilot. Pattison admitted being unfamiliar with the device and could offer no opinion on Smith's statement. However, he did lean towards attributing the cause "to a stall owing to lack of flying speed when the aircraft first left the ground." The matter, it seems, ended there.[83]

Among the aircraft to leave that same evening was Hudson T9465, a gift aircraft christened the "Spirit of Lockheed-Vega Employees," and piloted by Bennett. A current theory suggests that this aircraft, not T9446, crashed and burned at Gander that evening. In the interests of public relations and morale, goes the argument, a look-alike, or actualization of the original "Spirit," was hastily fabricated and sent overseas. [84] However, there is no evidence to support this claim. The RAF Watch Log, which recorded arrivals, departures, and crew surnames, identifies the crashed Hudson as Smith's T9446, and the "Spirit of Lockheed-Vega Employees" as departing Gander at 0032 hours on 29 December and arriving at Aldergrove at 1130 hours. Operations officer McGrath kept a diary of airport activities and in it likewise noted that Captain Smith's T9446, number six in the formation, "crashed and burned out – crew miraculously escaped." Finally, Pattison's report, with eyewitness statements, consistently identifies the aircraft as T9446, further confirmed by an addendum of crash photographs showing the serial number on the rear fuselage.[85]

Four days after the mishap, Captain W.C. "Penny" Rogers shuttled stranded crewmen Smith, Watt, and Loughridge back to Montréal aboard Hudson T9445. Rogers had in fact been fifth off the ground in T9445 the night of Smith's accident but returned several hours later with engine trouble.[86]

With the experimental flights of November-December 1940 behind them, the air ferry service and Gander prepared for its first full year of delivery flights. The year 1941 would bring further success to the ever-evolving ferry service with increased deliveries and the establishment of a Return Ferry Service to expedite the return of aircrews from overseas upon the completion of their ferry flights. The year would also be marked by organizational change and, regrettably, the air service's first ferry flight tragedy: one that would garner international headlines.

CHAPTER 2 | THE FIRST FULL YEAR

The year 1941 opened with the air ferry service having reassigned Squadron Leader Powell, who had been managing Gander's ground organization, to establish a base in Bermuda for Consolidated PBY (long-range maritime patrol bomber) Catalina deliveries.[1] Twenty-four-year-old Canadian civilian Lloyd Sampson then took over as CPR's station superintendent until Saint-Hubert Hudson instructor Captain Ian Ross, a Canadian and pre-war bush pilot and "pioneer of Ontario and Quebec far northern air routes," arrived in February 1941. Sampson remained at Gander for a few months as assistant station manager.[2] Ross, along with his wife and daughter, moved into the Eastbound Inn, a new hotel for transient aircrew that opened in December 1940. Under him was a small but ever-growing contingent of fifty civilian staff, from engineers and mechanics, to stenographers, clerks, janitors, and cooks.[3]

One of the stenographers, Newfoundlander John Murphy, arrived from St. John's by train late in January 1941, having secured employment with the CPR air service. He walked the short distance from the railway station to the Eastbound Inn, where he met Jack Lush, chief steward for the facility. The seventeen-year-old set up office in the inn. In those early days, "we did all the clerical work and helped load airplanes – we did almost everything," Murphy recalled. He soon became Ross's private secretary, and subsequently, confidential secretary to each of the ferry service's wartime commanders at Gander.[4]

Frustrations Abound

During the second week of January, five Hudsons arrived from Montréal. During one landing, no less than seventeen spectators had crammed inside the control tower. McGrath was annoyed and suggested that "everyone except [the] staff on duty should be banned." Pattison happened to be there too when an air force tractor crossed the runway just as Hudson T9441 came in on final approach. The tractor driver had a red light but ignored the signal "and sailed blissfully on." He presumably got the message after Pattison discharged a signal pistol and "put [a] red Very shell almost in his cab."

The five Hudson crews waited days at the Eastbound Inn until someone "discovered at this late date," said an incredulous McGrath, that the aircraft were too overloaded with mail and freight to make the crossing. The Overseas Air Movements Control Unit in Gloucester, which handled non-operational flights outside UK airspace, including those from North America, then issued further instructions. No Hudsons were to depart without certain engine modifications. The aircraft were to return in pairs to Montréal, where a maintenance team at Saint-Hubert would work on the engines. The crews were "disgusted," said McGrath, and one pilot, Captain Joseph C. Mackey, so "fed up" having been two weeks delayed at Gander that he resigned on the spot, at least temporarily it turned out. He left Gander at his first chance with two other Hudsons, contrary to orders that he leave the next day, paired with another Hudson.[5] With all aircraft recalled to Montréal, Gander dispatched no overseas ferry flights that January.

Moving forward, there would be no group or formation-type departures as with the flight experiment of November–December 1940. Although successful, these flights also demonstrated that North Atlantic weather was too severe "to make formation flying a practical arrangement." Getting all the aircraft ready at once proved difficult too.[6] Ground personnel would now ready individually arriving aircraft for flight and, weather pending, send them on their way one by one.

The next successful overseas flight came on 10/11 February, although the crew's patience was again tested leading up to it. After several days awaiting good weather and then having to replace a faulty autopilot with a unit borrowed from the RCAF, Captain R. Allen finally got underway in Hudson T9464. The airport had been experimenting that winter, as it had the winter of 1939–1940, using rollers to compact snow on the runways. The surface was hard this day, but there were soft spots on runway No. 3 that caught the Hudson's tail wheel and prevented the pilot from gaining sufficient flying speed. The next day, Allen and Pattison drove out to inspect the runway. It was no better, and even their car sank in the snow. The compaction "was not up to last year's standard for some reason," observed McGrath, blaming "either poor workmanship or less frost than last year." That evening, "a beautiful clear night," Allen made a "skillful" take-off using a suitably frozen runway No. 1. Ten hours and forty-four minutes later, he landed at Prestwick in Scotland, which would become the ferry service's key European terminus. On this lone Atlantic flight, First Officer Arthur Bruce Watt finally got to complete his first transatlantic crossing.

Five days later, two of three departing Hudsons returned to Gander, one due to excessive gas consumption and autopilot system problems and the other with carburetor trouble. The last of the trio, Captain Donald Anderson's Hudson T9453, landed at Prestwick in an elapsed time of eleven hours and eighteen minutes, and within ten minutes of its ETA.[7]

The Banting Crash

Sadly, the night of 20/21 February would mark the first fatal accident in Newfoundland since ferrying operations began. Hudson T9449 was the last of five Hudsons to lift off that night. Thirty minutes later, the pilot asked Gander for a QDM, or magnetic bearing to steer back to base. After that, silence. Several days passed with no word before search aircraft spotted the battered Hudson and its lone survivor near the shoreline of a frozen pond. If not for the passenger carried on board, the incident would likely have been little publicized. Instead, it garnered worldwide media attention.

When Hudson T9449 arrived at Gander on 17 February, surprised civilian and military personnel witnessed none other than Sir Frederick Grant Banting emerge from the Hudson's rear fuselage door. Banting, the Canadian co-discoverer of insulin, for which he and John Macleod shared the 1923 Nobel Prize in Physiology or Medicine, had arranged passage overseas to discuss matters of scientific research with his British compatriots.[8] While anxious to get overseas, Banting was seemingly unaware of the fledgling nature of ferrying operations. It came as a "severe shock," he wrote while at Gander, upon learning that the service had made only a small number of Atlantic crossings "during the past three months." The layover gave Banting time to get acquainted with his pilot, thirty-three-year-old Captain Joseph C. Mackey. At a party on the evening of the eighteenth, Mackey "was tight," wrote Banting, and confessed "to me that he promised never to take a passenger across the Atlantic." Nevertheless, said Mackey, he was pleased to take the Canadian scientist. "I take him to be a hard drinker, hard flyer, & if in a box a hard fighter," Banting jotted in his notebook. "He should be in the movies for he has dash, poise, nerve & nothing phases him."[9] Mackey probably fit the bill. The American had led a varied career in aviation before joining the CPR ferry service in September 1940. During the 1930s, he completed several short tours while serving as a second lieutenant in the US Army Air Corps Reserve. A popular barnstormer, he became a staple at air shows and authored books on skywriting and acrobatics. He represented the US in an acrobatics exhibition in France and participated in cross-country and pylon races at the National Air Races in Cleveland, Ohio. His last job before joining the ferry service was instructing students at the air corps' advanced flying school at Kelly Field in San Antonio, Texas. He arrived in Montréal with fifteen years' flying experience and more than twenty-five hundred hours flying time.[10]

For the next few days, the Hudson crews at Gander awaited favourable weather, killing time at the Eastbound Inn. Banting took in a picture show and visited the control tower with ferry pilot "Penny" Rogers for a weather report. Rogers, "with whom I have become friends," wrote Banting, took him inside one of the Hudsons, explaining "all the gadgets & mechanism[s]." Banting spent time rubbing elbows with other airmen too, gaining "more & more confidence in both the machines and the men," he wrote, and learning "a lot about aviation" and the problems associated with high-altitude flying at northern latitudes. Around noon on 20 February, the sun appeared and it began to clear.[11] A few hours later, McTaggart-Cowan gathered all the captains and navigators and, using the latest synoptic charts and meteorological information, gave a complete flight forecast. All in attendance agreed that conditions for a flight to the UK looked good. "It looks as tho[ugh] tonight was [sic] the night! The boys are packing," wrote Banting. "Coffee in thermos flasks has been ordered." At around 2000 hours local time, the crew of T9449 got underway. Mackey ran up the engines, and not until he was ready to taxi did Banting climb aboard.[12] A light snow was falling from the night sky as one by one, four Hudsons piloted by captains Adams, Rogers, Harmes, and a Flight Lieutenant Butler took off at roughly ten-minute intervals.[13] Another Hudson in the group never got off the ground. The ill-fated aircraft "bumped and swerved off [the] strip," wrote McGrath, and ran towards the south ditch, stopping just in time. The pilot cancelled due to engine trouble. Mackey was next. McGrath watched from the tower as he used the entire runway before pulling up sharply and disappearing into low cloud. Altogether, said McGrath, "an exciting series [of] departures."[14]

Some twenty-five minutes out, trouble began. First, the Hudson's port engine failed. Mackey immediately turned back and requested and received radio bearings from Gander. He pressed the feathering button for the dead engine, which would align the blades with the airflow to reduce aerodynamic drag, but that too failed. "The next thing that happened," he later explained in sworn testimony, "was severe smoke pouring out of the control box at my side. Whereupon I ordered the entire crew to the rear to throw out baggage and don parachutes." At about five thousand feet, the starboard engine suddenly lost power and the Hudson dropped to twenty-five hundred feet. Mackey then called his radio officer, William Snailham, "and gave him orders for everybody to jump ... He acknowledged the order," Mackey later testified.[15] A discernible change in the aircraft's balance suggested to him that they had abandoned the Hudson as instructed.[16] Quickly losing altitude on one malfunctioning engine and unable to leave his seat to don a parachute, Mackey exercised his only option and in darkness and zero visibility "rode the ship in for the crash." Mackey was conscious of hitting some trees and shut down the only running engine while trying to keep the aircraft straight. He had no memory of the final crash and awoke from unconsciousness an hour later. Exiting his seat, he started back to the cabin and "was completely surprised" to find the dead bodies of William Snailham and navigator William Bird, both wearing parachutes. Also in the cabin was Banting, still breathing but with a serious head injury and a broken arm. For unknown reasons he was not wearing a parachute. Banting spoke incoherently, and "at no time was he conscious of having been in an aeroplane crash and he was constantly dictating letters of a medical nature," said Mackey. Banting, his face bruised and eyes swollen shut, expressed no pain at any time, but had a terrific desire to undress and go to bed. "He had the idea in his mind that he was home," explained Mackey, who spent the first night trying to keep the stricken doctor comfortable and covered up on a bunk in the cabin.[17]

Not until noon the next day could Mackey get Banting to sleep. He then set out on foot for help, believing that the doctor would need immediate medical attention to survive. Using improvised snowshoes, Mackey walked about two miles, but having found no help, returned to the aircraft to discover Banting missing. Exhausted and in pain from his own injuries, Mackey rested until he regained strength enough to search the area. In the brush some twenty-five feet from the doorway of the aircraft, he found Banting's body "in a half reclining position. One of his shoes was off. He was otherwise dressed but without a top coat. He had obviously been dead for some time," observed Mackey. "I returned to the ship and took his coat and put it over him. He remained there until found by searchers."[18]

When word of the missing Hudson reached Don Bennett in Montréal, he immediately called Mackey's wife and asked whether she believed her husband to be alive. She gave a convincing "yes." It was a rather unorthodox approach, but Bennett "had heard in my various experiences in aviation of a number of occasions when through telepathic effects wives had been able to tell when their husbands were alive in doubtful circumstances." With that, Bennett set out for Gander. The RCAF, he claims, had taken over the search and denied ferry aircraft participation. Some of his crews, "furious that they had not been permitted to search for their colleague," went out anyway. Bennett smoothed things over with RCAF officers and airport authorities, and all hands decided "to carry out a land search and a limited sea search."[19]

On the fourth day at the crash site, a frustrated Mackey decided to leave the Hudson for good, having failed to attract the attention of overhead search aircraft. He set out carrying a pack with survival gear and dragging behind him the aircraft's compass on a piece of aluminum engine cowling, intending "to take a westerly direction thinking myself nearer the railway than the coast." Mackey's friend and Hudson ferry pilot Jim Allison had been two hours searching that morning when "a wisp of smoke" drew his attention. He first spotted the downed Hudson, and then "Mackey on the middle of the frozen lake," waving madly. Allison immediately radioed Gander his position, then came in low and dropped a message that help was on the way. Within minutes, other search aircraft converged to drop provisions.[20] Bennett was in the air too, and during one of his supply runs spotted two men crossing a nearby lake by dog team. "We wrote messages on paper" giving directions to the crash, "wrapped them up in packages," and threw them to the men below. Back at Gander, Bennett was pleased to find Fox Moth VO-ADE on the ground. The pilot, Captain Fraser, immediately left with Bennett and "did a good job of getting us down close to the wreckage." To Bennett's surprise, there was no sign of life.[21] The two men he had earlier messaged, Dalton Abbott and Walter

Hicks, along with their trapping companions Harold Hicks and Tobias Mouland, had been quick to the scene and already taken Mackey by sled to Musgrave Harbour, a distance of ten miles. The bodies of Banting, Snailham, and Bird were still at the crash site, but townspeople, having also received airdropped messages, shortly moved them by sled to the local Loyal Orange Lodge.[22] Several days later, three ski-equipped aircraft flown in from Canada landed at Gander with the deceased men and an injured Mackey. The next evening, Mackey gave a party for all those who aided in the search. "He appeared for a few minutes," said McGrath, "and didn't look too bad." On 2 March, an RCAF Digby patrol bomber flew the bodies of Snailham and Bird to Dartmouth, Nova Scotia, for burial in Halifax. Also that day, a ferry service Hudson took Mackey to Montréal for hospitalization. Another carried the body of Banting to Montréal and then to Toronto for a public funeral.[23]

Meantime, news of Banting's death had created a media frenzy. Rumours were swirling. The *Ottawa Citizen* repeated a story published in the *Toronto Evening Telegram,* claiming that Banting had bandaged Mackey's injuries before dying "on a bier of broken branches." Another story on the same page told erroneously how all four occupants had been wearing parachutes.[24] Several weeks later, Mackey clarified the facts in a firsthand account to the *Montreal Star* newspaper: "There have been various speculations by others that might be dealt with. One was to the effect that Sir Frederick had dressed my injuries. This is, of course, not true for at no time was he in a condition to do so. He was unconscious when I found him ... He never at any time recovered normal consciousness." Mackey donated the proceeds from his lengthy exclusive story to Snailham's three children.[25]

Late in March, the New York *Herald Tribune* told of a story "current in aviation circles" and attributed to unnamed but "reliable informants," that someone had sabotaged the Hudson by introducing a small amount of sand and grass into the oil supply of each engine. The article's credibility took a nose-dive when it reported that one saboteur had been caught and shot in Canada "and that another was lured over the border from the United States and dealt a similar fate." The newspaper admitted that this rumour had received "little credence in responsible quarters," but they published it nonetheless.[26] Indeed, when Banting's biographer, Michael Bliss, interviewed Captain Mackey's widow in the 1980s, she repeated a similar tale, saying that two ground crew at Gander had confessed to putting sand in the Hudson's oil and were subsequently executed. Another of Bliss's sources claimed that the saboteurs were buried in unmarked graves in Newfoundland.[27] A media release from London in April 1941 likely heightened suspicion when it reported that Lord Beaverbrook had disclosed to the House of Lords that to date, Banting's aircraft was the only one lost in the transatlantic ferry service.[28] There had been, of course, the loss of T9446. Several months later, the same newspapers reported that a fatal B-24 Liberator crash in Scotland had claimed Captain Joseph Mackey. A retraction the following day explained that his name had been confused with that of another pilot in the casualty list. Mackey was playing golf in Ireland and awaiting a flight back to Canada when news of his "death" reached his wife in Montréal.[29] Misinformation and media misreporting kept the rumour mills turning.

The time was ripe for some fact-finding. In February 1941, operational responsibility for Gander airfield still rested with Newfoundland civil authorities, although negotiations were underway to transfer control to the RCAF. Nevertheless, that arrangement gave rise to a magisterial inquest into the deaths of Banting, Snailham, and Bird. The inquest, headed by Magistrate Malcolm Hollett, gathered witness depositions and reported on the cause of death. Knowing that the Canadians were soon to start an official accident investigation, Hollett did not inquire into certain technical aspects of the case. However, in his submission to the Newfoundland government, he did call attention to one deposition wherein witness Jerome Coulombe, CPR's chief aircraft maintenance engineer at Gander, revealed that, "To my knowledge there was no special guard put on this [Banting's] machine."[30] This remark eventually gave rise to rumours of lax and even non-existent security. Gander resident Rod Goff, staff member at the airport weather office in February 1941, was among the last to see Banting alive. Writing on the crash to the Gander *Beacon* sixty years later, he addressed this rumour and subsequent allegations that, as he put it, "the Hudsons were vulnerable to an act of sabotage." Goff pointed out that both the hangar, where ground crew serviced the aircraft, and the administration building, "were guarded by Canadian Army soldiers [of The Royal Rifles of Canada] who were fully armed."[31]

The Royal Rifles' war diary for February–March 1941 shows that the regiment's A, B, C, and D companies moved interchangeably between Gander and Botwood on defence duties, with two companies at a time guarding either location. Each newly arriving company received airport orientation and learned the positions of runways one to four, all the main buildings, and each of the nine sentry posts. When "A" company assumed sentry duties on 9 February, they were "determined to maintain and if possible raise the already high standards of guarding competency," records the war diary. "All possible avenues of danger are discussed and the means of combating them determined," continued the writer. "Our men are confident that they can combat anything from sabotage by individuals or small organized groups to a large bombing raid." That the regiment meant business became evident early that month when an unidentified prowler, either man or animal, was heard moving in the brush by the new powerhouse. After refusing to halt or give their name, the interloper retreated after a sentry opened fire. On 18 February, the regiment was "greatly pleased" to be visited by Sir Frederick Banting. A week later, company duties were extended beyond airport security to include guard duty at the crash site, pending the arrival of Canadian investigators.[32]

Among the young army guards to be carried to the site by a ski-equipped RCAF Fairchild FC-71 were Corporal Edward Sauson and rifleman Oscar Robertson. The men gathered firewood, built a lean-to from poles and brush, and settled in to keep watch. Over the next few days, some trappers, a United Church minister, and a police constable arrived from Musgrave Harbour. The Fairchild brought in reporters from the *Toronto Star Weekly* who photographed the guards and asked them questions about their duties.

The investigators came next, and then RCAF mechanics arrived to remove certain instruments from the Hudson. One day, rifleman Robertson was inside the wreck when something on the floor caught his eye. It was a smoking pipe bearing the initials "F.G.B." on the bowl and the date 1931 on the stem. "I, of course, jumped to the conclusion that these initials must be those of the late Sir Frederick Banting," said Robertson. "I will always cherish it as a souvenir of my interesting experience," he continued, and "you can be sure I am going to take great care of it."[33] After their service at Gander, the Royal Rifles shipped out to defend Hong Kong. The British colony fell to the Japanese in December 1941. Among the casualties was rifleman Robertson, while Corporal Sauson was taken prisoner and died in captivity.[34]

During his inquest, Magistrate Hollett identified issues with certain paperwork by ground engineers, noting that no one had signed the inspection sheet or completed a certificate of airworthiness. The circumstances and reasoning behind these omissions were nonetheless explainable. Coulombe's civilian assistants had completed a routine inspection of Mackey's aircraft, filled out the necessary check sheet, and declared the machine airworthy. Presumably, neither Coulombe nor his assistants signed the document, and instead of issuing an airworthiness certificate, Coulombe told Mackey verbally that his aircraft was airworthy. This practice was hardly unusual, as Coulombe had not been issuing certificates regularly since arriving at Gander.[35] Ultimately, the absence of signatures and certain paperwork was more a breach of administrative protocol, assuming one existed at the time, than an airport security matter.

Writers have likewise made an issue over the absence of the report of the official court of inquiry, despite concerted efforts by researchers to locate any of the four copies distributed to the governments of Newfoundland, Canada, and the UK, and to the chairman of the CPR Air Service Department. Nevertheless, while the official inquiry report remains elusive, other archival documents specific to the matter are not. To begin with, when a dispute arose over Banting's life insurance policy, his executors requested a copy of the accident inquiry. In communication with Canadian Secretary of State for External Affairs, Prime Minister Mackenzie King, Newfoundland Governor Walwyn advised against this for security reasons as the inquiry revealed information about the aircraft itself and procedures of the inquiry proceedings. However, the governor did not object to having the executors told "confidentially [that] the conclusions of the Court showed [the] accident to have been due to certain technical failures, and contained no suggestion that failure might have been caused by sabotage." The governor then issued a media communiqué that the findings of the court were exclusively technical and publication was not in the public's interest.[36] This reluctance to release specific details likely stimulated sabotage theories.

Perhaps the most revealing document was another communiqué from Walwyn to Prime Minister King. Early in March, inquiry president Air Commodore G.V. Walsh, RCAF, and court members Wing Commander Adams, RCAF, and Stuart Graham of the Canadian Department of Transport, inspected the crash site and sat at Gander for almost a week of discussions. Following further sittings in Montréal and Ottawa, they reported their findings, which Walwyn shared with King by telegram on 2 April 1941.[37] The court identified engine failure as the immediate cause of the accident, and the underlying cause as "failure of [the] port engine oil cooling (broken tension adjuster ring in thermostatic unit) followed by failure of feathering motor on port airscrew and subsequent seizing of [the] engine ... In the absence of direct evidence, but after obtaining expert opinion in evidence," the court was of the opinion that the "partial failure of [the] starboard engine was due to ice accretion in [the] carburetor system."[38] Captain Bennett sat in on much of the inquiry as an observer for the CPR and MAP. In his own report, Bennett concurred with the court's findings but gave an expanded and technical explanation of how a fractured lug, "to which is attached the thermostatic control spiral of the oil cooler," caused the thermostatic control to vibrate "into the 'closed' position by passing the oil direct back to the tank, cutting out all cooling." The failure of the feathering system he attributed to either particles of metal in the oil or the high oil temperature jamming the feathering pump. Consistent with the court's findings, and "in view of the symptoms and the lack of any evidence to the contrary and [due] to the fact that the pilot was running on hot air in temperatures where he would better have been on cold air," Bennett agreed that carburetor icing had most likely caused the starboard engine to fail.[39]

One purpose of any inquest or inquiry, among other things, is to identify deficiencies in the system and, as King suggested to Walwyn at the time, "to furnish recommendation[s] to prevent [the] reoccurrence of similar accident[s]."[40] Both the court of inquiry and Hollett's inquest did just that. The crash of Hudson T9449 occurred in the ferrying program's formative period when flying the Atlantic in wintertime was still fraught with unknowns. In time, Gander would become a strategic overseas refuelling and maintenance stopover, but this was hardly a foregone conclusion in February 1941. There were bugs to work out both in the air and on the ground, as revealed by engineer Gilmore's work repairing and modifying Hudsons at Saint-Hubert. Pioneer Canadian bush pilot C.H. "Punch" Dickins, now vice-chairman of the CPR Air Service Department, acknowledged as much when he told Air Commodore Walsh that current conditions had made it difficult to "get an organization set up in Newfoundland which will function smoothly and easily." The inquiry prompted Walsh to ask the CPR a series of fourteen questions that Dickins replied to individually on 25 March 1941. The questions were multifarious and perhaps not unexpected given the fledgling nature of CPR's air service operation at Gander and elsewhere. In response, Dickins addressed matters surrounding aircrew emergency procedures and medical examinations, cockpit drills, and the introduction of additional aircraft survival equipment. To address any clerical or paperwork oversights, the CPR hired a new maintenance superintendent to reorganize the system of maintenance records and the supervision of staff. Under point twelve, Dickins spoke specifically on T9449's technical malfunction, explaining that the CPR had grounded all Hudson aircraft "as soon as it was known that the adjuster ring of the thermostatic unit had shown signs of failure." The rings in all

Hudsons remaining in Canada and Newfoundland were switched out to steel rings, he added, and a quantity of like rings ordered for aircraft previously delivered to the UK. Dickins's letter likewise revealed concerns with the arrangement of the oil cooler and the "matter of ice free operation of the injection type carburettor" as fitted on Pratt and Whitney and Curtiss-Wright engines, which "we believe is receiving the attention of the National Research Council [of Canada]," the engine makers, and the Lockheed Aircraft Corporation.[41] (Documents in Ottawa confirm that the Department of External Affairs lent a copy of the inquiry proceedings to the National Research Council for review.[42]) "The matter is being vigorously followed up," Dickins concluded, "especially with the technical section in Washington and the writer is proceeding there tonight in order to follow up the various technical difficulties which have arisen in the operation of these particular engines."[43] At no time did Dickins reference or even suggest sabotage as an explanation or possibility.

Absolutely no hard evidence has surfaced to suggest that the Banting crash was anything but an unfortunate accident. "The sabotage story is in fact wildly implausible, utterly undocumented, and unnecessary to explain the crash," argues biographer Michael Bliss. Such stories persisted, he adds, "because flyers, like most of the rest of us, resist the thought of being the victim of random accidents."[44] Banting's status as a preeminent scientist gave reason for many to think much the same, and thus gave rise to the spread of rumours.

Wartime conditions and the impulse to interpret events meaningfully often fostered such rumours. Facts become scarcer due to military secrecy and censorship, so rumour acts as a substitute, filling in the gaps in one's knowledge. They become believable too, because they simplify matters, put two-and-two together, and make sense out of puzzling questions.

Parting Ways With CPR

Early in March 1941, the ferry service underwent reorganization as MAP took over direct responsibility for delivery work "and the

CPR ceased to have any part in the organization."[45] Many of CPR's flying, ground, and administrative civilian personnel stayed on under the officially named Operating Division of the Ministry of Aircraft Production. However, the term more commonly used among employees was Atlantic Ferry Organization (ATFERO).[46]

The organizational changes to the ferry service in March set in motion an April visit to Gander by Air Chief Marshal Sir Hugh Dowding, former commander-in-chief of RAF Fighter Command during the Battle of Britain. Dowding arrived from Montréal aboard a Hudson piloted by Don Bennett and carrying Joe Gilmore and "Punch" Dickins. He made a brief tour of the airfield and returned the same day.[47] Dowding was in Canada "as a special emissary of Lord Beaverbrook" to both appraise ATFERO efficiency, and "to discuss American plans for ferrying" medium- and long-range aircraft from the US to the UK by way of Greenland.[48] This proposed northern air route would have implications for Labrador too, with the Americans, led by Captain Elliott Roosevelt, son of US President Franklin D. Roosevelt and an intelligence officer at Gander with the US Army Air Corps' 21st Reconnaissance Squadron, commencing ground and aerial surveys for a suitable aerodrome site. The Canadians did likewise that spring, sending out surveyor Eric Fry with the Dominion Topographic Survey. The two parties met up in Labrador in July, shared notes, and after a joint ground survey, recommended to their respective governments a raised sandy plateau between the west end of Goose Bay and the Hamilton River, known locally as "The Berry Bank."[49]

The Return Ferry Service

Following the lull of January 1941 and the problems of February, deliveries began in earnest. In addition to some dozen Hudson crossings, March and April saw the first overseas deliveries of an LB-30 Liberator (AM259), an unarmed variant of the multi-engine Consolidated B-24, converted as a long-range cargo transport, and a Boeing B-17 Flying Fortress (AN534). The spring weather brought increased ferrying of Hudsons, B-24s, and B-17s, with totals for May reaching fifty.[50]

Not every flight went smoothly. A frightening incident that month saw one Hudson go into a spin a couple of hours out while over the North Atlantic. Captain Daniel J. Duggan regained control and radio operator Laing sent out an SOS and advised Gander that they were returning. The crew became lost on the return flight and was no doubt relieved when the airfield came into sight. Duggan got away again a week later, this time landing at Prestwick without incident.[51]

All the deliveries had consequences for the ferry service too, with many of the aircrews now overseas and temporarily unavailable. To expedite deliveries and avoid backlogs, ATFERO needed an air passenger service to fly these crews back to Montréal for further assignments. Sending men by sea on a slow-moving ship was time wasted. Still, there was the problem of the prevailing west to east winds, which created a headwind that made westbound flights harder and longer. "At the beginning of 1941," writes Sholto Watt in his early history of the Atlantic air ferry service, "transport aircraft judged fit to conduct a two-way Atlantic Ferry were not in existence."[52] This changed once the first LB-30 Liberator cargo transports became available. The ferry organization had seven such transports further modified to accommodate passengers on a Return Ferry Service, including the aforementioned AM259. To operate the service they turned to BOAC. It was a logical choice as the state-owned airline boasted a nucleus of experienced pilots and management personnel from the former Imperial Airways, which had earlier flown the experimental transatlantic flights into Botwood using Empire flying boats.[53]

Early in May 1941, Captain A.B.H. "Jimmy" Youell brought Liberator AM260 in for a landing at Gander carrying seven passengers, marking the arrival of both the Return Ferry Service's and the airfield's first east-to-west flight. Eastbound that same day was Liberator AM258 bringing Dowding back to the UK.[54] Piloted by Captain Bennett, the Liberator arrived over Gander from Montréal with the nose wheel jamming on the doors and unable to extend.

"Whilst the aircraft circled, under the control of the second pilot," recalled Bennett, "I had therefore to climb down into the nose and have him retract and then extend the undercarriage a number of times whilst I tried to hold the doors clear for the nose wheel to go down." The wheel did eventually go down, but not before Bennett injured his hand in the process.[55] After a four-hour lay-over, Bennett was off again, delivering his important passenger to Prestwick ten hours later.

The Return Ferry Service filled a gap for the transportation of important persons of various stripes. Indeed, several days after Bennett passed through carrying Air Chief Marshal Dowding, Gander welcomed General Władysław Sikorski, Prime Minister of the Polish government-in-exile, and his political adviser, Dr. Józef Retinger, both returning to the UK aboard ferry Liberator AM916, following a visit to the US.[56] Gander's ground personnel would handle about ninety east and westbound Return Ferry Service transatlantic flights in 1941.[57]

A Marine Base at Gander Lake

Early in 1941, through Squadron Leader Powell's efforts, the air service began ferrying Catalinas to the UK by way of Bermuda. This made for a long flight, with the aircraft dangerously over-loaded with fuel and equipment, "affecting their flying qualities" and reducing the safety margin, reported the air service's vice-chairman Dickins. The shorter North Atlantic route through Gander was preferred for all but wintertime flights, so the ferry service had Ian Ross supervise the development of a marine base at Gander Lake. The initial setup amounted to one scow, a slipway, six moorings, one marine foreman, and five marine assistants.[58] Ross's marine staff came to include Newfoundlanders Corwin Staples, Russ Yarn, Harry Young, and Bill Locke.[59] Early in June, Catalina W8428 arrived from Bermuda at the hands of Squadron Leader Albert A. Case and crew, becoming the first transatlantic flying boat to use the new marine facility. Following a short lay-over, after which the crew was "taken out to the aircraft in canoes, as launches were not then ready for use," the Catalina was airborne again and landed safely at Greenock, Scotland, almost fourteen hours later. The first of the large flying boats to use the marine base, a Boeing 314A Clipper named *Bristol* with British registration G-AGBZ, arrived on 18 July from Foynes, Ireland, piloted by BOAC captain John C. Kelly-Rogers.[60]

Ferry Flights and Famous Visitors

The steady flow of Hudson and Liberator bombers, and a small number of Catalinas, continued into June and July. Shortly after midnight on 18 June, Hudson AM790 arrived from Montréal carrying radio operator Richard Coates and pilots Captain Grafton Carlisle and American "aviatrix" Jacqueline Cochran. The idea that Cochran should fly a bomber overseas originated with US Major General Henry "Hap" Arnold, in hopes that the anticipated media attention would dramatize the need for pilots. The proposal created a stir among the male ferry pilots who protested the move and threatened to strike. Compromise averted any potential crisis. Cochran, as co-pilot, "was permitted to fly the Atlantic and take the controls during the flight," but Carlisle would handle the take-offs and landings. After an eighteen-hour layover at Gander, they boarded their fuelled-up Hudson carrying "plenty of sandwiches, boiled eggs and tomato juice," said Cochran. The eleven-hour ocean flight ended uneventfully at Prestwick, with Cochran soon garnering newspaper headlines in Britain and North America as "the first woman to fly a bomber across the Atlantic."[61]

A record-setting day on 8 August saw twenty-four Hudsons dispatched overseas, representing the largest number to depart the station in any one day. On 10 August, Lord Beaverbrook himself arrived from the UK by Liberator and "left by freight train for other parts of the island. The visit is extremely secret," recorded the RCAF station diary.[62] Indeed, Beaverbrook's transport aboard the slow-moving "Newfie Bullet" rail system took him to the new American naval base at Argentia. Beaverbrook, having resigned as Minister of Aircraft Production, now held the office of Minister of

Supply. Anxiously awaiting his arrival at Argentia was British Prime Minister Winston Churchill aboard HMS *Prince of Wales*.[63] Moored nearby, the USS *Augusta* carried American President Roosevelt. Here in Placentia Bay, the two leaders conferred aboard ship. Out of that meeting evolved the later-named Atlantic Charter, a joint policy statement expressing the war aims of the two countries, one at war and the other still neutral.

Back at Gander, the first local ferrying accident since the Banting tragedy occurred when on 15 August, Hudson V9181 crashed on take-off for the UK, due to starboard engine failure. The aircraft was damaged beyond repair, but its Australian pilot, Wing Commander Norman G. Mulholland, along with crewmen Sergeant John K. Cleeve and John G. Gascoigne, escaped uninjured. The trio was back again one week later with another Hudson that they flew to Prestwick without incident. Theirs was one of one hundred Hudsons safely delivered to the UK in August.[64]

Things went smoothly for the next several weeks, although a small number of Hudsons returned to Gander mid-flight due to engine or radio trouble. However, three losses would abruptly end what had otherwise been a successful and mostly accident-free six months. It started on 21 September when Hudson AE545 disappeared en route to Prestwick, piloted by twenty-five-year-old Flight Lieutenant Robert F. Leavitt, RAF, and carrying Sergeant Elwood W. McFall, RCAF, navigator, and civilian radio operator Robert D. Anderson. A week later, Hudson AM940 likewise vanished over the Atlantic with its three-man crew, Flying Officer Harold W. Oldham, RCAF, Sergeant William R. Lance, RCAF, navigator, and civilian radio operator Cyril H. Small of St. John's, Newfoundland, one of Gander's original radio staff. The bad luck continued into October when Hudson AM951 went missing on its eastbound flight to Prestwick with the loss of its all-civilian and multi-national crew, William J. Guy of Great Britain, American William A. Herron, and Canadian Clinton L. Larder.[65] Notwithstanding the regrettable losses, delivery totals for September and October eclipsed one hundred, the vast majority Hudson bombers, with a dozen LB-30 Liberator transports in the mix.[66]

Of note was the September 1941 visit by His Royal Highness Prince George, Duke of Kent. The prince was returning to the UK following a six-week Canada-wide tour of air bases and training centres. Accompanying members of his party that arrived by Return Ferry Service Liberator included Air Chief Marshal Bowhill and the Honourable Malcolm MacDonald, British High Commissioner to Canada. During his ten-hour stay, the prince inspected the Guard of Honour and station facilities, dined in the officers' mess, and officially opened the RCAF hospital, named Sir Frederick Banting Memorial Hospital.[67] The prince would die in 1942 when the Short Sunderland flying boat on which he was travelling to Iceland crashed into a Scottish hillside.[68]

As winter set in at Gander, inclement weather over the North Atlantic curtailed ferry operations, although some forty aircraft, the majority type being LB-30s, followed by a couple of Catalinas and Hudsons, safely crossed in November and December.[69]

Notwithstanding the organizational changes and the unfortunate loss of eleven aircrew, one famous civilian, and several aircraft, the first full year of ferry operations at Gander qualified as a success. Ferry crews had safely delivered some five hundred aircraft through the airfield. Hudsons represented the majority of deliveries at eighty percent, followed by Liberators, Flying Fortresses, Catalinas, two Lockheed Lodestars, and one BOAC-purchased Curtiss CW-20 (G-AGDI),[70] a prototype from which evolved the C-46 Commando transport aircraft. Concurrent with these delivery flights, changes were afoot on the ground at Gander.

CHAPTER 3 | THE BIRTH OF BEAVER CENTRE

As ferry operations quickly evolved after January 1941, the need for separate and expanded facilities at Gander became more acute. Such requirements gave rise to a new building programme to develop a site for servicing aircraft and housing personnel.

In January 1941, Gander's key infrastructure amounted to the original civil hangar (then shared between the ferry service and the RCAF), the administration building, and the thirty-room Eastbound Inn, which was simply inadequate "to handle the volume of large aircraft proposed during 1941."[1] In conversation with Lord Beaverbrook during a visit to England, C.D. Howe, Canadian minister for munitions and supply, had offered to "render any assistance he could in connection with" the growing transatlantic delivery program. The pair continued to communicate after Howe's return, and as a result, Beaverbrook had MAP representative Morris Wilson prepare a statement detailing their requirements.[2] Wilson's February 1941 memorandum to Canadian Minister of National Defence for Air C.G. Power identified the CPR air service's immediate requirements at Gander as two additional hangars and new quarters for at least 150 people. "Contractors have the Newfoundland projects in hand" but had been unable to start because a priority RCAF building programme had limited the quantity of lumber and materials available, stated a concerned Wilson. The proposed solution was to have the RCAF detach twenty-five percent of the labour "and to release sufficient materials to allow the contractor to start at once on quarters which are most urgently required."[3] In the meantime, other transient quarters were ready by summertime, adjacent to the Eastbound Inn and called the Gander Inn. Combined, the two inns could accommodate 110 people, while the Eastbound Inn also provided dining facilities, two small recreation rooms, and a bank branch.[4]

Canada Takes Control

These developments came as control of the airfield changed hands. In April 1941, the Newfoundland Commission of Government relinquished control of the airfield and the Botwood seaplane base to the RCAF, agreeing to lease to the Canadian government for fifty years the lands occupied by hangars, works, and buildings constructed at Canada's expense. The transfer agreement likewise held that on the termination of hostilities, Canada would return control to Newfoundland, which intended to operate the air bases "primarily as civil airports and in accord with their original purpose for the development of trans-Atlantic aviation."[5] Several months earlier, the US War Department, anxious to establish an air garrison in Newfoundland for operational training, American neutrality notwithstanding, put forward the idea of a lease of land adjacent to the airport and an alternative of having Canada provide the facilities on an informal basis.[6] The Canadian government, then in discussions with Newfoundland to assume control of the airfield, approached the matter cautiously. At the time, Canada was unable to "provide adequate air defence" in the area, admitted air defence minister Power in welcoming the presence of additional military forces, even though the US "would not be committed to come to our assistance," he added. Still, Canada did not want any permanent American-owned facilities "at or near the airport," said Power in rejecting the lease proposal, and the US was unlikely to contribute financially "without some share of jurisdiction and security of tenure," he cautioned.[7] Ultimately, Canada agreed to incur the cost of erecting additional buildings to accommodate some 1,350 American personnel and seventy-three aircraft.[8] This made for a unique arrangement, with US forces occupying Gander essentially as guests of the Canadians.

The UK, on the other hand, was less restricted in its activities. The Canadians agreed to make available facilities at the base and the civil hangar as required "for delivery by air of military aircraft across the Atlantic."[9] With the RCAF moving into its own newly built hangars, the air service took over the civil hangar (identified as Hangar 20) in mid-April, although "nobody knows where the door key is," said airport operations officer McGrath that first day.[10] The transfer agreement also allowed the "Atlantic Ferry Organization of the Ministry of Aircraft Production and its agents" to provide itself with "such buildings and other facilities as the Newfoundland and Canadian governments may agree to be reasonably required." To allow for this, the two governments agreed to provide the UK with suitable ground space for the erection of hangars and other buildings. In future, commanding officers at Gander's ferry unit need only notify the RCAF of their specific building requirements before carrying out construction themselves.[11]

The transfer of control also made Pattison's position as aerodrome control officer redundant, although he stayed on for a few months during the transitionary period. Newfoundland then appointed him to the permanent and pensionable post of Air Representative at Gander of the UK and Newfoundland governments. Pattison took control of the wireless organization that, for the time being at least, the Air Ministry continued to operate. Additionally, he acted as a liaison between the ministry and Canadian and American authorities at the airfield and as an advisor to Newfoundland on air matters.[12]

Construction Complications

By mid-1941, construction of ferry service facilities was underway on the east side of the airfield, supervised by John Schofield, chief architect of the Canadian National Railway, with the assistance of an experienced engineer, J.H. Norris. Schofield, praised by Wilson in correspondence with Colonel John Moore-Brabazon, Beaverbrook's replacement as Minister of Aircraft Production, "built all the TCA [Trans-Canada Air Lines] facilities across Canada and … has had a very wide experience in the design and construction of hangar accommodation."[13] Still, the state of progress suggested that the concerns expressed by Wilson in February remained largely unaddressed.

Concurrently, the ferry organization was about to undergo significant changes. Delays in the delivery of American-made aircraft from the factories had caught the attention of the Roosevelt administration. The situation "was apt to grow worse as production reaches an accelerated rate," warned the president in May 1941. Consequently, Roosevelt offered "to direct the army and navy to assume full responsibility of [the] transfer of American built aircraft from factory to [the] point of ultimate take-off," but under the condition that a military rather than civil authority accept the aircraft.[14] The British happily accepted, but satisfying the president's wishes required a reorganization of the ferry service, and a man to do it. For this, the Air Ministry appointed Air Chief Marshal Sir Frederick Bowhill.

One of Bowhill's first tasks that June before taking up his appointment was to visit North America and "to determine what modifications are required in existing arrangements."[15] On 15 June, he and William P. Hildred, Principal Assistant Secretary in the MAP, arrived at Gander from the UK by Liberator and held a joint conference with RCAF and US officers, including Captain Roosevelt.[16] Their discussions, reported conference attendee Sir Wilfrid W. Woods, Lodge's replacement as Commissioner for Public Utilities, invariably followed a line of inquiry that questioned whether the airport's facilities were sufficient to meet the needs of the ferrying organization. The busy and focussed activity of the Canadian building programme at Gander, which now included American requirements, left Bowhill concerned that aircraft ferrying had taken a backseat to Western Hemispheric defence initiatives.

This, and the Canadian and American officers' insistence on the inadequacy of Newfoundland's road and rail communications and their tendency to overstate climate difficulties, observed Woods, set Bowhill to thinking of starting delivery flights elsewhere in Canada. Squadron Leader Pattison quickly intervened and corrected the climate concerns, but the discussions revealed to Woods "a disposition that the presence of the Canadian and United States forces ... just about exhausted the capacity of the airport in regard to facilities."[17]

Surprisingly, there was little discussion on the progress, or lack thereof, to fulfil ATFERO's construction requirements, said Woods, who had previously pointed out to the RCAF's Air Commodore A.E. Godfrey that cooperation between MAP contractors and those handling the RCAF-US building development was hardly adequate. With Woods's approval, airport authorities had earlier given the Canadian-hired contractors a near-monopoly on the use of airport machinery and the local quarry. That decision had now proven problematic. Woods even intimated that this apparent unwillingness to assist ATFERO had been ordered by Ottawa and reflected how Canadian and American officers concentrated "unduly" on Western Hemispheric defence projects "to the possible prejudice of delivery flights." In conversation with Bowhill, Woods discovered that he too was conscious of this tendency. When asked of any political repercussions in Newfoundland should there be more attention given to delivery flights, Woods assured the air chief marshal that local sentiment would welcome any plans that would expedite aircraft deliveries to the UK. The people of Newfoundland have "no Western Hemispheric defence complex," assured Woods, and nothing really mattered to them "except the survival of Great Britain as the centre of the empire."[18]

Regardless, the situation suggested an absence of any immediate drive to build the required hangars and accommodations. No planes had been delayed in Newfoundland for want of facilities, assured Woods in June 1941, but with increased deliveries, "planes and crews will begin to accumulate in numbers beyond" ATFERO's capacity. Furthermore, the arrival of winter was likely to delay or halt construction, and the absence of buildings would "make it impossible to handle more than a few planes daily." Woods again approached Air Commodore Godfrey, asking that he make representations to Ottawa in hopes of inducing higher authorities to "ease their embargo on assistance to the ATFERO contractors." At Hildred's suggestion, the commissioner notified the Dominions Office of the situation as Hildred felt sure that neither they nor Air Ministry officials were aware of the low priority that Canadian and US officers at Gander assigned to delivery flights.[19]

Soon after the Gander visit, the Dominions Office notified Newfoundland that the matter of ATFERO requirements had been discussed with Canadian air defence minister Power, Chief of Air Staff L.S. Breadner, and Bowhill. The difficulty, explained the Dominions Office, lay with the RCAF's commitment to US authorities, which had absorbed all their resources of manpower and equipment. The RCAF could help, they said, but only if relieved of some of these obligations. They left it to Bowhill to seek a sympathetic ear from the Americans.[20] Power, evidently, bent somewhat on the matter and agreed to have his developers loosen their grip at Gander, but when ATFERO manager Harold Long visited the airfield early in July, he complained that cooperation from the RCAF still fell short of what was urgently required. "I foresee a really disastrous situation," Woods warned the Dominions Office, especially in light of the anticipated winter delivery agenda, "unless ATFERO's building programme is much accelerated." At any rate, the support required was "absolutely indispensable" and unlikely to materially affect Canadian commitments to the US, added Newfoundland Governor Walwyn. On 11 July, Walwyn further suggested to the Dominions Office that minister Power, then visiting London, should be urged to communicate these concerns to Ottawa.[21] The approach presumably worked. Before month's end, Sydney de Carteret, Power's deputy minister, had conferred with representatives of the RCAF and the ferry organization and its project contractor, Belmont Construction. The Canadians agreed to make crushed stone and sand available, and further instructed their director of works and buildings at Gander to exercise "discretion in authorizing a certain amount of interchanging of equipment and workmen between the two projects."[22]

The Gander project, known as Beaverbrook Centre, for Lord Beaverbrook, or Beaver Centre for short, could now forge ahead. Meanwhile, Bowhill had concluded deliberations at Gander, Montréal, Ottawa, and Washington, and became the air officer commanding-in-chief at Montréal of the new RAF Ferry Command, which took over from ATFERO on 20 July 1941.[23]

The Evolution of Beaver Centre

Belmont established a temporary work camp adjacent to the construction site and started on two side-by-side hangars, designated as numbers 21 and 22. Still, progress depended on the availability of services from the RCAF, themselves behind schedule, reported former ATFERO and now Ferry Command Assistant Operating Manager Captain Arthur Wilcockson in September 1941. Indeed, as of that date, the hangars were only fourteen percent completed, with work pending on the hangar apron, aircraft parking area, and two taxi strips.[24] Conversely, work on accommodations for civilian and military personnel had progressed swiftly, with one building almost ready for occupation. Of concern too, Bowhill pointed out to de Carteret, was whether the water, sewer, and power services that Canada agreed to provide would be available once the buildings were ready. Some personnel were living in tents, but with winter approaching, such an arrangement was untenable, stressed Bowhill, and "we must utilize our new building immediately it is ready."[25] In response, de Carteret assured Bowhill that works and buildings staff at Gander were determined to provide these services. Meantime, a temporary water line installed from nearby Deadman's Pond provided sufficient supply "pending completion of our pumping system from Gander Lake." The Canadians had also taken steps to secure two power-generating sets for Ferry Command use and anticipated having them installed by mid-October. In addition, de Carteret expected a new sewage disposal plant to be operational soon after.[26]

October closed with Belmont having completed three two-storey H-block structures next to the hangars, identified as Buildings A, B, and C.[27] The RAF permitted spouses of military personnel to live on base, but only if their wives were already residing on this side of the Atlantic.[28] They extended the same courtesy to civilian personnel. Apartments in Building B, for example, housed the families of RAF civilian employees. The Eastbound Inn rented family apartments and the Gander Inn provided additional accommodations. Hotel department staff at the RAF Gander unit managed both establishments, although located outside the designated MAP construction area. Building A housed RAF officers and other ranks in separate wings on the lower floor, and in time, some twenty female Morse code operators on the upper floor, two to a room. Building C housed permanent male residents, some of them also Morse operators. At one time or another during the war, Buildings A and C also provided various conveniences, such as a library, canteen, recreation room, and barbershop.

Once completed around mid-November, Hangar 21, the larger of the two, was linked to the administration building by teleprinter and contained three aircraft bays and a workshop as well as stores for the aircraft maintenance department (and later a billiards room). Eventually, clerical staff at the Eastbound Inn moved their offices to this hangar. Two-bay Hangar 22 likewise contained a workshop and stores, and later, a recreation room for aircrew and a cobbler shop that offered services to both military and civilian personnel.[29] A small boiler house connected the two hangars, piping underground steam heating throughout the RAF base.

The commanding officer's residence, located behind the H-blocks, counted among the few single-dwelling homes in wartime Gander. Locals called the quaint, two-storey wooden structure "The Barn," for its gambrel roof. Throughout the war, "The Barn" was a veritable VIP guesthouse, where the presiding commander entertained countless visiting military and civilian dignitaries from the Allied nations. Transient visitors included Rear Admiral Leonard W. Murray and Vice-Admiral Percy W. Nelles of the Royal Canadian Navy (RCN); Air Marshal Sir John Slessor, Air

Officer Commanding-in-Chief, RAF Coastal Command; senior RAF commander Air Chief Marshal Sir Trafford Leigh-Mallory; American general Barney M. Giles; radar developer Sir Henry Tizard; Henry H. "Hap" Arnold, Commanding General of the United States Army Air Forces (USAAF); Clement Atlee, who later replaced Churchill as prime minister; and numerous other generals, admirals, air commodores, colonels, air vice-marshals, governors, and government officials.[30]

Later in the war, officers' quarters for the Women's Auxiliary Air Force (WAAF) relocated from a building near the Eastbound Inn to the RAF side. The WAAF officers arrived from England on postings of six months to a year. The WAAFERY, as base personnel called it, was directly behind the H-blocks and between the base water tank and pump house and the cafeteria stores. The building fronted on Ross Avenue, named for Captain Ian Ross. (Eventually, the streets in the RAF sector assumed the names of people prominent in Ferry Command and in the development and operation of the Gander unit.) Other infrastructure included barracks and ancillary buildings for personnel of the works and buildings and motor transport departments, barracks for security section personnel, a carpenter shop, a paint shop, a high-frequency radio direction-finding station, and a cafeteria that occasionally doubled as a dance hall.[31]

The Social Scene

Still, the RAF sector was a bare minimum operation. In time, a scheduled bus service between Beaver Centre and the larger RCAF and USAAF sectors allowed personnel to attend church services, shows, and performances, or visit the Post Exchange and other conveniences. A scheduled service also bussed children to and from school and staff to and from the transmitting and receiving stations.[32] If Tchaikovsky, Mozart, or Wagner was your thing, you could attend the weekly "Symphonic Hour," a program of recorded music presented at the Canadian Women's Division lounge.

Phyllis Locke, wife of Ferry Command employee Bill Locke, recalled that they lived in "lovely apartments" in Building B. Wooden boardwalks connected this and other buildings in the RAF sector. At the American Red Cross, civilian housewives knit for the troops overseas, but most entertainment was homemade, remembered Locke. "Everyone ran in and out of each other's houses and there was always a party or game of cards going on somewhere." Aside from card parties and dances, "the main entertainment of the women living at Gander ... was to go to the movies. The cost was 17 cents on the American Side and that's where everyone went. The Canadian movies were much more expensive – 22 cents. All of the features were first-run shows."[33] Although this was the economical choice, adult civilians standing in line at the American cinema were "admitted only after the U.S. personnel were inside," recalled Ferry Command employee James Reid. The same restriction applied to USO performances, where Reid saw Hollywood celebrity Joan Blondell.[34] Gander-based Ferry Command wireless radio operator Roland Masse had his own Hollywood run-in while lined up at the theatre. "I happened to turn around to see a tall American pilot. I am twisting my brain, trying to identify that man. I knew him from somewhere but could not recall." Suddenly, it hit him; it was actor Jimmy Stewart, now a captain and squadron commander in the US Army Air Forces.[35]

To foster esprit de corps among its personnel, the RAF formed non-public unit funds to provide recreation, entertainment, and benevolent services for civilian and military personnel. Civilians pledged a small monthly sum to the RAF Welfare Fund, and military personnel contributed to the Service Institute Fund. The funds helped others outside the unit too. The Welfare Fund, for example, donated to the Bonavista North Fire Sufferers Fund, the Newfoundland Patriotic Association, the Women's Patriotic Association, and the Permanent Marine Disasters Fund, while military and civilian personnel alike contributed to a subscription drive opened by the unit's commanding officer to provide beds for the Twillingate Hospital. The unit addressed its own medical needs using a scheme that enabled civilian personnel and their wives and children to receive free treatment at the RCAF's Banting Memorial Hospital for a small monthly fee per person, with a maximum rate of two dollars per family. Membership was voluntary and extended to domestic servants and ancillary services like the meteorological section, Shell Oil, which handled refuelling for the unit, and staff at the soon-to-be-established piggery. Other initiatives included a Suggestion Committee, which awarded monthly prizes for the best-submitted suggestion, the Gander Discussion Club for public speaking, and the Tarmac Club for civilian personnel, which opened its own building near the runway apron by Hangar 22.[36] There was also the RAF Gander Sailing Club with its single-spar Snipe sailboats. The boats, recalled John Murphy, were "built from scratch in the hangar" and used on Gander Lake.[37] When the unit commanding officer "complained mildly that the progress was slow," the builder, a man from Fortune Bay, "said the work would go faster" if he had his own axe. With that, both men were off to Fortune Bay in the unit Catalina. They returned with both axe and a supply of live lobsters, so the commander "was able to satisfy King's Regulations by reporting his admirable addition to the food supply of the base."[38]

Late Year Logistics

Gander's wireless organization (Gander radio VOAC), or "Signals" to use the British term, underwent a managerial change in October 1941 when the Air Ministry transferred control to RAF Ferry Command to provide point-to-point (between stations) communications, ground-to-air communications, weather information, and radio direction-finding services.[39] The transfer agreement between the RAF and the Air Ministry also came with a proviso that signals continue to give service to civil aviation.[40] Henceforth, Gander signals "continued to look after the flying boat service, which operated each summer through Botwood." Englishman Frank L. Ratcliffe, an established Air Ministry civilian employee at Gander since December 1938, took charge as VOAC's radio superintendent.[41]

This development relieved Pattison of a large part of the duties he performed for the UK government, but Bowhill had something else in mind. With the ferry service now under military control, he suggested bringing Pattison back into the RAF fold with the rank of group captain and putting him in charge of the Gander operation. Newfoundland did not object at first, thinking Pattison could continue as their air representative, but balked once they became aware of the full extent of his expected RAF duties. A recall to the RAF would only weaken his position as air representative, argued Commissioner Woods in a telegram to Bowhill, and his services were too valuable to lose.[42] Newfoundland's position was agenda-driven too, as they needed Pattison to keep them closely in touch with the civil side of transatlantic operations, "which would be invaluable after the cessation of the present hostilities." Bowhill evidently conceded, and under a new arrangement, Pattison continued in his liaison role at Gander under the title Newfoundland Air Representative, and later in the war became the government's director of civil aviation.[43]

Goose Bay, Labrador

The year 1941 ended with Beaver Centre's key infrastructure ready for occupation. Moving forward, 1942 promised to be even busier both in the air and on the ground, but with this came concerns. Officials recognized that increased deliveries might create a bottleneck at Gander, especially in wintertime with inclement weather delaying crossings, so the Labrador surveys by Eric Fry and Captain Roosevelt's men took on added importance. As well as facilitating the movement of aircraft along a network of northern airways, a landing field in Labrador would alleviate congestion at Gander and "provide greater security for crews and equipment." With pressure mounting from the Americans to get the project moving, and Washington voicing its willingness to take it on themselves, the Canadians agreed to finance and construct the airfield and to provide the required facilities "as soon as possible." Work at the site jointly recommended by Fry and Roosevelt thus commenced in August 1941, supervised by the Canadian Department of Transport. The Canadians acted quickly, bringing in men, machinery, and supplies by ship and working around the clock.[44] On 3 December, Goose Bay airfield welcomed its first landplane, Quebec Airways' de Havilland DH.89 Dragon Rapide CF-BFP.[45] The chartered ski-equipped Dragon "arrived with little pomp and less ceremony," wrote Wing Commander W.J. McFarlane, who later commanded the RCAF detachment at Goose Bay,[46] as pilot Lucien Gendron set down on the airfield's snow-compacted runway, carrying Department of Transport airways inspector Stuart Graham, who earlier sat as a member of the Banting Hudson crash court of inquiry.[47] By year's end, Goose Bay was operational and its three temporary runways "ready for the largest type of aircraft."[48] This would help relieve some pressure at Gander, but the demand would remain heavy.

John Joseph Gilmore

Clearly then, only a core ground crew with the necessary experience and leadership, based at Gander, could sustain the continuous and ever-increasing flow of medium and heavy bombers through the field. This leadership arrived late in 1941 in the form of forty-one-year-old Saint-Hubert engineer John Joseph (Joe) Gilmore, Ferry Command's new superintendent of maintenance at Gander. Gilmore's name would soon become synonymous with Gander's Ferry Command operation as the unit's resident and reliable aircraft salvage specialist. Joe Gilmore knew planes, and he could fly too, piloting countless search and rescue missions in the unit's soon-to-be-acquired Fox Moth VO-ADE, and later Noorduyn Norseman FR405. In time, the intrepid engineer and flyer would gain a reputation in nearby rural communities, accessible only by boat or aircraft, for his daring mercy flights, evacuating stricken men, women, and children to hospital at Gander. If the situation required, he might even deliver a nurse or doctor to their doorsteps.

Joe Gilmore's aviation career began in his native Ireland. Born in east Belfast in June 1900, but raised in the fishing village of

Ardglass, County Down, Gilmore took an interest in engineering and attended Downpatrick Technical School. He opened a garage in Ardglass in the early 1920s and shortly after got involved briefly with the Irish Republican Army (IRA). In July 1923, authorities arrested Gilmore and he spent time in custody for helping a wounded IRA prisoner escape to the Irish Free State. Continuing his chosen profession, he tinkered first with automobiles and then aircraft, building aircraft engines in Belfast, and further practiced his trade while employed with the Irish Free State's Army Air Corps at Baldonnel Aerodrome southwest of Dublin. Not satisfied with a ground job, he learned to fly, and in 1932 earned Irish Free State licence No. 23. The following year, at Baldonnel, he made the country's first parachute descent from an aircraft and subsequently carried out further exhibition jumps before thousands of air show spectators. Recognizing his expertise, Imperial Airways hired him in 1933 as their commercial aircraft engineer. Three years later, they chose him to be chief engineer for an experimental flight to Yemen on the Arabian Peninsula. When the airline looked to establish a transatlantic air service, they again turned to Gilmore, transferring him to their Atlantic division in 1938. Before the outbreak of war, he helped set up flying boat bases at Botwood and Boucherville, Quebec, for the experimental flights that followed. War postponed any possibility of a scheduled transatlantic commercial passenger service, and in August 1940, Imperial Airways transferred Gilmore to the recently formed CPR Air Service Department where he headed the ground engineers at Saint-Hubert.[49]

His engineering ability was also reflected in his penchant for inventing things. Among his creations, writes Gander historian Robert Pelley, was "a carburettor de-icing system and air intake shutters" for the Hudsons; a fuel-dump system for the BOAC Liberators; and, for ground operations, a "mobile generator-battery-pack to assist aircraft in start-up," an improved aircraft tow-bar, and a mobile hydraulic jack for raising airframes.[50]

A promotion to chief engineer followed in March 1941. Later that year, with the ferry service now reorganized as RAF Ferry Command, Gilmore arrived at Gander to supervise the aircraft maintenance and marine base department, and with his wife, Mary, and children, took up residence in Building B. This would be his home for the next three and a half years.

Bigger things were in store for Gander too. Demands on the airfield would continue to grow, especially with America's entry into the war in December 1941. A subsequent increase in ferry flights would require a more coordinated effort between US and RAF forces at Gander. This, and the overall progress and success of the Ferry Command unit, depended on leaders, both civilian and military, and on a committed workforce. Fortunately, Gander had both.

CHAPTER 4 | WORKING TOWARDS A COMMON CAUSE

During 1942, the need for closer cooperation between the RAF unit and US forces at Gander became increasingly apparent. Prior to America entering the conflict, the US Air Corps Ferrying Command, formed in May 1941, had been operating a transatlantic shuttle service through Gander, delivering passengers and diplomatic mail. American neutrality restricted the Air Corps from delivering aircraft to Europe. This was left to RAF Ferry Command. However, in June 1942, with America now at war and preparing to send air combat groups to the UK, the Air Corps Ferrying Command, having gained valuable experience with its overseas shuttle service, was renamed Air Transport Command, and broadened its responsibilities to include transatlantic delivery flights.[1] The shared RAF-US function at Gander in supporting overseas ferrying operations led to new working arrangements in the areas of communications and pre-flight briefings, but more especially air traffic control, which underwent major reorganization. Equally important too, were the people who operated these services, essential to the safe delivery of aircraft overseas.

The year opened with Ferry Command civilian administration and ground support employment numbers at Gander having tripled to 150 since manager Ross's arrival in February 1941. By mid-1942, that number had swelled to 334, with half working in the cafeteria, hotel, commissary, works and buildings, and motor transport departments. Their occupations varied, from general labourers, cooks, stewards, busboys, and clerks, to electricians, carpenters, heavy equipment operators, and motor pool mechanics. Aircraft maintenance and signals made up a third of the civilian workforce, while flight operations counted among its early civilian staff dispatcher E.P. "Ted" Watson, his assistant, Newfoundlander Frank Corbett, and several Newfoundland government air traffic control officers.[2]

A Guiding Hand: Controller Tom McGrath

For the first year of ferrying operations, these civilian controllers had tracked and guided each aircraft overseas from a transatlantic control centre inside the administration building. The building also housed a signals traffic room with a female cypher officer, traffic clerks, and messengers to handle coded messages for the control officers, sent over the teleprinter circuit from the wireless receiving station as it communicated with transatlantic air traffic.[3] Although the transmitter site was several miles away, radio operators at the receiving station could send transmissions remotely.[4] To maintain the efficiency of this essential arrangement, the managerial changes that saw the RAF take over the wireless organization from the Air Ministry in October 1941 likewise applied to transatlantic air traffic control. That same month, the RAF sent Flight Lieutenant D.E. O'Bryen to assist the "hard pressed" civilian control staff. O'Bryen thus became "the first RAF officer to be posted to Gander," and the senior flying control officer. A second RAF control officer, Flight Lieutenant P.J. "Paddy" Dundee, joined O'Bryen the following month. Henceforth, all control officers in flight operations would be RAF, and came to include within their ranks airport operations officer Tom McGrath.[5]

After Canada assumed control of Gander in April 1941, Tom McGrath continued as a civilian operations officer under the RCAF, but not for long. Ferry Command recognized his talents too, and more especially his "unique knowledge and experience" in connection with the transatlantic flights by CPR and ATFERO.

"It was vital," stressed Newfoundland Commissioner Woods, "that his services should be available to whatever organization was responsible for Atlantic flights." To allow civilians to carry out their duties as uniformed members, the RAF created the Civilian Component (CC) commission. On Pattison's recommendation, and with Woods's consent, McGrath accepted a CC commission with RAF Ferry Command in December 1941.[6] Now, as flying control officer, Flight Lieutenant McGrath joined Gander's transatlantic control unit (interspersed with short assignments at Goose Bay and Bermuda).[7]

Working as a controller presented a great opportunity for young McGrath. Occasionally, unit control officers did temporary duty overseas to observe and report on the various phases of control activity at other airfields. When McGrath's turn came in September 1942, he took a ferry Liberator to Prestwick and spent two weeks in the UK visiting airfields and speaking with control, signals, and meteorological officers. The system in operation at Transatlantic Air Control in Prestwick was especially eye-opening. His visit there led McGrath to recommend four modifications to Gander's control organization: installation of blackboards to track inbound and outbound flights; adoption of Prestwick's system of recording aircraft signals and wireless bearings on small slips of paper called "chits" that were then passed to the control officer and filed on a special rack (controllers were then recording information on a control sheet); installation of a weather board showing hourly conditions at airports in Newfoundland and the Maritimes; and construction of a large wall map showing all the transatlantic air routes. Control could also use the map to plot wireless telegraphy bearings. A simple but effective procedure employed at Prestwick for plotting an aircraft's position, explained McGrath, required little more than a string attached to each transatlantic direction-finding station (each with compass rose) and a pin at one end. Compass bearings received from these stations were "plotted by aligning the string and pushing the pin in the map." Where the strings intersected marked the position of the aircraft.[8] In correspondence with Dorval, which replaced Saint-Hubert in the fall of

1941 to become the "western hub of transatlantic ferrying,"[9] the unit commanding officer supported McGrath's proposed modifications, arguing that they "would increase the efficiency of control," especially during emergencies when mechanical problems or bad weather forced aircraft to return to base. The problem, however, was that the control offices in the administration building lacked sufficient wall space for all but the weather board, installed in short order at the commander's behest. The remaining modifications would have to wait, and with Dorval's approval, he added, be "put on hand" at such time that control, weather, and signals staff relocated from the administration building to Beaver Centre.[10] This was soon to happen, but with certain alterations to the control unit due to the start-up of American ferrying operations.

The Need for Integration

After the US entered the war in December 1941, activity at Gander intensified dramatically. Added manpower began to arrive and facilities in the American sector of the field expanded to accommodate impending US ferrying operations. With three military organizations, Canadian, American, and British, now sharing the airfield in separate sectors, some duplication of services was unavoidable. This arrangement rankled one US commanding officer at Gander, who saw it as "incompatible with the desired war effort." In April 1942, speaking specifically on joint operations with the RCAF, he argued that manpower and costs were doubled because of the installation of separate weather bureaus, radio ranges, telephone and teletype lines, and hospitals. Such criticisms of ground arrangements were "few in number," wrote Gander's US base unit historian, but the need for cooperation in regards to transatlantic ferrying operations would eventually demand closer collaboration with RAF Ferry Command.[11]

In August 1942, with plans already in the works for a combined RCAF-USAAF-RAF operations building for meteorological staff, air traffic control, and communications, British, Canadian, and American commanders at Gander agreed to establish a transatlantic briefing room in Hangar 9 in the US sector. A significant movement of US transatlantic air traffic anticipated any day, said Lieutenant Colonel Arthur Fickel, the American commander at Gander, in explaining this development, required "certain special facilities" for the "control of our tactical functions." The American-operated briefing unit served to brief and instruct complete crews for the US ferrying organization and commercial carriers BOAC, PAA, and American Export Airlines (AEA). Briefing officers spoke on emergency procedures, emergency alternate airfields, navigation and communications, and used maps, charts, photographs, and film footage to describe the air routes.[12] Hangar 9 also housed an American weather organization, but not until spring 1943 did it have the personnel and equipment to take over the forecasting for US transatlantic ferry flights.[13] In the meantime, a forecaster from the Canadian meteorological service office at the administration building provided transatlantic weather briefings at the hangar. The service was also booked as needed by RAF Ferry Command crews as an adjunct to the limited briefing facilities offered in Hangar 21 at Beaver Centre.[14] Within a couple months of the US organizing its new briefing unit in Hangar 9, the RAF began an expansion project at Hangar 21 to address the spatial limitations to its briefing services. Inside an annex attached to the hangar, the airmen's stand-by room was enlarged, and the pilot and radio operator briefing rooms expanded to each accommodate one hundred aircrew.[15]

Until such time that the US developed an independent communications system at Gander, the RAF signals section continued to handle all transatlantic radio traffic. In addition, the Ferry Command unit at Gander assigned radio callsigns for all aircraft proceeding on transatlantic flights (identified as external flights), irrespective of their service organization. Aircraft inbound (internal flights) to Gander from Dorval or US ferrying bases such as Presque Isle, Maine, used different callsigns, issued at their departure points. Aircraft using the northern routes might communicate with a series of ground stations along the way, so it was impossible to conceal their presence from a listening enemy. "What should be concealed," stressed RAF Group Captain G.H. Randle in discussing these procedures with US officials, is the "nature and identity of the aircraft concerned." As principal departure points on the North Atlantic ferry route, Goose Bay and Gander each had a block of callsigns from which they selected and issued one callsign to each aircraft entering that route. Aircraft flying direct to the UK retained their callsigns until reaching their final overseas destination. Aircraft proceeding to Iceland, however, were allotted new callsigns for the Iceland to Prestwick leg. Coded movement messages sent by Gander signals for air traffic control staff in the UK provided basic details, such as type and number of aircraft, serial numbers, destination, ETA, and callsigns. As a unique identifier, a callsign helped reduce the length of in-flight messages, thus speeding up the "passage of signals between the parties concerned" and serving as a "preliminary method of authentication."[16]

The function of transatlantic air traffic control at Gander, on the other hand, followed a different pattern, with RAF controllers at the administration building and an air traffic control office for American ferrying operations incorporated into Hangar 9.[17] The Hangar 9 set-up, implemented in August 1942, coincided with the expected large-scale overseas movement through Gander of B-17 Flying Fortresses and B-24 Liberators from North America flown by US combat crews, which got underway in September 1942 under the code name Bolero.[18] The Bolero plan, "formulated in the early spring of 1942," writes historian Samuel Milner, "called for the dispatch of an American expeditionary force, including ground and air forces, to the United Kingdom for operations against enemy-held Western Europe." Gander was among the airfields to assist with this aerial movement plan. The first Bolero aircraft arrived at Prestwick in July 1942 using the northern route through Goose Bay, Labrador, two newly operational US airfields in Greenland, one at Narsarsuaq near the island's southern tip, code-named Bluie West 1 (BW-1), and the other, Bluie West 8, at the head of Søndre Strømfjord on the northwest coast, and lastly, RAF Station Reykjavik, Iceland.[19] As the staging unit for the northeast ferry route, explained General Harold L. George, Commanding General of the US Air Transport Command (USATC), which handled aircraft ferrying and the transportation of cargo, personnel, and mail, the US contingent at Gander was responsible for clearing all aircraft. This meant servicing and maintenance, briefing of flight crews, communications, and weather forecasting.[20] Fortunately, collaborative arrangements between the Americans and their RAF Ferry Command counterparts on the other side of the airfield had allowed for the sharing of many such services.

The following year promised to be even busier with the US committed to increasing aircraft deliveries over the North Atlantic for their UK operations.[21] The complications inherent in having two ferrying organizations using the same air routes demanded further inter-Allied cooperation, best achieved with the integration of control for transatlantic traffic. Consequently, Bowhill and George appointed a board consisting of three RAF Ferry Command members, one each representing communications, aircraft control, and meteorology, and three equivalent USATC members. The board then set out to examine control, communications, and weather reporting services at each of the major airfields along the North Atlantic air routes, with a view to establishing joint liaison and control centres to coordinate the movement of aircraft overseas.[22]

In December 1942, Gander welcomed British board representatives meteorologist Patrick McTaggart-Cowan, Wing Commander James G.H. Jeffs, chief control officer at Dorval, and Wing Commander George C. Cunningham, chief signals officer at Dorval, along with Lieutenant Colonel Tallmadge L. Boyd (control) and Colonels Ivan L. Farman (communications) and Arthur F. Merewether (meteorology) for the Americans.[23] Bowhill had determined in advance of the board's arrival that communications and other facilities then in place in Montréal put the RAF in a "superior position so far as the main route through Gander is concerned." With this in mind, he added, Dorval briefed the RAF board representatives beforehand to push for Beaver Centre as the location for a joint liaison unit, "against which we would be prepared at Goose [Bay] to go into the American quarters."[24] Once at Gander, the board quickly determined that the existing physical layout of the airport and its control offices and meteorological and communications services made it impractical to establish the ideal control centre with all the various functions in juxtaposition. Therefore, the board decided, presumably with RAF encouragement, to build a joint control room inside Hangar 21, and recommended as well that the Canadian meteorological service be moved there from the administration building.

The decision to use Hangar 21 had no major impact on the briefing unit set-up in Hangar 9 in the American sector. With living quarters for permanent and transient US personnel located nearby, the board agreed, for reasons of practicality, to leave the existing briefing room, radio communications, and meteorological services at Hangar 9. The only exception was the air-ground radio operating staff and equipment pertaining specifically to transatlantic flights, which the board suggested be moved from Hangar 9 to a room adjacent to the planned joint control room in Hangar 21. Close liaison between the two weather services, and between the proposed control room and the existing radio transmitting and receiving sites, required that telephone and teletype equipment be installed and that USAAF communications and meteorological officers be on duty at the joint control centre.[25]

Following several days of discussions at Gander, that were "favourable to us," said control officer McGrath, the board flew to its next stop, Goose Bay.[26] In the months that followed, the board convened at airfields along the North Atlantic air routes, and later the South Atlantic routes, during which time, changes to its composition saw Group Captain Bryan D. Nicholas and Major William L. Day replace Cunningham and Farman, respectively.[27]

The Canadians were now worried about the effect this proposed joint arrangement might have on the combined RCAF-USAAF-RAF operations building then under construction in Gander's Canadian sector. The building had been planned and designed before the US contemplated large-scale ferry operations, which had triggered discussions on the integration of control. But the building was in any event impractical for a joint control centre, reported Air Commodore K.M. Guthrie, RCAF.[28] Regardless, the Canadians pushed forward with construction, as did USATC and

RAF Ferry Command officials with the joint control set-up at Beaver Centre. Structural work got underway at Hangar 21 early in 1943. The contractors made good progress, building offices and installing telephones, electrical wiring, and heating. The US Army Signal Corps provided control cables of various lengths and sizes to allow signals staff remote control of the radio transmitting and receiving equipment from inside the hangar.[29] By May, the new centre was ready for occupation and the two services opened the temporary joint RAF-USATC control room. Meteorology and signals section staff joined them as well. It made practical sense now to move the RCAF-operated control tower from the administration building to Beaver Centre. In late summer 1943, the RCAF commenced work on a new tower alongside Hangar 21 and staff transferred there in February 1944.[30]

The set-up inside Hangar 21 was similar to that of the joint operations units established at other airfields on the Atlantic air routes, such as Prestwick, Reykjavik, Lagens in the Azores, and Nutts Corner in Northern Ireland. These centres housed a large control room, a briefing room and dispatch counter, offices for supervisory, cypher, and meteorological staff, a room for ground-to-air radio operators and another for operators to communicate with other stations using wireless or teletype.[31] Gander's signals section adopted Prestwick's paper chit system, which used different coloured chits depending on the nature of the message. The operator on ground-to-air watch recorded an aircraft's destination, pilot's name, and departure and arrival times on a pink chit. Bearings went on yellow chits and messages received and sent on white and green, respectively. Inside Gander's control room, USATC and RAF controllers sat side-by-side at desks where they filed the chits on racks. This gave them a complete and readily available record for each aircraft. For tracking purposes, staff recorded flight details on a wall-size "movements" chalkboard.[32]

Gander's control centre guided aircraft eastbound overseas on the direct route until they reached longitude 30° west. At this position, Prestwick assumed control duties, provided that communication was satisfactory on long-range ground-to-air wireless radio frequency 6500 kcs (kilocycles per second). Similarly, Gander took control of aircraft westbound from Prestwick at the same position.[33] In keeping with the RAF's commitment in October 1941 to continue air traffic control services for civil aviation, the Gander Ferry Command unit sent a control officer to nearby Botwood when the flying boat season opened in springtime and commercial carriers BOAC, PAA, and AEA began their transatlantic operations. The airline companies, in turn, kept representatives in the control office at Gander when flights were due.[34] With no scheduled transatlantic passenger service as such due to the war, these airlines operated under government contract, carrying cargo, mail, diplomatic passengers, senior military personnel, and other VIPs. It was easy to detect the military personnel, said one Botwood radio operator. In the interests of secrecy and security, "they simply took off their officer's cap and tunic and put on a sweater or sports jacket to make believe they were civilians."[35]

The Men and Women of Signals

Early in 1942, Gander's signals section employed a predominately Newfoundland staff of twenty-eight that included twenty wireless operators, five radio supervisors, two radio engineers, and one radio operator.[36] Indeed, in the early days of ferrying operations, five of Gander's original operators resigned their positions to join Ferry Command as aircrew radio operators. Four gave their lives on air duty.[37] In March 1942, with Gander signals now under the auspices of Ferry Command, radio superintendent Ratcliffe received a CC commission with the rank of squadron leader and an appointment as senior signals officer. Long-standing Air Ministry employee Cecil Brant took a position in signals as radio maintenance officer with a CC commission as flight lieutenant (later squadron leader).[38] The section continued to grow with the arrival of more ground radio staff. The men and women of signals provided a critical communications link between stations on both sides of the Atlantic and with east and westbound transatlantic flights. This included American ferry flights until the fall of 1943 when the US had improved its own Army Airways Communications System station at Gander to the point of self-sufficiency.[39]

Roland Masse's Story

One cold winter's day in March 1943, Ferry Command wireless radio operator Roland Masse arrived by air from Dorval to join Gander's VOAC operating staff. His first stop was the security office for photos and fingerprints. He was then handed a mini-passport and told to carry it at all times. He made his way to his new address, the Eastbound Inn, and there met some familiar faces from the Dorval signals station. His work schedule began the next day with instructions to await transportation by the inn's main door. "The following morning," he recalled, "I boarded the bus and took a seat a few rows back. As we drove on, we came to a road curve – I saw a car coming towards us and we are not getting out of his way. I braced myself, waiting for an accident – but nothing happened! I was reminded that in Newfoundland vehicles drive on the left side of the road. My fellow passengers laughed their heads off."[40]

The bus deposited Masse and his fellow radio operators northwest of the field at the receiving station in front of a large building called the receiving house. "The main floor was the VOAC communication center," he wrote, with desks "large enough to stack two receivers. The lower one was a GE all band receiver, while the top one was an HRO National, considered top of the line in those days. The upper floor housed the station manager [Newfoundlander James Dempsey] ... Our job was to establish communications between ground station and planes, plus our other circuits specifically used to assure that airports located in the North Atlantic would receive up to date weather reports, on the hour, so crews getting ready to take off were made aware of the best routes." His time at the receiving house was short-lived, however, for in May 1943, the signals section moved to Hangar 21 at Beaver Centre. The ground-to-air room offered a "much more functional setup," recalled Masse. "We now had an RAF oversize English issue telegraph key, installed at the table's edge. Another improvement over the old receiving house was that the ground to air circuit was caged in a glass office, which served to eliminate white noise heard on speakers or headphones." The new station had two circuits to Dorval and one each to Prestwick and Ireland, with coded weather reports representing the bulk of traffic between Gander and Dorval. Eastbound aircraft needed accurate weather information from the flight-plan office, "so VOAC radio receiving the right information within the shortest possible time frame was the key to giving the green light to take off or not. Even the Americans were using VOAC radio control." Once airborne, Gander's ground radio operators could contact individual aircraft by Morse code using their assigned callsign and communicate using three-letter "Q-codes," each representing short questions, requests, or phrases. For longer, confidential messages, operations issued departing aircrews with Syko cards, used to code and decode messages. A Syko machine substituted plaintext words with a number of different cypher letters and numerals. The cypher groups changed daily and were never used again.[41]

One summer's day in July 1943, Masse witnessed a first for Gander when more than one hundred B-17 Flying Fortresses associated with US ferrying operations in the American sector of the field left for the UK. It made a lasting impression:

> They took off at one-minute intervals. The flight plan said they would fly in four-plane formations. To make sure the ships could get into position, they flew a large spiral until the first plane reached 9000 ft, where it took a sea bound direction. The second plane flew a shorter loop to position itself behind the lead plane, as did the 3rd and 4th. The spiral idea was designed to ease your way into a four plane formation, so when all planes had reached the altitude, you had a global formation of twenty-six 4-plane flights, which was quite a sight!
>
> Two or three planes had to turn back, and I saw another first for me, a huge 4-motor bomber with only one motor running, one propeller turning and the other 3 frozen. Imagine the pilot with only the outboard motor running on the left wing – he had to find a way to keep the ship flying a straight line. It looked awkward coming in on one motor and I guess I said a hundred prayers!

Masse's eventful day did not end there:

> Upon reaching altitude, each plane's wireless radio operator turned on the radio transmitter and using Morse code, began to transmit their identification. At the VOAC receiving station, you can imagine the noise Morse code characters sent by fifty or more transmitters sounded like in our earphones. It was identical to a philharmonic orchestra before a concert when musicians tune their instruments. The ground operator got very excited, completely at [a] loss, without the faintest idea how to advise these boys to stop transmitting. The officer in charge did not have a solution either. But he knew I was the most experienced operator at hand, so he came to me hoping I held the magic baton to end that symphony. He requested I take over.
>
> Now I needed someone to take care of the log. I turned to my old friend André Pepin, who had extraordinary handwriting, like that of a notary public of yesteryear. I was to handle the telegraph key. The nervous ground operator was anxious to know if we had some procedure in mind, so we quickly answered: "None"! I would simply wait until transmissions quieted down a bit and would then take control. The planes had just began an eight-hour flight or more – so we had plenty of time to complete the roll call.
>
> Finally the frequency is quiet. I sent out a three-word message QRT, meaning no more sending. I began by calling the lead plane. André was logging and we got answers from all of the remaining hundred or so planes remaining on mission. The original arrangement was only the lead plane of each group had to report every thirty minutes while flying over the ocean. But in case of trouble any plane can break radio silence ... We fellows in the radio room had lived through quite a day and it remained a subject of discussion for quite a few days![42]

Just as control officers did temporary duty at Botwood during the summer flying boat season to fulfil their commitment to the civil airlines, so too did Gander's signals section radio operators. Masse arrived there one August on loan to PAA, AEA, and BOAC. "This was quite a change from the busy life in Gander," he admitted, as you were in service only when an aircraft departed. This occasionally allowed him a day or two off between flights. "The receiving station was just a small wooden construction inside an RCAF base compound ... connected to Gander via teletype machine, and all coded messages coming from the clippers were typed directly to Gander." Masse could do 35–40 words per minute in code, and this speed may have led to his selection for the job, he surmised.

One day, as a clipper was inbound, Masse noticed that radio traffic was unusually heavy. He said as much to the RAF liaison officer, but the man was strangely quiet. The clipper docked and its passengers disembarked. Masse was leaving the radio shack as one of the passengers walked towards the RCAF building, lighting a long cigar as he shuffled along. "He looks at us and gives us the V sign with his right hand while puffing on his cigar." Masse was stunned. It was Prime Minister Winston Churchill.[43]

Hazel and Gloria Do Their Part

Hazel B. Fausak (née Bjornstad) and Gloria Lindsay (née Durham) were each determined to do their part in the war effort. Both enrolled in the Radio College of Canada in Toronto, learning Morse code and radio repair. Following graduation, they were recruited by Ferry Command, and after honing their craft at Dorval for a time, shipped out by air for Gander.

Inside the radio room in Hangar 21, which was separate from the ground-to-air room, Fausak, Lindsay, and other operators, male and female, worked around the clock, handling the point-to-point circuits connecting Gander with Dorval, Prestwick, New York, and Foynes. "The messages were all coded," explained Fausak, "so we never knew their contents, except that weather reports and forecasts were all in groups of five figures. Letter messages were in five letter groups. For both weather forecasts and letter messages, the first group was a letter with four figures. For example, R1234: This gave the setting of the cipher machine to decode the messages received or encode messages to send. The messages were graded with no letter if it was an ordinary message, "P" for important, "OP" for very important and "O" for emergency." Outgoing messages were brought from the cypher office, which was run by WAAF officers, to the radio-room front-office desk. Here, they were logged and given to the operator working the target station. "We sat at a desk with a radio, a set of ear phones, typewriter, sending key, and a basket of messages," Fausak recalled. "Most of the stations were busy all day. It was, however, early in the times of radio communications so sometimes a station might fade out or be completely overshadowed by static or other interference. It was remarkable though, how that Morse signal could penetrate the noise and be audible. If we chose, we did have the option of re-routing the messages through another station that may have better contact with the first."[44]

Change of Command at the RAF Gander Unit

For more than a year beginning in February 1941, Ian Ross had managed the unit staff at Gander, but in April 1942, his term ended after BOAC requested his release for flying duties on the Return Ferry Service. He was a "prince of a man," praised John Murphy of his outgoing boss, "and admired by all the staff." Murphy even prepared Ross's farewell letter to the heads of each department wherein he expressed "my very deep gratitude to you and all the men under your command for the splendid loyalty and co-operation you have shown … I shall leave Gander with a feeling of having accomplished something towards the war effort by organizing the facilities at this airport for the Ferry Command."[45] Ross went on to head up the test department for aircraft manufacturer de Havilland Canada and later tried to wrest Murphy away from Gander to accompany him on test flights and keep statistics. Murphy gave it serious consideration, interviewed in Toronto, and completed high altitude testing at an air force unit in the area, but ultimately decided to stay in Gander.[46]

Group Captain Sidney Joseph "Jack" Cottle next assumed command of the Gander Ferry Command unit, albeit for a short few months, and became the first commanding officer to take up residence at "The Barn." As a pilot with the Royal Flying Corps in the first war, Cottle scored fourteen victories, mostly in Italy, while on operations with 45 Squadron, earning the Distinguished Flying Cross (DFC) in 1918. "He is a determined leader of patrols," reads his citation, "and conspicuous for devotion to duty."[47] Cottle's assignment at Gander marked a shift from what was essentially a civilian command under Ross, to one which reflected the ferry service's reorganization under the RAF banner. The transition would require some adjustment by the staff, warned Ross before he left, "as it is most difficult for a Service Officer to fully appreciate the view point and problems of civilians ... and you will be called upon to use tact, patience and perseverance in order to make possible the smooth running of this organization."[48] Still, while some regular RAF people arrived, the civilian population at the unit remained high at about ninety percent.[49] In keeping with military protocol, Cottle began his tenure on 12 April by issuing the first serial of routine orders or directives to unit personnel. All subsequent unit commanders did likewise every day or so, posting them in a conspicuous place for staff to read. Such orders commonly identified personnel on temporary or permanent duty, and announced promotions, new committees, social events, security regulations, and bus, cafeteria, and pay parade schedules.

Cottle's replacement, and as it turned out, the unit's longest serving commanding officer, Group Captain David F. Anderson, arrived in August 1942. Anderson would become directly involved in local flying activities and became a popular figure at the unit and throughout rural Newfoundland. Anderson's military career began in the First World War when he joined the Royal Artillery. Wounded and gassed, he returned to the UK to convalesce and then joined the RAF in 1918 at age twenty-two.[50] As a flying officer, he attended the School of Technical Training in April 1921 and six months later arrived in Iraq, attached to No. 1 Squadron. While there, he was decorated by King Faisal, friend and protégé of T.E. Lawrence, more commonly known as Lawrence of Arabia. His efforts during aerial operations in Kurdistan in 1923 earned him the DFC, and he again distinguished himself when Afghan rebels advanced on Kabul in November 1928. The RAF evacuated all the British legation staff and their families to India in one of aviation's first major airlifts, crossing mountains averaging ten thousand feet in severe winter weather. Anderson carried out eight evacuation flights and for his part received the Air Force Cross. Once, engine trouble delayed him at Kabul for five nights. Only by "hard work and ingenuity" under harsh conditions, reads his citation, did he manage to return to Peshawar carrying a full load of passengers.

The early 1930s saw Anderson posted to No. 27 Squadron at Kohut, India, where he flew as personal pilot to the Viceroy of India. In 1934, he competed in the London-to-Melbourne MacRobertson Trophy Air Race. Then, at Martlesham Heath airfield in the UK, site of the Aeroplane and Armament Experimental Establishment, he headed up the experimental test flights on the Hawker Hurricane and Supermarine Spitfire fighters, before the RAF accepted them. His steady rise in the ranks continued with a promotion to squadron leader in 1936, then wing commander, and in 1941, group captain.[51] Leaving behind his post as Assistant Air Attaché to the British Embassy in Washington, Anderson arrived at Gander with his American-born wife, Alma, in August 1942, assuming command from Group Captain Cottle.[52] His wife came to assume a role at the unit too, recalled one Gander-based Ferry Command pilot, acting as a "mother hen" to the "young, pretty, and unmarried" WAAF officers. She kept the men out of the WAAFERY and made sure "her chicks were home at a reasonable hour. The fact that her chicks worked around the clock didn't make her job any easier."[53]

Gander's Maintenance Men

As with signals, the aircraft maintenance department employed a large number of Newfoundland civilians. Among the native-born mechanics, mechanics' helpers, inspectors, and crew chiefs were men like Sam Blandford, Harry Young, James Warren, Frank Adams, Richard Gaul, John MacDonald, John Dawson, Michael Noonan, Larry Mills, Claude Burry, Gordon Locke, James Reid, and John J. "Jack" Fennell, department foreman and Gilmore's right-hand man.[54] Fennell, praised Gilmore, "could weld a steel band around a cigarette without burning the paper."[55] Some of these men entered Ferry Command as apprentices and learned their trade at Gander. Angus Steele, on the other hand, was a mechanic before the war and "the first Newfoundlander to receive a ground engineer's license." Starting in 1934, Steele worked with Captain Fraser and with the Newfoundland government's air service, and in 1940 joined the CPR. Even Gilmore's private secretary, Gerald Wakeham, was a local St. John's boy.[56] Maintenance staff from outside the former dominion included William Anderson, Charles Kane, Douglas Mitchell, Norm Linington, Leslie Musker, Vic Maki, Harold "Shorty" Foster, and Sammy Hudson.[57] Under Gilmore's direction, these men kept the ferry flights moving, working with five crews of about half a dozen men each and one crew chief. Most of the crew chiefs were Canadian, said Richard Gaul, but with time and experience, several Newfoundlanders, among them Sam Blandford, took on the job. During the busy times, said James Reid, each crew worked twenty-four hours on, twenty-four hours off, with a couple of rest days in their work rotation.[58]

When an aircraft went down, Gilmore's men jumped into action. Theirs was no easy task, as they contended with heat and mosquitoes in summer, rain and cold in fall, and snow, wind, and freezing temperatures in winter. A series of salvage operations in 1942, some occurring simultaneously or extending into subsequent years, attest to the arduous and selfless work carried out by the maintenance men of Ferry Command at Gander, as described in Chapter Five.

CHAPTER 5 | MISHAPS AND SALVAGE SAGAS

The year 1942 would prove to be a busy one for Gilmore and his maintenance team as they laboured to salvage six downed Ferry Command aircraft, and in an unusual twist, one RAF Coastal Command aircraft, their locations scattered throughout Newfoundland. Fortunately, no lives were lost in any of the seven mishaps. Unfortunately, however, two fatal accidents near the airfield, another in the Gulf of St. Lawrence, and the disappearance of twelve aircraft over the North Atlantic would stand as sober reminders of the risks associated with ferrying operations. Transoceanic flying and ferrying in general was, in the apt words of Ferry Command historian Carl Christie, "no piece of cake."

And so it was that 1942 opened with a pair of aircraft losses. Just off the Newfoundland coast on 9 January, American-born pilot Flight Lieutenant James L. Mitchell, RCAF, Pilot Officer Keith P.S. O'Donnell, RAF, navigator, and RAF radio operator Sergeant Francis Garrity, encountered mechanical trouble in Hudson V9125 and reported that they were diverting to Goose Bay. The crew kept asking for bearings but was unable to read Gander's signals, said control officer McGrath. Their last message was "SOS ENGINE DEAD." Multiple aircraft from Gander took up the search but sighted nothing. Two weeks later, some six hundred miles out from Gander, Captain Robert W. Whitmore's Hudson AM932 reported flying on one engine. An hour later, all communication with Gander failed. No SOS was received from AM932. Again, the search effort came up empty. When the RCAF sighted a man with a fire burning on an island in Notre Dame Bay, hope was renewed, but the man did not attempt to signal the aircraft for help. It turned out to be a local hunter or fisherman, and Gander heard nothing further of the missing aircraft or crewmen Whitmore, Egyptian civilian pilot Baha E. Hosny, Squadron Leader Edward D. Chantler, RAF, navigator, and Canadian civilian radio operator Horace G. Meyers.[1]

Clearly, the odds were against anyone attempting a water landing in the stormy North Atlantic at any time of the year, but especially in wintertime. Surviving the landing was one thing; being found by a ship or search aircraft among that vast ocean swell was another. Not surprisingly, the chances of survival and rescue were markedly higher if the aircraft went down on land. Search and rescue at Gander was often an informal cooperative effort using available Canadian, British, and American resources in both manpower and aircraft. Whether an aircraft went down near the airfield or some rural coastal community, or perhaps in some remote corner of the Newfoundland wilderness, the first priority was to locate and rescue the crew, or in some unfortunate instances, recover their bodies. Salvage, whether in whole or in part, was secondary and left to maintenance department personnel. Aircraft were expensive, not to mention essential to the RAF's war effort, so once Joe Gilmore assessed the condition of a downed and damaged aircraft and determined how best to proceed, his men set to work.

Hudson FH235

On 16 March 1942, engine trouble forced pilot Captain Jahaziah Shaw Webb, an American flying for the RAF Ferry Command, to land Hudson FH235 wheels-up on a snow-covered barren hill in western Newfoundland with his two-man crew. The aircraft's wireless continued to work and the uninjured crew, New Zealander Gordon A.L. Webby, navigator, and radio operator Louis A. Caldwell, reported the Hudson as undamaged. Blowing snow hampered visibility and the men initially thought they were on the Magdalen Islands, but a search aircraft from Charlottetown on Prince Edward Island quickly ruled that out. The following day came word that the crew had pinpointed their position as behind the town of Codroy in an area known locally as Brooms Hill. With this information, search aircraft soon spotted the downed aircraft and the RCAF airdropped supplies. The captain and crew then set out on foot for Codroy[2] and soon happened upon a local man, Isaac Kendall.

The arrival of three men in full flying gear at Albert Samms's home startled young Albert, then just a six-year-old. Kendall had brought the airmen there, Samms recalled years later, to see his mother, Lottie, who as local postmistress and Aircraft Detection Corps observer, could report their arrival by telegraph. A volunteer organization set up by the RCAF, the civilian corps had observers like Lottie who watched for aircraft in distress or anything of a suspicious nature.[3] Soon, Hudson FH235 was under guard by a member of the Newfoundland Ranger Force, which provided policing and other government services in isolated parts of the country. The fate of the aircraft thereafter rested in the capable hands of Gander's superintendent of maintenance.

Gilmore wasted no time. Within two days of the forced landing, he was westbound by train to Codroy with the necessary tools and equipment and a team of civilian Ferry Command mechanics and mechanics' helpers, among them Sammy Hudson, "Shorty" Foster, Bill Locke, Vic Maki, and Norm Linington.[4] On 21 March, Gilmore arranged with locals to have four teams of horses take them the five miles to the crash site. The horses managed only three miles in the deep snow, so the men covered the remaining two on foot. Gilmore made a structural assessment of FH235 and resolved to salvage it entirely. To facilitate the removal, he looked to both his mechanics and the people of Codroy, and that evening made plans for a morning return using both dog and horse teams.

The "expedition left Codroy village at 08:30 am," Gilmore jotted in his notebook, and "changed all gear to dog teams at 3 miles. Arrived at plane 10:30. Great difficulty in jacking – gave up jacking and decided to dismantle in position." Severe cold, high winds, and freezing hands made for slow and tedious progress. The men got back to Codroy around suppertime and stored their equipment in a shed for the night. The following morning, 23 March, Gilmore and his men set out again, but a snowstorm forced them back. They made a second and successful attempt that afternoon. Gilmore's crew managed three hours' work, removing the flaps and tail assembly and returning to Codroy at dark. Next day, the men removed the port and starboard wings and pumped fuel from the Hudson's tanks into barrels. A blinding snowstorm came on before further work could be done, so they walked back to Codroy, arriving drenched and fatigued.

The next morning, Gilmore's men removed the twin Wright air-cooled radial engines and along with the barrels of fuel, had them taken to Codroy on horse-drawn sleighs. Workers meanwhile pulled the fuselage and wings to the edge of a wooded area, and an "arrangement [was] made for lots of help in the morning," Gilmore noted with satisfaction. For the next five days, Gilmore, his crew, and men and boys from the area laboured to remove the dismantled aircraft. The fuselage proved the most challenging and required the use of mules, horses, dog teams, and brute force. The men attached ropes to the fuselage and dragged the aircraft downhill on a sleigh-like frame, jury-rigged from timber cut at the site. Thick woods and snow five feet deep slowed progress, making the going extremely difficult. In places, trees were cut to widen the trail and the fuselage was pulled over long wooden poles or skids positioned at intervals on the deep snow. The snow proved too soft the first day and the men gave up after two hours, hoping that overnight frost might harden the surface. The men pulled the fuselage one-half to one mile daily until reaching Codroy.[5] There, the Hudson's landing gear was jacked down and the aircraft left at Codroy to await the spring thaw when it was shipped by sea to Montréal for repairs. The aircraft bore one minor alteration. Mindful of Charles Lindbergh's famous "Spirit of St. Louis" aircraft, and to honour the work done by the people of Codroy, the salvage team stencilled the words "Spirit of Codroy" on the Hudson's nose.

The efforts of local authorities and townspeople did not go unrecognized at the command level. Writing from Montréal in April 1942, Air Chief Marshal Bowhill acknowledged to Newfoundland Commissioner for Justice and Defence, the Honourable Lewis E. Emerson, "the valuable work rendered by Ranger F. A. Thompson, both to the crew of the Hudson ... and to Mr. Gilmore."[6] Bowhill also expressed "great appreciation ... to the people of the village of Codroy" for their "extremely valuable help" in all aspects of the salvage operation.[7] Hudson FH235 was subsequently repaired to flying condition and re-entered service, only to be destroyed in a fatal crash near Wilmington, New York, in February 1943.[8]

Besides salvaging a vital piece of military hardware, the effort at Codroy also served to inspire a local lad, the aforementioned James Reid. A teenager at the time, Reid remembered "vividly [mechanics] Hudson and Foster for they put the bug in my ear to give up school and seek a job in Gander with the Ferry Command, for in their words, 'The future is in aviation.' " Mindful of this, Reid gathered his belongings and in July 1942 entrained for Gander where he immediately found employment. "I was eager to learn, kept my eyes open, and [was] given opportunities to do things. As one was given bigger jobs, an inspector would check out the completed job." In time, he became a mechanic's helper – "And I had a complete toolbox to prove it!!"[9] Like most single men in maintenance, Reid took up residence in Building C, sharing a room with Norm Linington, who, "being senior, got the top bunk."[10]

Other Losses

The month of April saw two more ferry flight losses, bringing the year's early tally to four, including the two Hudsons lost in January. Hudson FH246 disappeared on 8 April with American Richard G. Miller, a civilian pilot with almost two thousand hours of flying experience, Flying Officer William Murray, RAF, navigator, and Canadian civilian radio operator Nathan Frankelson. When and where the crew ran into difficulty was unknown, as

Gander made no wireless radio contact with the aircraft after take-off. Then, on the twenty-fifth, Liberator 41-1119 went missing en route to Prestwick, piloted by Group Captain Herbert R. Carefoot, RCAF. The aircraft carried a "most experienced crew," reported Bowhill, including Canadian civilian Hamish I. Douglas, "the best Flight Engineer in the employment of the Ferry Command." Also lost were the Liberator's first officer, Wing Commander Mervyn J.C. Stanley, RAF, Pilot Officer William G.J. Woodmason, RAF, navigator, and Canadian civilian radio operator Leo B. Doherty. Dorval's theory held that the aircraft had flown south of its track and encountered severe headwinds. Then, with the UK coast in sight and the crew believing they had enough fuel to make landfall, the aircraft ran its tanks dry at low altitude, leaving insufficient time for the pilot to carry out proper ditching procedures or the radio operator to send a distress signal. Whatever the case, search efforts from Gander for both missing aircraft came up empty.[11]

Early in May, Captain Leon Segal's Lockheed Ventura AE711 went missing while outbound from Gander for Goose Bay. Ferry Command aircraft searched unsuccessfully between the two airfields when word came from Montréal that a lighthouse keeper reported an aircraft crash in Bradore Bay on Quebec's Lower North Shore in the Gulf of St. Lawrence. An American Grumman Goose recovered the body of the Canadian navigator, Pilot Officer James Watson, and returned to Gander. Neither American civilian pilot Segal nor British civilian radio operator Martino M. Paggi were ever found. Padre Flight Lieutenant Taylor and Bishop Abraham conducted a funeral service for Watson in RCAF Hangar 5, and the airman became the first Ferry Command casualty interred at Gander cemetery.[12] The need for a military cemetery had become apparent the previous year following the fatal crash of an RCAF Digby aircraft. That accident coincided with a visit by deputy minister of National Defence for Air de Carteret, so he, together with Pattison, selected the cemetery site.[13]

The bad luck continued several days later when a signal from outbound Hudson FH269 advised that the crew was aborting its overseas nighttime flight and returning to Gander due to engine trouble. A message from Grates Cove on Newfoundland's Bay de Verde Peninsula told of a passing aircraft five miles offshore and a bright light that lit up the sea and fell into it. However, an organized search by multiple aircraft revealed nothing of RAF Wing Commander Charles F. Herrington's Hudson. He, along with Pilot Officer Richard J. Sotham, a navigator from New Zealand, and RCAF radio operator Alexander R. Montgomery, were presumed lost at sea.[14]

Ventura AE689

The next incident, although not directly related to Gander, ended on a happier note and is deserving of mention. On the evening of 23 May, Ferry Command Ventura AE689 left Dorval for Goose Bay carrying food supplies when the crew got off course and became lost. Low on fuel, the pilot force-landed in some then-unknown location, shearing off both wings in the process. The radio remained functioning and the first radio direction bearing put the aircraft in the area of Hamilton Inlet, Labrador, but a later bearing correctly showed the location as Belle Isle, an island at the entrance to the Strait of Belle Isle. Goose Bay meantime instructed the pilot to conserve his batteries and come on the air every half hour for three minutes. Search parties were organized and the equipment section at the Labrador base busied themselves overnight preparing rescue kits for dropping. Canadian aircraft out of Gander flew over the island and photographed the crash, but how the rescue unfolded was not recorded in the station diaries of either Gander or Goose Bay, while Dorval's Ferry Command operations record book made no mention whatsoever of the incident.[15] However, one story published later tells how Belle Isle lighthouse keeper Fred Roberts found the crew. The light station was located on the northeast end of Belle Isle, but this day Roberts decided to visit the marine radio station on the island's west end. He hitched up his dog team and sled and set out, covering some six miles when from atop a ridge he spotted a wrecked aircraft at the bottom of a rocky valley. Two crewmembers approached Roberts as he pulled alongside the Ventura. The third crewman, the pilot, was injured, so they put him aboard the sled, wrapped him in a blanket, and set out with Roberts on foot for the marine radio station, several miles away. Radio operators at the station got word out about the crash and crew's location and relayed the information to authorities across the strait in St. Anthony.[16] A US Grumman OA-9 Goose then went out and brought in the crew.[17] Roberts, meanwhile, had "more practical plans in mind. He and his assistant keeper returned to the crash site the same evening and rescued fresh meat, onions, juice, and spices; they would be able to serve bottled [preserved] meat, and plenty of it, throughout the spring and summer."[18] The Ventura crew was indeed fortunate, but May ended on a sour note nonetheless when Hudson FH465 went missing out of Gander carrying Pilot Officers Raymond P. Dezall (RCAF pilot) and David G. Gatehouse (RAF navigator), and RCAF radio operator Sergeant Arthur Scarth.[19]

Ventura AE862

The four-man crew of Ventura AE862 fared much better. For the pilot, Albertan Pilot Officer Harold A. Stackhouse, this would be his first ferry flight. Likewise for Pilot Officer Austin R. Vatcher, the crew's Newfoundland-born radio operator, recently finished training in Canada as a wireless operator/air gunner. He and fellow crewmembers navigator Scott and Sergeant Vernon L. Pearson likely qualified as Ferry Command's "one-trippers," earning passage overseas by delivering an aircraft. The crew left Dorval on 6 July, bound for Gander where they would refuel. The port engine failed while they were over the Gulf of St. Lawrence some sixty miles off the west coast of Newfoundland. With the port propeller now feathered, Stackhouse maintained flight on the starboard engine, until that one suddenly started to sputter, "causing an immediate loss in altitude." The crew unfeathered the port prop and tried unsuccessfully to start the engine. With Vatcher sending messages to Gander, Stackhouse scanned the coastline below for a place to land. Spotting "a small field not far from the beach," writes Gander aviation historian Frank Tibbo, he "planned the forced approach, however, just prior to reaching the field the one remaining sick engine died completely and the aircraft crash landed." The stricken machine came down on the shoreline near the community of Mainland on the Port-au-Port Peninsula. The crew escaped serious injury and Vatcher walked to Mainland and telephoned the Newfoundland Ranger in Stephenville.

The following day, a jeep from the American base at Harmon Field in western Newfoundland arrived over rough terrain to collect the stranded airmen. A Flying Fortress flew them from Harmon to Gander, and from there they hitched a ride back to Dorval on Ferry Command Hudson FH316, arriving one week after their unexpected and unscheduled visit to Mainland.[20] A salvage crew stripped the Ventura of useful parts, but the fuselage was left on the seashore to succumb to the salty ocean swell. All that remains in Mainland today is a salt-corroded engine and section of wing, removed from the beach years after the crash.

Two More Losses

The next loss came on 12 July when Hudson FK413, piloted by Flight Lieutenant Robert D. Crofton, RAF, disappeared on its Atlantic flight with Sergeants Raymond E. Wylie and Elton D. Brabender, navigator and radio operator.[21] Then, several weeks later, Gander control reported Ventura AE917 overdue and believed lost off the coast of Ireland. The radio operator's last SOS message told that the aircraft had an engine out. Based on the meagre evidence, Dorval speculated that the crew had trouble changing over gas tanks and starved the engine of fuel. Added to the list of Ferry Command missing were three RAF men, Pilot Officer Charles De Cardonnel Findlay, captain, Sergeant Rhys M. Alexander, first officer, and Pilot Officer John McCubbin, navigator, as well as Royal New Zealand Air Force radio operator Sergeant Francis A. Weaver.[22]

Hudson AM844

The month of July also found Gilmore and his men headed to another isolated location for their next major salvage operation. The forced landing of Hudson AM844 that summer presents circumstances unique to wartime Newfoundland and Labrador in that the aircraft, although RAF, was attached to neither the Ferry Command nor the Return Ferry Service; and nor was it en route to the UK when the mishap occurred. The aircraft had indeed crossed the Atlantic, but with the flight originating in the UK.

The chain of events that brought AM844 to North America began when the US declared war on Japan following its attack on Pearl Harbour on 7 December 1941. On 11 December, Japanese allies Germany and Italy declared war on the US. Germany quickly initiated Operation Paukenschlag (Drumbeat), sending U-boats to attack shipping along America's Atlantic coast. Operation Neuland (New Land) followed, extending Germany's submarine warfare into the Caribbean Sea in February 1942. United States air and naval antisubmarine warfare measures proved mostly ineffective, allowing the U-boats to inflict massive damage on Allied shipping. German submariners called it the "happy time," while German submarine commanders referred to it as "American shooting season." The "happy time" lasted until about August 1942, by which time Allied countermeasures were taking shape.[23] These measures included help from the British, who sent naval vessels and antisubmarine aircraft from 53 Squadron, RAF Coastal Command.

Number 53 Squadron's orders to proceed to the US came late in June 1942. The main objectives, explains squadron historian Jock Manson, were to "familiarize the Americans with ASV [Air-to-Surface Vessel] radar and anti-submarine procedures and also to reinforce the rather inadequate resources currently facing the U-boat menace on the other side of the Atlantic." The squadron's Hudsons were "painted white all over for this operation."

Early in July, the first three aircraft left the UK. The trio stopped en route at Iceland, Greenland, Goose Bay, and Montréal, and after a four-day journey reached their destination at the US

Naval Air Station at Quonset Point, Rhode Island. Flying operations commenced two weeks later. Back in the UK, other squadron aircraft prepared to join the advance party at Quonset Point.

Westbound Hudson AM844 departed Reykjavik on the evening of 25 July on a flight leg to Goose Bay. The Hudson made landfall but got off course and headed for Gander instead. Low on fuel and unable to reach the field due to bad weather, AM844's Australian captain, Pilot Officer Alan A. Morris, scanned below for a suitable landing place. Morris spotted some flat open ground among the thickly wooded countryside and executed a wheels-up belly landing on marshland. Their location, it turned out, put the crew about 120 miles west of Gander, but close to the railway and only ten miles east of the town of Deer Lake. Morris, his observer Sergeant A.W. Darlington, and wireless operators/air gunners Flight Sergeant Cook and Sergeant Hancox, escaped injury and were soon located and rescued.[24]

The landing had severely damaged Hudson AM844 and its future lay in doubt. "A local contractor invited to tender for the salvage," recorded the Ferry Command Gander unit diary, "quoted $15,000 for the salvage and delivery, with engines, wings and all components packed in crates F.O.B. Corner Brook." Being transported F.O.B., or Freight on Board, meant that subsequent shipping and rail charges would apply. In considering this, and the risk of damage in transit, "it was decided that unless the aircraft could be repaired 'in situ' and flown off, the only parts worth salving [salvaging] were the engine, instruments, and the radio equipment."[25] To evaluate this possibility required air and ground surveys. In mid-September, Gilmore and the unit's new commanding officer, Group Captain Anderson, took aerial photos of AM844 from a Hudson piloted by Lester E. Schaffer, himself soon to be the subject of a search and rescue operation.[26]

Late in September, an infantry party from the Gander-based Prince Edward Island Highlanders headed west by rail for Deer Lake with Gilmore, four mechanics, and two Bren gun carriers. The infantry-operated carriers were meant to transport Gilmore and his men to the crash site to complete a ground survey. The carriers ultimately proved unsuited for navigating bogs and only "with great difficulty got back to the railway." Gilmore nevertheless reached the crash and a week later was back at Gander, firmly convinced that with a new engine, two airscrews, and a pitot head mast, the aircraft could be made safe for flight.[27] In any event, this project would have to wait as immediate attention now turned to another downed Hudson.

Hudson FK559

While Gilmore was away that September inspecting AM844, Ferry Command Hudson FK559 out of Dorval appeared unannounced over the small coastal community of Boat Harbour on the Northern Peninsula. The bomber flew in low, the local story goes, its wheels lowered and the pilot intent on landing in what he thought was a meadow. It turned out to be a marsh, so when the aircraft touched down, the wheels dug in. The Hudson cartwheeled and broke into pieces but luckily did not catch fire. Startled residents, unsure if the interloper was friend or foe, greeted the injured crewmen with rifles drawn. It came about that Captain Charles B. Smith and his crew had become lost and force-landed when their fuel ran low. Locals tended to their injuries and at the schoolhouse showed the wayward airmen Boat Harbour on a globe. Townspeople next took the pair for medical attention at nearby St. Anthony, where Group Captain Anderson picked them up in an RCAF Consolidated Canso amphibious aircraft. Gilmore and his men were shortly on the scene and determined that the Hudson, although irreparable, was salvageable. Work began immediately. An RCAF Canso flew in supplies, as did Catalina FP532, sent from Dorval to assist and flown by renowned Canadian bush pilot Clarence Alvin "Duke" Schiller, now employed by Ferry Command. Portable wireless equipment and a radio operator arrived by air, and two-way communication was established between Gander and Boat Harbour.[28] Soon, Gilmore's men would attach one of Hudson FK559's usable parts to Hudson AM844. The tail section of FK559 remained in Boat Harbour, where it became a playhouse for children like Tamsey Woodward. Sixty years later, she recalled her community's role in the salvage effort:

> My grandfather, Thomas Woodward, had a storage shed that served in the summer as a kitchen for himself and his family and his sharemen. In the summer, the shed had a stove and everything my grandmother needed to cook with. In winter, it was used as a place to store wood, water, and barrels, and this is where they stored the cargo that was taken off the plane.
>
> People here, they had to watch over the military cargo and nobody was allowed in there; even the ones that guarded it didn't know what was in that shed. My mom's brother, Garfield, says he was one of a number of boys that were paid to watch the supplies after the crash, and he said they didn't get paid very much, but he was only a young boy at the time, so I suppose that's why they didn't pay him much.
>
> Later, the military came to Boat Harbour in float planes and picked up the cargo. Uncle Garfield told me there were no wharves they could come into on account of the depth of the water, so they made rafts from 45-gallon drums and put the supplies on the raft and floated it out to the planes.[29]

October's Activities

In October, repair work at Hudson AM844 near Deer Lake got underway. A full-page précis in the Ferry Command Gander diary told how the unit had salvaged "an engine from a Mk. VI Hudson … from Boat Harbour, Strait of Belle Isle, and it was decided that this could be used, provided airscrew and wiring differences between Mk. V and Mk. VI Hudsons could be reconciled." Maintenance subsequently worked out any conflicting nuances between the models, while a party of five men and a winch-equipped bulldozer brought in the engine from the rail line. The winch proved "invaluable in the bush" and enabled the bulldozer to "pull itself out of the bog."[30] The work would continue for the next couple of months.

Overseas departures for October totalled fifty-six, the majority being Douglas DB-7 Bostons, the first of this type to arrive for Atlantic delivery. Catalinas were a close second, followed by a lesser number of Liberators, Flying Fortresses, Venturas, North American B-25 Mitchells, and Martin B-26 Marauders. Not all crossed successfully. Gander made no radio contact with Ventura

AJ450 after its departure on 8 October carrying RAF Sergeants Derick Wallsh and Thomas G. Knowles, captain and first officer, Sergeant Dennis F.J. Jupp, RAF, navigator, and radio operator John R.W. Grant, RCAF. One week later, B-25 Mitchell FR369 likewise disappeared after Flight Lieutenant Ronald L. Moss, RAF, aborted the flight and turned back. Lost on this flight too were Pilot Officer Francis J. Pook and Sergeant Michael J. Gardner, RAF, navigator and first officer, and British civilian radio man Leonard R.J. Vine. On 20 October, radio trouble forced FR368 back to Gander, but the B-25 lost its port wheel on landing and the undercarriage collapsed. The mishap left the Mitchell badly damaged, but the crew escaped unhurt.

The first delivery of Bostons did not go smoothly. Boston BZ205 returned with electrical trouble and BZ196 with propeller problems. Another made two failed crossing attempts, aborting due to fuel consumption in the first case, and with radio trouble in the second. On 25 October, staff at Gander believed BZ200 to have force-landed at sea.[31] The crew had indeed made landfall, only to crash-land in County Mayo, Ireland. Two airmen escaped, but Norwegian pilot Nils B. Rasmussen was killed after the aircraft flipped over in a bog.[32]

Abner Knee to the Rescue

Bostons continued to trickle in at Gander in November, but poor weather allowed only half of the thirty on the ground that month to depart for overseas. A like number of Flying Fortresses also made the crossing. Unlike the Fortresses, however, not all the Bostons reached their destination. On 10 November, eight Bostons set out from Gander. Hope was lost when BZ215 failed to reach Reykjavik, but two days later, wireless operator Abner C. Knee, a Newfoundlander with Gander's signals section, picked up the aircraft's faint SOS transmission coming from, of all places, the Greenland ice cap. Poor weather grounded Gander's search Catalina FP532 for several days. Finally, on the seventeenth, FP532 was loaded with supplies and search personnel, including Group

Captain Anderson and RCAF medic Flight Lieutenant Wilson, who volunteered to drop by parachute if necessary. Wilson was fitted with a harness and "provided with two parachutes, one a seat type and one a lap type." The preparations were all for nought as the Catalina crew, in the midst of a crosswind run-up, received word that BW-1 in southern Greenland had closed in. The timing was perhaps fortuitous, as twenty-four hours later the Catalina crew would be needed close to home to rescue the occupants of a downed Ventura. Gander could meantime do little for the stranded airmen in Greenland. Happily, on 26 November, two weeks after the forced landing, BW-1 sent word that an American ship had picked up the men on the Greenland coast. For his efforts, commanding officer Anderson later presented wireless operator Knee with a suitably inscribed silver tankard.[33] The marooned Boston crew recognized Knee's efforts too. It took several months for navigator Albert Nash to find out who had picked up their signal, assuming all along that it was Goose Bay. An officer at Dorval eventually put Nash on the right track. One day in June 1943, during a delivery flight on the South Atlantic route, Nash was at the Royal Victoria Hotel at Nassau in the Bahamas enjoying warmer climes when he penned a letter to Knee. "We had no chance out there without your help," acknowledged Nash, "so I'm very very thankful to you." Nash hoped to fly through Gander at some point and thank Knee in person, and invited the radio operator to look him up after the war should ever he be in Winnipeg, Manitoba.[34] Abner Knee stayed on to live in Gander for years after. He passed away in 2004 at age ninety-three. His tankard is now part of the collections of the North Atlantic Aviation Museum in Gander.

Ventura AJ471

The eighteenth of November 1942 found Ventura AJ471 bound from Dorval to Goose Bay at the hands of Captain A.F.J. "Bud" Scouten. The twenty-five-year-old had taken up flying in the mid-1930s, and as his first job, airlifted freight and passengers into northern mining areas for Starratt Airways and Transportation in his home province of Manitoba. In 1939, at age twenty-two, he joined TCA, becoming their youngest-ever captain.[35] Two years later, he was with Ferry Command, gaining valuable experience on both the North and South Atlantic ferry routes. His crew assignment card gives some indication of a ferry pilot's busy schedule.

On 24 August 1941, he left Gander for the UK in Hudson V9221, completing his first overseas delivery flight. Four days later, he returned to Montréal as a passenger aboard a return ferry Liberator and picked up another Hudson. Before month's end, he was back at Gander waiting to complete an impressive second transatlantic crossing in a week. During the first half of 1942, Scouten delivered both a Liberator and a Flying Fortress overseas before embarking south in July on a series of special flights in Liberator FL919.[36] His aircraft did not leave Dorval empty, however, and on arrival at West Palm Beach, Florida, disembarked a cargo of B-26 Marauder flight crews for overseas ferrying assignments via the South Atlantic route.[37] For the next two weeks, Scouten flew roundtrip to Cairo, stopping en route at Trinidad, Belem and Natal on the Brazilian coast, Ascension Island in the South Atlantic Ocean, Accra in western Africa on the Gold Coast (now Ghana), Kano in north-central Nigeria, and Khartoum in then Anglo-Egyptian Sudan. He flew a similar route during the last two weeks of August, starting instead at Miami and bypassing Trinidad to make Borinquen Field in Puerto Rico his first stop. This time Scouten's flight plan did not include Cairo but terminated at Accra. Two days later, he landed FL919 at West Palm Beach.

Scouten returned to Montréal late in August, made two flights to Bermuda, and finished September with trips to Goose Bay and Gander. His busy schedule continued into October with a train ride to a Liberator waiting at Houlton, Maine. His ferrying assignment from Houlton included Gander for yet another successful transatlantic trip to the UK. He arrived back at Montréal by Return Ferry Service on the last day of October.

November opened with a return flight from Dorval to Goose Bay via Mont-Joli, Quebec, and then two same-day direct flights from Dorval to Goose Bay on 12 and 16 November, all in Ventura aircraft. Such non-delivery flights, commonly called milk runs, likely carried mail, freight, or passengers.[38] His next milk run from Dorval to Goose Bay on 18 November in Ventura AJ471 would not run as smoothly. When poor weather closed the Labrador airfield, Captain Scouten altered course for Gander where, as it turned out, visibility was little better. Then, while he was making a blind approach on instruments, the fuel-starved engines started to sputter. Scouten broke cloud at a few hundred feet, skimmed the treetops and belly-landed on a bog several miles east of the field. His efforts under these challenging circumstances later received praise in Bowhill's monthly operational activities report.[39] The crew and passengers, including some Canadian army personnel, were uninjured. Group Captain Anderson quickly initiated a search in Catalina FP532 and soon located the missing aircraft. In darkness, searchers dropped two emergency containers with food and sleeping bags. Scouten and army Captain Connelly had meantime left on foot for Gander. The pair plodded westward through woods and over bogs in darkness and continuous rain until reaching the airfield seventeen hours later, exhausted and functioning on only three hours sleep in the bush. The remaining stranded personnel now became priority, so Anderson took off again carrying Gilmore and four others to reconnoitre the area for rescue possibilities. A test water landing on Home Pond just north of the downed aircraft proved successful, so Anderson returned to Gander for waders, food, and other supplies and returned to the pond, beaching the aircraft on the south shore. Steering by compass, the rescue crew reached the crash an hour and a half later. Although suffering from exposure, the men at the Ventura were fit to travel and followed their rescuers back to Home Pond. They arrived in pouring rain and a ceiling of only two hundred feet, but Anderson got the Catalina safely to Gander and three of the rescued men to hospital.[40]

In addition to passengers, AJ471 also carried the eagerly awaited Goose Bay mail, left behind during the rescue. A week later, Sergeant Vanderburgh of the RCAF and another airman were assigned to collect this important postal freight. They reached the Ventura on foot with some difficulty, leaving from a bombing range several miles due south on the shores of Soulies Pond. The pair was unable to return before nightfall and spent the night in the woods, supplementing their rations with tinned corned beef from the aircraft and returning the next morning to Gander with the mail.[41]

Two months passed before a maintenance crew attempted to salvage AJ471. This time, however, the unit's newest staff aircraft Fox Moth VO-ADE would provide transport. The Newfoundland government first loaned the Moth to the RCAF, but by late 1942 it was in the hands of Gander's Ferry Command unit, rebuilt by maintenance using dismantled parts supplied by the RCAF. Gilmore's men replaced the wheels with skis and installed blind flying instruments, and after several successful test flights, deemed the machine airworthy. On 11 January 1943, Gilmore set out in VO-ADE with mechanics Sammy Hudson and Angus Steele. The passengers had left their luggage behind after the forced landing, so the men loaded it aboard the Fox Moth. Gilmore flew back to Gander with his cargo, leaving the two mechanics to dismantle the Ventura's radio and other equipment. Gilmore returned a few hours later with mechanic Richard Gaul for extra help. He was taxiing close to the Ventura when the Moth's undercarriage suddenly collapsed, leaving one wing tip resting on the snow. With no transport or communications, their options were few, so the four men plodded westward on foot, leaving the message "walking back" written in the snow. An RCAF Canso spotted the message that same day, but no aircraft were available to drop supplies. The men had no choice but to overnight in the woods and fend for themselves.[42]

Back at the Ferry Command hangar, Charles Kane of maintenance set to work making supply-dropping parachutes to Group Captain Anderson's design, using parachutes extracted from Wiley flares, slow-burning droppable flares used during emergencies to light up the terrain below. The next day, an RCAF North American Harvard from 127 Squadron with Kane aboard located the men on foot three miles from Gander. Downward from the Harvard, attached to Kane's contraption, fell thermoses of hot soup, sandwiches, and survival gear. A ground party quickly got underway, leaving from Radio Range Road north of the base as the Harvard guided them to Gilmore's location. Searchers led the exhausted men back to the road. Two went direct to hospital suffering from frostbitten feet and exposure,[43] which was no surprise since the average minimum temperature during their two days in the bush was minus fourteen degrees Celsius.[44] In the morning three days later, an RCAF Norseman flew Gilmore back to VO-ADE with two mechanics. That afternoon, Gilmore landed the partially repaired aircraft at Gander, less his two mechanics. They awaited a planned pick-up back in the wilderness by the Norseman, but now that aircraft had become unserviceable. Gilmore, unwilling to leave his men stranded again, took the Fox Moth out through snow squalls and brought them in.[45]

The ordeal was enough to convince Gilmore to suspend further attempts to salvage AJ471. A maintenance crew waited until summer 1943 to tackle the downed Ventura. Among the crew was mechanic's helper James Reid, the lad from Codroy. Years later, he recalled his first salvage operation:

> In July 1943 several of us were sent to the crash scene to salvage what we could. It meant taking the train to Benton, then a boat up the pond, then a couple hours walk through a rough trail with sleeping bags, etc., on our backs, living in a tent for a couple of weeks, and trying to survive the flies. They almost carried us away!! And it was hot!
>
> Sam Blandford was the [Crew] Chief. I know Jack Dawson and Mike Noonan were there and myself. I think Larry Mills, Dick Gaul and George Blandford were there ... There was also an old fellow who did the cooking whose name I cannot remember. He was not Aircraft Maintenance; I never saw him before or after that salvaging operation around the Ferry Command. We dismantled engines, wing tips, ailerons, rudder, flaps, cockpit equipment, including radio equipment of course. I cannot remember if we took off the wings themselves … All the exterior items only required a Phillips Screwdriver to do the job. The interior was taken care of by the experienced mechanics…
>
> Gilmore made a couple of flyovers in our Norseman and parachuted food on the marsh for us. We also had made a rig to communicate ... no cell phones then! ... 2 poles about 25 feet apart. Sam would write his notes and rig it on a line across the poles, and Joe would make passes over it until he succeeded in

hooking our string with a line (hook attached). Somebody in the Norseman manipulated.[46]

The salvage work did not end there. A party of four under Sergeant Rogers returned the following winter to recover the engines. Gilmore made several trips to nearby Soulies Pond, bringing in provisions for the crew. The work took two weeks, but the crew got the salvaged Pratt and Whitney R-2800 radial engines to Gander for shipment to Dorval.[47]

Hudson FK693

While the crew and passengers aboard Ventura AJ471 in November 1942 escaped unscathed, the same could not be said for those aboard Hudson FK693, piloted by Pilot Officer Albert M. Carey, RCAF. Late in November, the aircraft disappeared between Gander and Reykjavik carrying civilian first officer Joseph P. Kiernan, and RCAF crewmen Pilot Officer Norman A. Allen, navigator, and Flying Officer Irwin E.S. Robinson, radio operator.[48]

Boston BZ277

Two days later, on 30 November, Squadron Leader Robert E. Morrow in Boston BZ277 ran into trouble over the North Atlantic and desperately attempted to nurse his aircraft back to the Newfoundland coast.

Twenty-six-year-old Morrow, a native of Crossfield, Alberta, had been two years flying Hurricane fighters overseas. He had commanded the RCAF's 402 Squadron and completed many operational sorties, earning a DFC for "his brilliant leadership and skill … On one occasion he led the squadron in a low level attack on five enemy destroyers," reads his award citation. "Squadron Leader Morrow has destroyed one and assisted in the destruction of another hostile aircraft."[49] He returned to Canada in September 1942 on thirty days' leave before taking command of a fighting wing. "After that leave," he explained years later, "I undertook to 'working' my way back to the UK by flying an aircraft."[50]

Morrow arrived at Gander from Montréal early in November, and following a three-week delay, set out for BW-1 with Flight Sergeant J.C. McLaughlin, radio operator, and Pilot Officer C.W. Tamblyn, navigator. After setting course, Morrow climbed to thirteen thousand feet. He maintained this altitude for some three hours until, in his own words, "the cloud layer broadened into continuous light cloud with thinly defined layers, and icing was encountered." Morrow reversed course, hoping to clear the icing, then climb over the cloud tops and proceed to BW-1. Regardless, the aircraft "iced to a dangerous extent," and the de-icing paste applied to the wings at Gander had no effect. The next frightening four hours Morrow later related in detail to Group Captain Anderson:

> The aircraft was flown in high blower, full throttle and in excess of 2,000 RPM, however, it stalled several times at speeds up to 190 MPH but was stopped from spinning by application of full power and diving. I endeavoured to gain altitude but was unable to do so. No definite course was kept as it was necessary to follow cloud breaks to prevent further icing. Finally at 12,000' the a/c [aircraft] stalled and spun … I recovered from the spin and the aircraft then fell off into a spiral dive with little or no control. At approx. 3,000' altitude and at 350 MPH I recovered from the spiral dive. As I had passed through solid icing cloud from 12,000' I decided that the only hope of getting clear lay in going down to sea level on the chance of getting warmer air. Accordingly I continued to dive the a/c towards the sea. At 1,000' I eased off the dive as speed was then in excess of 400 MPH. At the same time warmer air was encountered and the ice began to break off the leading edges. At about 100' contact was made with the sea, and I followed cloud and fog breaks at sea level for approx. 20 minutes. During the time at height when the aircraft was becoming uncontrollable I instructed the radio operator to send S.O.S. as I thought there was little or no chance of survival.
>
> After 20 minutes at sea level the ceiling began to lift and I started to climb, hoping to top cloud at 13,000' as on the way out. I followed cloud breaks during the climb and was thus unable to fly correct courses. My courses varied from 230 to 330 [degrees]. During the climb back to height unavoidable icing was encountered. I topped cloud at 18,000', with some ice on the wings and set course for Gander. During this flight … I could only maintain height at 185 MPH by using high blower, full throttle and 1800 RPM.[51]

Three hours after turning back, Morrow made landfall somewhere on the Labrador coast. A lack of visible terrain made it impossible for him to pinpoint an exact position. Gander sent several QTEs (compass bearings estimating the position of the Boston), but they left the crew doubtful as none showed their position as being near land. Indeed, Morrow later estimated that all the bearings were some twenty-five degrees off, putting the Boston east of its real position. Morrow set course from the landfall position to Gander at seven thousand feet. An hour later, low on petrol, Morrow assumed he was over Newfoundland and let down through the cloud, making contact at seven hundred feet near an unknown coast. Further QTEs from Gander helped little, and zero visibility in snow squalls made flying inland impossible. Morrow was running out of options:

> At 1840 the last QTE was received giving a bearing of 358° T[rue]. We were then near Conche, which bears 338° T[rue] from Gander. At 1845 GMT I had exhausted the bomb bay tank, the port aux[iliary] tank, reduced starb[oard] aux[iliary] tank to about 15 gals and each main tank to about 10 gals. I searched the coast for a position to land and selected a position behind Conche, which was far from good, but the best I could find. At 1850 hrs the navigator bailed out over the town at an altitude of 600'. He was positioned in the nose compartment and I considered it unsafe to land with him there ... I approached into [the] wind, wheels up, at 110 MPH. The a/c flew through two fences, hit on the belly and slewed to starboard. I swung around 90 degrees on the starboard main plane and then skidded to port, breaking the port wing root. The port tail plane crumpled but prevented the aircraft from turning over.[52]

The unexpected landing rattled dishes and kettles in the town, but Morrow and McLaughlin, although shaken, escaped serious injury. Tamblyn had meantime floated down safely at nearby Berry Head and made his way to Conche.[53] Twelve-year-old John Bromley was in school when he first heard the plane and then spotted it through a window. Despite the teacher's efforts to keep the students in their seats, Bromley was out the door and running towards the downed bomber with a sprinting Father William Hennebury at his heels.[54] Hennebury, the Roman Catholic priest at Conche, took the crew to his home. Shaken by the ordeal, they quickly consumed his winter supply of brandy.[55] Morrow found accommodations at the priest's residence and Tamblyn and McLaughlin at the home of Ambrose Flynn.[56] They immediately contacted Gander using a wireless set in the town, powered by a battery from the wrecked Boston.[57] The next day, Group Captain Anderson with Captain Louis Bisson and crew attempted to pick up the men, but stormy weather forced the Catalina back to Gander.[58]

Morrow, Tamblyn, and McLaughlin started salvage operations and were soon joined by the crew of the RCAF supply ship *L.K. Sweeney*, sent at Gander's request. Using local labour, including that of young John Bromley, the salvage team removed the engines, loaded them onto log skidders, and dragged them one mile over rough ground to the shoreline. The engines were transferred to the *Sweeney* along with radios, instruments, seven machine guns, seats, and other loose and detached equipment. Morrow made provisional arrangements with Father Hennebury to supervise the dismantling of the remaining airframe for shipment at a flat rate of one hundred dollars and recommended that Ferry Command, should they wish to proceed with the work, supply the local labour with hacksaw blades, rope, and axes. Ferry Command, it turned out, had no interest in the damaged airframe.

Flight Lieutenant Braithwaite, paymaster aboard the *Sweeney*, paid all local expenses connected to the salvage and damages done by the aircraft. The total payment came in at $281, which covered hired labour, property damage, and the replacement of 195 feet of fence belonging to Leonard Bromley. As well, James and Ambrose Flynn were appointed to guard the aircraft. Morrow recommended a financial arrangement of five dollars weekly for their services and a similar amount for Leonard Bromley on whose grazing land the aircraft rested.[59] "My part in it was hauling on a rope," said John Bromley. He got seven dollars for his efforts and gave the money to his father.[60] The *Sweeney* then brought Morrow and his crewmates to the "Grenfell Mission hospital in St. Anthony for treatment of superficial injuries," and from there to Dartmouth, Nova Scotia.[61] Final word on the performance of Boston BZ277 during the flight rested with Morrow:

> The aircraft was flown for 7.25 hours plus 30 minutes ground running, after which there remained approx. 25 gallons of usable petrol. This high consumption is explained by the fact that the engines were run for long periods at full power, due to wing icing. The bomb bay tank failed after about 3 ½ hours flight. It is not known whether all the petrol was used or not. The tank gauge showed about 60 gallons remaining. This could not be measured after landing as the tank was ripped open. The feed stopped and the booster check light went out which suggested failure of the booster pump.[62]

Morrow continued his service in the RCAF and survived another crash the following year while commanding the RCAF "X" Wing in Alaska.[63] Postwar, he became a successful lawyer and businessman and directed several Canadian companies, including the Anglo-Newfoundland Development Company. Morrow passed away in 1998 at age eighty-two.[64]

A few weeks after the Boston crash, Conche resident John O'Neill found Tamblyn's headset in a clearing near Berry Head. The family kept it as a keepsake for years after.[65] Someone, presumably the maintenance staff at Gander, decided not to salvage the remaining airframe. Today, the wreckage still rests at Conche and is fenced off with interpretative signage. In 2007, the town had it formally recognized as a registered municipal heritage site.[66]

Airfield Congestion

Overall, November 1942 had been a poor month for deliveries on both the North and South Atlantic routes and included the "longest weather delay that this Command has experienced," reported Bowhill. A month-long stationary weather system over the UK had produced headwinds for half of the flight journey. In addition, some delivery aircraft were without long-range tanks and therefore had to use the Greenland to Iceland route, "where the short hours of daylight added considerably to the delays." As a result, Gander became congested with aircraft and personnel; so much so that US forces there had to house some of the crews.[67] Still, the aircraft kept coming.

Hudson FK690

The congestion continued into December, which opened with forty-two aircraft, mostly Bostons and Hudsons, grounded because of poor weather, and eighty-four aircrew and passengers accommodated at the US Army barracks.[68] Not until the night of 5/6 December did the weather allow Gander to dispatch one Flying Fortress and eight Hudsons. One Hudson, FK690, crashed right after take-off. The fully loaded bomber lifted off from runway 27 carrying two Royal Australian Air Force men, Flying Officer Ronald G.S. Burrows, pilot, and Sergeant Jack E. Fazel, radio operator, and two RAF men, Pilot Officer Graeme H. Thomson, navigator, and Sergeant Douglas P.C. Simmons, co-pilot. The Hudson started a left-hand turn at three hundred feet, losing height steadily until it crashed into heavy timber southeast of the end of the runway, taking the lives of all four. A funeral service was held two days later in RCAF Hangar 5, attended by Group Captain Anderson and thirty-six officers and airmen of the Ferry Command unit. Also present were The Prince Edward Island Highlanders and a large contingent of RCAF personnel with a firing party and escort. Following the service, the Highlanders led the procession to the cemetery, where some 250 people, civilians included, witnessed the committal services.[69]

After the funeral, news of Burrows's death reached his wife by telegram in Darlington, a small town in the Western District of Victoria, Australia. Reverend W.E. Moorhouse, Vicar of St. Paul's Church of England in nearby Camperdown, followed up with a condolence visit. "She seemed grateful for the visit," Moorhouse wrote the Australian Air Board. "I found that like nearly all the women she had taken the sad news well and was presenting a brave face to the world. Naturally she is anxious about the future of her two sons, and I promised all the help that lies in my power."[70]

Boston Delivery Woes

Personnel at the Ferry Command hangars had their hands full on 8 December with twenty-four Bostons, eight Hudsons, and two

Venturas on the ground at Gander. Among the arrivals that cold, wintry day was Boston BZ295, which Captain Schaffer landed in the early afternoon from Dorval. The brakes gave out on landing but Schaffer kept the Boston under control. However, when taxiing from the administration building to the Ferry Command hangars, Schaffer ran into a ditch at the end of the taxiing area, damaging the undercarriage, airscrews, and a wing. Schaffer also lost the belly tank, installed to carry extra fuel on medium-range aircraft flying overseas direct from Gander. The crew escaped injury, but the accident marked the beginning of a disastrous day at Gander and for Ferry Command operations in general on the North Atlantic.[71]

The weather throughout the day had been variable in both overcast and visibility, allowing six Boston bombers to depart eastbound. Only two of that number would arrive safely. Bostons BZ248 and BZ304 were not long out when engine trouble forced them back. Flight Lieutenant James E. Steel's Boston BZ222, airborne for over thirteen hours and low on fuel, completed the crossing only to crash near Martlesham Heath in Suffolk, but not before the crew managed to bail out. Captain Arnold Cowitz's Boston BZ247 left Gander early that morning on 8 December with Pilot Officer Raymond R. Hustwaite, RAF, navigator, and Canadian civilian radio operator Robert L. Abernethy, and was last heard from five hours later while over the North Atlantic.[72] The aircraft and its three-man crew vanished without a trace.

Boston BZ294

Conditions worsened that evening and for several hours a heavy snowstorm caused zero visibility at Gander. With the storm in force, two Bostons arrived from Dorval and circled the field in darkness trying to land. Boston BZ319 diverted and eventually got down safely at Harmon Field, Stephenville. The crew of Boston BZ294 decided not to divert but to attempt a final approach from the east. From inside the aircraft, the lights at Gander were visible several miles away. Suddenly, the crew "felt a series of ever increasing shocks culminating in a terrific crash."[73] Boston BZ294 was down somewhere in the snowy Newfoundland wilderness.

For twenty-three-year-old Flight Lieutenant Douglas Gordon Chown, Boston BZ294 was his first scheduled delivery. Since joining the RCAF in January 1940, the Winnipeg native had been training in Canada, first with the Hamilton Aero Club in Hamilton, Ontario, where he began preliminary instructions, and then under the British Commonwealth Air Training Plan (BCATP). The BCATP would eventually graduate more than 131,000 aircrew from training schools across Canada. Under the BCATP, Chown earned his wings at Advanced Flying Training School and progressed to Service Flying Training School, learning to operate more powerful, technically advanced aircraft with retractable undercarriages. Late in October 1942, with four hundred hours of flight time on both single- and multi-engine aircraft under his belt, Chown reported to Dorval on temporary duty with the RAF Ferry Command.[74]

Chown's navigator that day in December 1942 was Pilot Officer Kenneth Herbert Wells, a married man from Victoria, British Columbia. The twenty-four-year-old Wells trained entirely under the BCATP, moving through a succession of schools and courses until receiving his air observer's badge (air observers were later renamed navigators). He then completed courses in astronavigation at air navigation school, the final step for air observers.[75] A posting to Dorval followed, where on 8 December he boarded BZ294 with pilot Chown and radio operator Flight Sergeant Fred Richard Coates for an overseas ferry flight.

Gander tower had been in contact with the Boston that evening as it circled the airfield and then approached from the east over Soulies Pond and near Benton, a small logging town on the railway line. After the tower abruptly lost contact and the Boston did not reappear over Gander, it became evident that BZ294 had crashed. The search, a disjointed affair as it turned out, began immediately with Group Captain Anderson, RCAF medic Flight Lieutenant Wilson, and civilians Corbett, Kerr, and Blandford proceeding by rail to Benton, eight miles east of the airfield, and arriving just before midnight. Anderson gathered local information and returned to Gander while the others set out on foot to search in the surrounding bush. A fire had meantime caught the attention of an overhead RCAF Canso. For several hours the Canso patrolled between the fire and the ground party, visible by their torch signals. Inexplicably, the pilot did not attempt to direct the search party to the fire, drop a message, or go below nine hundred feet. The Canso pilot returned to Gander and made "no written report and went to bed without realizing the implications of what he had seen." The ground search party arrived back in Gander fourteen hours later, having found no trace of the downed aircraft. On 9 December, with evening setting in, Corbett briefed Anderson, who immediately called a conference in the Canadian operations room with the Canso pilot present. Another aerial search commenced with Corbett and Kerr as spotters. They soon noticed a flashing torchlight from the bush and dropped supplies by parachute, but accuracy was impossible due to darkness and because the light was displayed only momentarily and at infrequent intervals. They later learned that the supplies came down half a mile from the flashing light and were unreachable because of thick woods and snow. As nothing more could be done this day, Anderson organized a further search for dawn the next day.[76]

The search had not long started on 10 December when an RCAF Harvard spotted a lone figure, assumed to be from the Boston, in the bush three miles southeast of the radio-range station. After the man spelled out "eat" in the snow, the Harvard came in low and dropped a small package of food wrapped in a blanket while a Norseman dropped a larger parcel by parachute. At Anderson's request, the Americans flew in a ski-equipped Taylor Cub from Argentia, but the aircraft was redirected to rescue a downed Canadian Hurricane pilot, based out of Gander and missing and without food for six days. Corbett set out from Gander with a ground party, walking a compass course to the lone man. A Harvard soon appeared overhead, diving and firing its lights as though identifying the man's location. The ground party headed in that direction but neither saw nor heard anything and returned to

Gander. Corbett's party set out again the next morning, this time with Anderson directing them from above in the American Taylor Cub. Anderson dropped a message to the lone man, asking his name. The man spelled his name in the snow as "Coates," BZ294's radio operator. Anderson then dropped another message, asking if there were other survivors. Coates spelled out "No. One killed. One died." Anderson had Gander forward this information to Dorval and patrolled the distance between Coates and the ground party. Corbett's men made good time, following a frozen brook near the range station. They found Coates sheltered on its bank and quickly got him to hospital, where he was found to be suffering from minor bruises and shock.[77]

At Gander, Coates recounted the sad events following the crash. The aircraft was already on fire when "with great difficulty," he pulled himself together and forced "his muscles to work enough to get him out of the machine ... He shouted out and heard groans coming from the pilot's cockpit." His recollections were hazy, but somehow Coates got pilot Chown to safety just before "one or more tanks exploded." The pilot was in bad shape with broken legs and internal injuries. Coates feared that Wells, "who was beside him at the time of the crash, must have been killed." He searched the wreckage and along the hundred-yard scar the downed aircraft cut through the trees but saw no sign of the navigator. He then lit a fire and tried to keep the injured pilot warm with his own body.[78] The diary picks up the story from there:

> When he saw the Canso coming over, he flashed his torch sending morse signals which, however, were not recognized by the Canso as being morse signals. He realized that the aircraft had seen his signals because parachute flares were dropped right overhead; it also blinked its landing lights. When nobody came to his rescue, he decided to try and walk for help but very shortly found he was back on his own tracks in the snow. He therefore returned to the pilot and stayed with him until he died at 1100 hrs in the morning. It is tragic to think that there was a doctor and rescue party within a mile of them from about 0100 hours onwards. After the pilot died, Coates started walking in what he thought was the direction of Gander but found he had little strength and although there were aircraft overhead all day none of them saw him or his signals. As soon as night fell, he climbed a tree and saw the lights on the Radio Range Station towards

which he started walking. Next time he climbed a tree, he found that he had gone round in a circle … This happened altogether six times, but while he was walking the Canso was overhead and he periodically flashed signals to it. When the commanding officer dropped the supplies by parachute, although he could not reach them, he felt very confident that he had been located and would be seen next day. He therefore stayed by the brook in the shelter of some trees from where he was finally collected at about 1400 hours, 11 December.[79]

Having recovered sufficiently a week after his rescue, Coates, to his credit, flew as an observer in an RCAF Harvard as they attempted to pinpoint the crash location. A few days later, he was up in another aircraft searching again. A party of Prince Edward Island Highlanders had arrived at Benton by rail and proceeded to the RCAF bombing range at Soulies Pond, ready to do a ground search. They notified Gander as soon as they arrived and a Harvard renewed the search with Coates aboard. Coates dropped two messages directing the party to the crash. Searchers located the bodies of Chown and Wells and brought them to Benton by toboggan and then by rail to Gander. At the funeral held on 23 December, Squadron Leader E. Turnbull represented Ferry Command's Air Officer Commanding-in-Chief, Sir Frederick Bowhill. Also present were Group Captain L.E. Wray, commanding officer of RCAF Station Gander, and two RCAF Women's Division officers. The Canadians provided the band, firing party, escort, and bearers. Both Protestant and Roman Catholic padres conducted the service. Chown and Wells were afterwards interred at Gander cemetery. More than a year later, unit aircraft twice dropped a salvage crew at Soulies Pond, but thick brush blocked their way to the crash site and they returned to Gander. Persistence paid off, and on the third attempt, they reached the aircraft and recovered some of the crew's personal belongings.[80]

December Closes

On 10 December, two days after the crash of Boston BZ294, Dorval authorized the remaining Bostons at Gander, twenty-one in number, to return there and proceed by the South Atlantic route at each captain's discretion. The aircraft were in any event not "winterized so far as de-icing arrangements are concerned," reported Bowhill. Nevertheless, he added, none of November and December's Boston losses had been definitively attributed to ice accretion, but the lack of de-icing equipment had dampened morale among the crews who were putting their lives at risk.[81] With that, ten crews returned to Dorval with their aircraft over the next two days. Two crews took their chances and crossed the Atlantic successfully on 12 December, but the remaining nine eventually accepted the alternate route option and made their way back to Dorval during the next week.

Christmas Day saw minimal airborne activity at the Ferry Command hangars. "Christmas fare was provided for all personnel, and there was a concert at the cafeteria in the evening," recorded the unit diary. Gilmore's maintenance men, on the other hand, laboured into the holidays in isolation and bitter cold biting wind near Deer Lake at the salvage site of Hudson AM844. Indeed, the weather had turned so cold that on one December day the heating system in the Ferry Command hangars failed, delaying the departure of two Return Ferry Service Liberators. Even the water fountains froze. Still, the crew working to salvage AM844 were not entirely overlooked by the season's festivities as a Hudson got through to airdrop food supplies on Christmas Eve. The year 1942 closed with only one delivery aircraft at Gander, a B-17 Flying Fortress.[82]

Churchill's Chariot

Among the aircraft to make the crossing in 1942 was Liberator AL504, a specially modified long-range passenger transport and future occasional visitor to Gander. The aircraft, nicknamed "Commando," was flown overseas in July of that year at the hands of American-born ferry pilot Bill Vanderkloot. His reputation as an "exceptionally cool and capable pilot and superbly competent aerial navigator" had earned him a special assignment.[83] For the remainder of 1942 and into early 1943, "Commando" became Prime

Minister Winston Churchill's private transport, and Vanderkloot his personal pilot, complemented by a mixed US-Canadian crew. The twenty-seven-year-old Vanderkloot, who had been one year with the Ferry Command and before that a pilot with the US carrier Transcontinental and Western Airlines (TWA), subsequently flew the prime minister to Cairo, Egypt, in August 1942, and then on to Moscow for diplomatic meetings with Joseph Stalin. Early in 1943, Vanderkloot flew Churchill to Casablanca in French Morocco for a conference with US President Roosevelt. The risk involved was immense as these trips often crossed over enemy-occupied territory.[84] In August 1943, "Commando" was further modified for transport duties and continued carrying VIPs over the North and South Atlantic until it disappeared along with fourteen crew and passengers near the Azores in March 1945.[85]

Success in Numbers

Despite the unfortunate loss of fifty-two airmen in fifteen accidents, the men and women of Gander's Ferry Command unit could point to the successful delivery of 670 aircraft in 1942 as a testament to their efforts. Indeed, Ferry Command delivered 848 aircraft in total to the UK in 1942 via the North and South Atlantic routes, which meant that nearly eighty percent went by way of Gander. The unit also handled nearly two hundred east and westbound transatlantic Return Ferry Service Liberator flights.[86]

Gilmore and his men had proven themselves as capable aircraft salvage specialists during 1942. The year 1943 would see the maintenance department presented with further challenges, while both Gilmore and Group Captain Anderson would be called upon to demonstrate their piloting skills in search and rescue and in providing medical aid to rural Newfoundland.

CHAPTER 6 | SEARCH AND RESCUE, SALVAGE, AND SWINE

The year 1943 was to present a hodgepodge of activities at the Gander Ferry Command unit. The unit's salient function to support aircraft ferrying operations remained unchanged, as did the maintenance section's dogged work salvaging downed aircraft. The year's successful operations at Beaver Centre were marred only by the tragic loss of a Return Ferry Service Liberator near the airfield. Mercy flights and a miraculous and inspiring survival story also lay ahead for the unit, as did an enterprising and initially contentious scheme by the commanding officer to establish Beaver Centre's very own piggery. Aircrews would continue traversing the North Atlantic in numbers in 1943, delivering mostly Liberators, Catalinas, and Mitchells, while major organizational restructuring at the command level due to increased air transport requirements would see Ferry Command come to an end, at least in name.

The year opened with Hudson AM844 close to ready following repairs at the site of the July 1942 forced landing near Deer Lake, although difficulty in starting the engines had prevented completion of any final adjustments. The handy bulldozer had meantime carved out a makeshift runway measuring 450 yards by ten yards. By mid-January, maintenance had sorted out all minor mechanical issues and readied AM844 for flight. A Hudson parachuted a large fire extinguisher and dropped covers to prevent frost, ice, and snow from forming on the wing surfaces, and Gilmore arrived by

RCAF Norseman with AM844's designated pilot, Captain Al Torrey.[1] Torrey was an American of Latin parentage, wrote Ferry Command pilot Don McVicar, whose "dark good looks reminded me of the actor Ramon Navarro."[2] Torrey fired up the Hudson's engines and began his take-off run. About one hundred yards "down the snow-covered improvised runway, the port wheel broke through the crust of snow, into a hole, snapped the left leg off at the root, and the aircraft, spinning around, smashed the port wing and bent the airscrew."[3] One can imagine the shock and dismay of the mechanics who had worked so hard for months. Dejected, Gilmore, Torrey, and the party of mechanics detrained at Gander the last day of January, having been stranded at AM844 since the unsuccessful take-off attempt. Gilmore and his men thereafter had to temporarily abandon all further salvage operations on AM844 and concentrate on an aircraft that had meantime force-landed some twenty miles to the east.

Birchy Lake Salvage

Ventura AJ459 had been en route to Goose Bay from Dorval on 7 January but diverted to Gander because of poor weather. Its fate remained a mystery all day until an evening radio transmission from the aircraft revealed that Captain Lester Schaffer had run low on fuel and crash-landed on a frozen lake somewhere west of Botwood. The radio signals were too weak to get a bearing and visibility too poor to send out search aircraft.[4]

The twenty-five-year-old American-born pilot was no stranger to Gander, having stopped over in a Hudson on his first overseas ferry flight in September 1941. Since then, Schaffer had made no less than six flights to the UK via Gander and Goose Bay ferrying Hudson, Ventura, Boston, and B-25 aircraft. In between assignments, he made numerous special flights back and forth from Dorval to Gander or Goose Bay carrying mail, passengers, and supplies, as well as a flight in September 1942 to photograph downed Hudson AM844.[5] Fortunately for Schaffer, his stay in the Newfoundland wilderness was short-lived. The following day, a bonfire and flares drew the attention of two RCAF Canso search aircraft that reported the Ventura down on Birchy Lake, one hundred miles west of Gander. Soon, a Ferry Command Liberator outbound from Gander to Goose Bay circled the downed aircraft and dropped two sleeping bags. Shortly after, a ski-equipped RCAF Norseman alighted on the snow-covered lake alongside AJ459 and soon had its three uninjured crew and four passengers in the comfort of a warm building back at Gander.[6]

Gilmore's men next entered the scene, with Frank Corbett from the unit's flying operations section and a mechanic arriving on 10 January aboard an RCAF Norseman to assess the damage. When the Norseman's engine failed to start, they too, were left stranded and did not return to Gander that day as expected. An RCAF Canso went out to investigate and received a radio message from the Ventura explaining the engine problem. Following some minor repairs to the Norseman and two days on the lake, Corbett and his mechanic were able to return to Gander having salvaged the passengers' baggage, a Lear radio, and the Goose Bay mail. Back at Gander, Corbett reported that big snowdrifts had begun forming around the downed Ventura and determined that the only feasible means of salvaging the aircraft was to fly in replacement airscrews and attach them on the spot. The job required a Norseman, but the two operated by the RCAF were occupied at the time on other salvage operations, and the recently flightworthy Fox Moth was limited to light transport work.[7] Ideally, the unit needed its own rugged utility transport. Early in February, this need was met when Norseman 2486 arrived on loan from the RCAF, piloted by Captain Elwood Palmer Walmsley, a Torontonian and naturalized American. The twenty-eight-year-old was new to Ferry Command, having the month before delivered his first aircraft, Boston BZ225, to the UK by the South Atlantic route. Once back at Montréal, he was given the task of ferrying 2486 to Gander.[8]

The unit put Walmsley and 2486 to work right away, flying Group Captain Anderson to Birchy Lake to make salvage arrangements. First Class Aircraft Inspector Jack Fennell and his maintenance crew were already at the lake. They were not about to go hungry, having supplemented their food rations with rabbits and trout. The Ventura had settled below the lake surface, filled with several tons of ice. On 10 February, Fennell's crew hoisted AJ459 from the lake's icy grip, but it started to sink again. The men quickly felled some trees and made a platform that they shoved underneath the fuselage to support the weight. Work then began to get the aircraft operational. The Ventura's undercarriage was fitted with skis as part of the salvage operation, and on 25 March 1943, the aircraft was flown off Birchy Lake and on to Gander.[9] Gilmore's men had done it again!

Gander's Return Ferry Tragedy

As the maintenance crew worked to hoist and secure AJ459 that February, search aircraft at Gander were on standby, awaiting a break in the weather. Overnight, Return Ferry Service Liberator AL591 had gone missing somewhere near the field carrying twenty-one passengers and crew. To this point, tragedy had not eluded the return service on the North Atlantic route. In August and September 1941, only months after the return service's inception, crashes in Scotland of Liberators AM260, AM261, and AM915 had claimed the lives of forty-seven ferry personnel and seven civilian passengers.[10] Among AM260's deceased was Nova Scotian John J. MacDonald, another of Gander's former radio operators.[11] Sadly, AL591 would increase by nineteen the number of lives lost on the return service.

On the morning of 9 February, Liberators AL591 and AL529 left Prestwick, Scotland, within minutes of one another, loaded with returning aircrew. Piloting AL529 this winter day was Captain W.L. "Geordie" Stewart, who had piloted Hudson T9434 during the second delivery flight of Hudson bombers out of Gander in November 1940. He transferred to the return service soon after its formation in May 1941. Stewart's counterpart in AL591 was Englishman Captain G.P.M. "Pat" Eves. Both were experienced trans-atlantic pilots. The thirty-two-year-old Eves had joined Imperial Airways in 1936 and regularly flew the Imperial air routes into the

Middle East, India, Australia, and Singapore. In 1940, he left the UK for Canada and joined the CPR Air Service Department. Like Stewart, he delivered a Hudson bomber on the second flight out of Gander in November 1940. He completed six months as the service's chief flying instructor and in November 1941 transferred to the BOAC Return Ferry Service.[12]

The westerly headwinds, caused by the then little-understood jet stream, were particularly strong this day, increasing the flight time and therefore fuel consumption. Indeed, "the adverse winds proved to have been double the strength of those forecast," later reported former MAP secretary William Hildred, who in 1941 was appointed Director-General of Civil Aviation at the British Air Ministry. The flight crews also had to contend with poor radio reception that day, and in AL591, stuck fuel gauges.[13] Once they passed their point of no return, that imaginary line over the Atlantic where an aircraft's reserve fuel was not sufficient to turn back, the two Liberators could only push onwards. At Gander, the "weather deteriorated towards the late afternoon eventually becoming zero zero," recorded the unit diary. Gander control therefore instructed westbound ferry aircraft to divert to Sydney, Nova Scotia.[14] Captain Stewart in AL529 "did not hesitate after he heard that Sydney had a ceiling of 1,000 with visibility more than 15 miles," said ferry pilot and passenger Don McVicar. Captain Eves in AL591, believing he lacked sufficient fuel to make Sydney, decided otherwise. Stewart flew onward to his alternate, "desperately worried" as he listened to his friend's transmissions. "He wanted to help," said McVicar, "yet all he could do was keep his radio off the air."[15]

Meantime, staff at Gander were "astounded when 591 said it was coming in here." Emergency procedures were immediately put into operation.[16] Eves arrived over the field in darkness and a ceiling of two hundred feet with a heavy fall of sleet making visibility poor. The Liberator circled the field several times at about 100–200 feet in an attempt to land, but Eves reported seeing nothing but a blur of lights.[17] Years later, Newfoundlander Walter Vivian, a civilian employee with Ferry Command, recalled seeing AL591's navigation lights as it passed overhead at low altitude. "I was in security there doing duty from one to six," said Vivian, "and I think it was between five-thirty and six [local] that she came over and we lost the sound of her and that was it."[18] A Canadian accident investigation officer, present at Gander on another matter, later gathered information, albeit unofficially, that the control officer had asked Eves to make a 360-degree turn while staff got a direction-finding bearing so the tower could verbally direct the landing by radio.[19] Shortly after, with Eves somewhere northeast of the aerodrome, the tower abruptly lost contact with the aircraft. Airborne sixteen hours and thirty-two minutes and having circled the airfield for one and a half hours, Liberator AL591 had exhausted its fuel supply of thirty-one hundred US gallons and dropped from the sky.[20]

The low ceiling and poor visibility that night kept search aircraft grounded. The next day's weather proved no better as search aircraft waited on standby. Just after midnight, a break allowed Captain Walmsley and Squadron Leader J.W. Powell to take off in the Norseman. The pair "flew for an hour and a half in an endeavour to find flames or lights from the missing aircraft. The weather was not at all pleasant and no lights were seen." February 11 brought better conditions. At daylight, three Ferry Command Hudsons, Norseman 2486, and Fox Moth VO-ADE commenced a search.[21] Flying Officer Walz and Sergeant Bockman from 127 Squadron, RCAF, also took to the air. The pair flew their Harvard on a course of 120 degrees magnetic to the north border of Soulies Pond and gently turned on a northern heading. Five minutes later, red flares appeared on their port side.[22] Below, on a snow-covered bog, two figures "were waving feebly as we passed overhead," Bockman recalled years later. "Six feet of the nose was buried in snow while the fuselage was broken in two behind the wing, hurling bodies out in all directions."[23] The tail section lay relatively intact. The sudden impact had broken the wings and dislodged the four engines from their mounts. The forward section had simply disappeared into the bog, along with five men.

The Norseman and Fox Moth landed alongside the wreckage and found three survivors, all passengers. The other eighteen passengers and crew had perished. The Moth immediately flew a seriously injured Sergeant Graham P. Pollard to Gander for medical attention. The remaining two survivors, Pilot Officer Cyril M. Abelson and Captain Kingsbury E. "King" Parker Jr., followed shortly. Group Captain Anderson flew in to assess the scene and returned to Gander to organize the salvage and recovery effort, which proceeded uninterrupted the entire day. Captain Walmsley operated the Norseman, while Anderson and Gilmore were in the Fox Moth. The two aircraft made a total of seventeen trips, bringing in thirteen bodies and various pieces of equipment.[24] Sadly, twenty-year-old Pollard succumbed to his injuries shortly after hospitalization.[25] A funeral service for Pollard and the thirteen recovered victims was held in the drill hall on 15 February with Anderson and his wife representing Sir Frederick and Lady Bowhill. The burial, noted the unit diary, "was attended by a large crowd of civilian employees." The next few days found Anderson flying members of the accident court of inquiry to the crash site and back. Maintenance and salvage personnel then took over. Their work would take weeks, with Anderson and Gilmore making multiple trips in the Norseman and Fox Moth.[26]

In mid-March, three army halftracks carrying demolition experts, security guards, and maintenance personnel attempted to reach the site. After several days, they "reluctantly abandoned the idea" and instead left behind a party of seven men under the direction of Flight Lieutenant E.C.P. Salt.[27] Among the seven was Walter Vivian, who had spotted AL591 that fateful night. Vivian recalled how the explosives expert "put down a few shots [in the bog] and we found clothing."[28] After much effort, they recovered the bodies of the last of the missing men: Captain Fortune A. Dugan, a passenger that night, and four of AL591's flight crew – radio officer John D. Jones, navigating officer Frederick J. Brown, co-pilot Captain Thomas R. Harmes, and Captain Eves. Their remains were airlifted to Gander and interred at the cemetery near the end of March with Anderson and his wife again in attendance, along with

J.V. Wood of BOAC, the Return Ferry Service manager at Dorval.[29] The loss of AL591 ranked among Ferry Command's most tragic and stood to become Newfoundland and Labrador's most fatal single accident of the war. In an instant, Ferry Command had lost thirteen returning aircrew, and the Return Ferry Service an entire five-man flight crew. Also killed was passenger Lieutenant-Colonel Lancelot T. Grove of the British Army.

Gilmore's maintenance department was not yet finished with AL591. Twice in April, Vivian and other unit staff made extended trips to salvage the undercarriage, which they eventually pulled on sleds to the edge of Jonathon's Pond, two miles southwest of the crash. In the spring, "after the ice went," Vivian recounted, "they flew us out there and we rafted her up to the other end of the pond and they got a horse and brought it into Gander. I guess they were going to use it [again] … Good rubber was scarce at that time."[30]

Gander's "Darling" Stowaway

February also witnessed both the disappearance of Captain Donald L. Annibal's Mitchell FR148 after Prestwick received an SOS that the port engine had caught fire,[31] and the only recorded stowaway case originating at the unit. Whether by accident or design, neither the RCAF nor the RAF Gander diaries mention the latter event, although a postwar list of unit incident reports reveals a case file entitled "Stowaway on FD.773 – Marion Darling."[32] Her story subsequently made headlines. While stationed at Gander with the RCAF, Leading Airwoman Darling, a native of Springfield, Massachusetts, slipped aboard a Ferry Command Douglas C-47 Dakota cargo plane, determined to join her RCAF pilot husband overseas. Lucky for Darling, American Captain Nat Tooker preferred to fly low over the ocean whenever possible, avoiding the intense cold and oxygen deprivation found at higher altitudes. Two hours from Scotland, Tooker's co-pilot went aft to get something and found Darling, in uniform, huddled among the baggage. Battling ice on his wings, a preoccupied Tooker gave little heed and focussed on making landfall. Besides, "it was too late to make her get out and walk," he joked, so they gave their stowaway some sandwiches and cocoa and sent her back to the cabin. Later in Ottawa, air minister Power, impressed by the "romantic spunk" of a member of his RCAF Women's Division, told media with a chuckle that Darling had received minor discipline and was told never to do it again. She reportedly found a job at RCAF headquarters in London.[33] It would seem, however, that the anticipated romantic reunion did not occur. Flight Sergeant Gordon Darling was no longer in the UK, and a month after his wife's unorthodox arrival, he disappeared on a photoreconnaissance flight out of Gibraltar.[34]

Humanitarian Services

Occasionally, Gander received urgent requests from the Newfoundland government or from outlying, isolated communities for emergency medical aid or evacuation. The men of Ferry Command were happy to oblige if practicable, as were their RCAF and American counterparts at the field. Two such requests came in February 1943, shortly after salvage operations at AM844 had been temporarily suspended and attention had turned to the Birchy Lake Ventura and Liberator AL591. The first, in mid-February, saw Anderson, Walmsley, and Dr. Noel Stewart Knapp, a physician with twenty years' service in rural Newfoundland and now practicing in Lewisporte, evacuate an eighty-four-year-old woman from Brown's Arm in the Bay of Exploits. The recently arrived Norseman 2486 flew the elderly patient to Gander for hospitalization with a fractured hip. Several months later, Anderson returned the fully recovered woman to Brown's Arm by Norseman.[35]

At the end of February, the Department of Public Health and Welfare sent word that another woman, Marjorie Pinksen of Wild Cove in White Bay, was in labour and experiencing complications. Late in the day, Walmsley left Gander in 2486 carrying Frank Corbett and radio operator Thomas Gavriloff from Dorval's signals section. The flight stopped briefly at Lewisporte to pick up Dr. Knapp and arrived over White Bay in fading daylight. Wild

Cove was unsuited for the ski-equipped Norseman, so the pilot instead landed five miles away at Seal Cove. Snow and ice in the cove made for a rough landing, and when 2486 finally came to its abrupt stop, a ski had been torn off and the aircraft left severely damaged. Fortunately, all aboard were unharmed. Locals whisked away Dr. Knapp by horse-drawn sled and dog team to attend to his patient.[36]

This time, as fate would have it, the rescuers needed rescue. It took eleven days, but on 9 March, an RCAF Norseman finally got through to Seal Cove and picked up the stranded men. So began another salvage operation. The damaged aircraft was taken ashore, and repair crews from Gander worked throughout the remaining winter months and into the spring, aided by two mechanically inclined locals, Frank Pinksen and Sidney Banks. Aircraft from Gander arrived periodically with parts and food supplies. Gilmore's men and their helpers replaced the skis with a wheeled undercarriage and repaired the engine mount and cowlings. With the help of townsfolk, hired for a reported fifty cents an hour, a makeshift runway was prepared, its path leading across several vegetable gardens, including one owned by Joseph Banks. Officials advised Banks to defer planting his garden for fear that it would be destroyed when the Norseman took off and compensated him financially for his would-be potato crop. He planted his potato garden anyway and "did have a good yield," goes the community story. By summertime, maintenance was done, and on 17 June 2486 made its long-delayed return flight to Gander at the hands of Joe Gilmore, leaving Seal Cove to rightfully boast of having its very own airfield.[37] Captain Walmsley, having spent an eventful few weeks at Gander after delivering Norseman 2486 early in February, hitched a plane ride back to Dorval a few days after returning from Seal Cove that March. Later that month, while carrying out another ferry assignment, he was killed on take-off at Nassau in the Bahamas, leaving behind a wife and two small children.[38]

As much as Group Captain Anderson wished to assist with such mercy flights, the Seal Cove incident had placed the unit in a bad predicament. Only days after the incident, public health and welfare was again asking for an air medevac, this one for a patient in the island community of St. Brendan's in Bonavista Bay. With the Norseman damaged and stranded at Seal Cove, the unit's remaining suitable aircraft was the Fox Moth, but Anderson declined to make it available lest it be needed for their own rescue work. Indeed, Anderson "expected to get a rap over the knuckles for the Seal Cove affair," he told the Newfoundland government, and should the Fox Moth "be used and damaged at a time when a ferry bomber crashed in the interior he could expect nothing short of the severest criticism." Ignoring his own concerns, Anderson flew the Fox Moth to St. Brendan's anyway to reconnoitre a potential landing place. He found nothing suitable and suggested that the government approach the RCAF for a different type of aircraft that could land in the bay.

In the meantime, and unbeknownst to Anderson and the government, someone had removed the patient by other means. This left the secretary for public works furious, as proper communication could have prevented Anderson's "fruitless flight." Besides, stressed the secretary, "such circumstances could very easily lead to the excellent cooperation now afforded by them being affected adversely." There was no formal procedure in place for mercy flight requests, nor was the air force, British, Canadian, or American, obligated to carry out such flights. The government recognized this, as well as the risks involved, so they had to tread carefully. Initially, the government intended that such requests "should be limited to cases of difficult confinement and appendicitis," although they were willing to "expand the qualifications upon which an emergency flight may be based." Moving forward, said the government, public health and welfare requests would have to constitute "a real emergency involving life or death."[39]

Ferry Command nevertheless continued to provide mercy flights when called upon, as did the RCAF's search and rescue specialist and commander of its one-man and one-plane mercy flight division, Flying Officer Horace "Jimmy" Westaway. His efforts at Gander earned him the Air Force Cross.[40] It happened too, that at the time Anderson was voicing his reluctance to the government over the use of the unit's Fox Moth, Gilmore was winging his way to Gander from Dorval with another RCAF loaner to augment the unit's search and rescue capabilities, Menasco Moth 4810.

Hudson AM844 Revisited

In April, attention again turned to AM844. The spring thaw had begun, so Gilmore's men had to act quickly. A bulldozer hauled in a new port wing, which the men had assembled in three days; a "remarkable achievement" claimed the unit diary. A similar repair job at Gander by TCA experts had taken ten days. (TCA began operating a mail and passenger service between Newfoundland and Canada in May 1942 and set up offices and a passenger waiting area in the administration building.) Hudson AM844 was ready for its second flight attempt. The problem now was that warming daytime temperatures made the runway usable only on certain mornings, "depending on the previous night's temperature." The men therefore prepared skids "on which the Hudson could be towed down to a frozen lake, half a mile below the runway, from which the take-off would have been simple, if the ice continued to hold." It turned out that the skids were not required. Captain Lowell J. Thompson, a "confident pilot and a bit of a dare devil," recalled John Murphy, had arrived at Gander from Dorval. At daybreak on 19 April, an RCAF aircraft landed with Thompson. Group Captain Anderson, delayed by a flat tire on the unit's PBY, alighted on the frozen lake just as Thompson roared down the narrow runway in AM844, made a skillful take-off, and set course for Gander.[41]

Final word on the feasibility and practicality of such salvage operations rested with the unit's diary wordsmith. Eight months had passed since AM844's unceremonious forced landing, during which time Gilmore and his men made multiple trips to and from the site. Their wages were in any case paid, the writer rationalized, "so that beyond a few hundred dollars for local labour, petrol, railway charges, etc., it would seem highly unlikely that the cost has exceeded $2,000.00, which for an aircraft valued at over $100,000 is very encouraging."[42]

Captain Thompson made several test flights and an ice survey flight early in May in Hudson AM844, and after that she was flown to Dorval.[43] Late in September, Don McVicar flew the aircraft west to Edmonton, from where he commenced survey flights for a northern ferry route. In the air, McVicar found the Hudson difficult to fly straight and level, and on landing, "she tried to swing as the tail came down." These tendencies he attributed to the "odd" replacement port wing. Early in October, McVicar began his take-off run from Churchill, Manitoba. "I eased the wheel back gently and broke into a cold sweat. The left wing wanted to fly. The right one didn't." In attempting to gain control and get the wings level, McVicar cut the power and put the nose down. "The wheels bit with a screech" and the Hudson swerved to the right and towards a 45-gallon steel drum. A kick of the rudder to avoid certain disaster took AM844 off the side of the runway and over a hidden drainage ditch, folding the undercarriage and damaging the props. What became of AM844 is unclear as a replacement Hudson collected McVicar and his crew six days later.[44]

A Case of Voodoo at Gander

In April, Gander welcomed an unusual visitor in the form of Waco glider FR579, under tow by an RAF Dakota. Piloted by Squadron Leader R.G. Seys and carrying Squadron Leader F.M. Gobeil as co-pilot, the CG-4A glider, nicknamed "Voo-Doo," discharged two thousand pounds of freight through its hinged nose, "which opens and closes with a jaw-like action," and then left for Goose Bay. The trial flight, a triangular Dorval–Gander–Goose Bay and return course, was a precursor to a broader experiment proposed by Bowhill to cross the North Atlantic and demonstrate the possibilities of an airfreight service.[45] After considerable investigative work and several trial tow flights carrying various loads, the expedition set off in June, flying in stages along the route between Dorval and Prestwick, stopping at Goose Bay, BW-1, and Reykjavik. The first glider to cross the Atlantic covered thirty-five hundred miles, spent a total of twenty-eight hours in the air, and delivered three thousand pounds of cargo to Britain.[46] Ultimately, however, the RAF never adopted the method due to a variety of technical and weather-related problems experienced along the way.

Organizational Restructuring

Reconfiguration at the command level in April saw further renaming and reorganization of the ferry service. All transport operations, including ferrying, now fell under the newly created RAF Transport Command (RAFTC), itself comprised of transport groups and worldwide staging posts. Ferry Command ceased to exist in name. Dorval became home to 45 (Transport) Group, which controlled two aircraft ferrying wings, No. 112 Wing at Dorval for North Atlantic operations, and on the South Atlantic, No. 113 Wing at Nassau in the Bahamas. Air Vice-Marshal Reginald L.G. Marix took command of No. 45 Group at Dorval while Bowhill returned to the UK as air officer commanding-in-chief of Transport Command. Later, the unit at Gander was renamed 83 Staging Post but otherwise continued to function as usual.[47] (As Carl Christie notes, "Members of the ferry service … continued to refer to the operation as Ferry Command, regardless of the period of the war," and this practice is followed here.[48])

Missing Parachutists

One of Newfoundland and Labrador's most intriguing survivalist stories began with a Ferry Command milk run flight from Goose Bay to Gander on 8 May 1943. Piloted by Sheldon Luck, Ventura AJ164 carried mail, cargo, and a group of passengers, including Newfoundland Ranger John Hogan. Luck's biographer tells how the Ventura was crossing the Strait of Belle Isle at about twelve thousand feet when a burning smell in the cockpit soon turned to smoke, emanating from between the rudder pedals under the pilot's feet. A later inspection revealed that the smoke had come from a broken exhaust pipe on the gasoline-fired cockpit heater. The radio operator checked that no passengers were smoking and returned to the cockpit when a sudden vibration through the aircraft suggested that someone had opened the cabin door. Luck ordered the radio operator back again to check on things. He shortly returned and in disbelief reported that the passengers were abandoning the aircraft. Luck immediately reduced power and pushed the Ventura's nose downward. The maneuver worked as the vertical g-forces pinned the remaining occupants to the cabin floor. Luck then levelled off, turned the controls over to his co-pilot, and went back to the cabin to investigate. The smoke, he discovered, had caused a panic situation, with passengers hurriedly connecting their parachutes to the harnesses they were wearing. Amid the confusion, three members of the RAF and Ranger Hogan had exited the aircraft. The Ventura continued on and safely landed at Gander.[49]

Captain Lowell Thompson, who was still at Gander following his recovery flight of Hudson AM844, left immediately in the unit Catalina, but fog covered the strait and forced him to return. Next morning, Group Captain Anderson searched until late afternoon in the same machine. The RCAF provided a search Canso and Goose Bay dispatched more aircraft. Thompson flew again three weeks later following a report of smoke coming from an island in the area.[50] In truth, the location of the aircraft when the passengers jumped was unclear. The Ranger force determined that the parachutists had come down either on the Canadian coast, near Flower's Cove on the Northern Peninsula, or most likely in the frigid waters of the strait. Ranger-organized ground parties searched the area around Forteau in southern Labrador, along the shoreline and inland near Flower's Cove, and inland from Englee and Jackson's Arm. Another report of smoke had the Ranger detachment member at Battle Harbour searching Chateau Bay on the Labrador coast. The Ferry Command unit meanwhile kept the Newfoundland government informed of its search for their Ranger and forwarded a suitcase and haversack that Hogan left behind in the Ventura. The parish priest in Carbonear, Hogan's hometown, notified the family that "he was missing, with indifferent prospects ... of being located."[51] The air search continued intermittently until month's end, but the effort revealed nothing of the missing men.

The first three weeks of June brought no news of the missing parachutists, but on the evening of the twenty-sixth, a message from Port Saunders on the Northern Peninsula told, incredibly, that Hogan and Corporal Eric Butt had been found, alive. Anderson left immediately in the unit's newest acquisition, Norseman FR405, taking medical supplies and RCAF medical officer Flight Lieutenant F.C. Barton. Gilmore had flown the Norseman from Boucherville, Quebec, to Gander on 1 June.[52] The aircraft soon sported a nickname, the "Flying Caribou," and some applicable artwork on its forward fuselage. The Norseman would prove to be the unit's workhorse for the next two years, and the loaner Menasco Moth and Norseman were returned to the RCAF.

Anderson landed float-equipped Norseman FR405 at Port Saunders and soon reported back that Hogan, although thin, "was in excellent condition," and that Butt, except for "frost-bitten toes, was also in good condition." Anderson flew the two men to Gander the following day.[53] When Hogan stepped from the Norseman at Gander, "he appeared spic and span," said the media, "except for being a little weak and much reduced in weight."[54] The description hardly betold what the men had endured. Corporal Butt was treated at hospital for malnutrition, exposure, and frostbite, reported the RCAF. Hogan was in good enough condition to travel on to St. John's.[55] In time, the Ranger told the story of their astonishing survival.

His departure from the aircraft started when he heard someone ask for a fire extinguisher. Amid the confusion and standing passengers, Hogan thought he saw flames in the cockpit. He remembered for certain seeing the co-pilot pointing the extinguisher towards the floor. An unknown voice said, "pack chutes," and then another passenger tried to open the cabin door. Butt lent a hand and turned the emergency release. With that, the door flew out, recalled Hogan, and Butt and another man, "almost immediately, went with it." Being next nearest the exit, Hogan jumped to make room for the others to follow. It was his first jump, but from the airmen's stories at Goose Bay, he learned that a parachute could be guided by manipulating its cords. By such manipulation, he landed on the shores of a small pond, well inland from Hawke's Bay and east of West Lake. The landing slightly injured his knee. An experienced woodsman and not one to panic, he stayed put that night and started a fire to dry out his wet boots and socks. For shelter, he trimmed some large branches into tent poles for the parachute canopy. Early the next morning he climbed a hill to get his bearings. Eyeing the sea and possibly Hawke's Bay, he broke camp and headed eastward, discarding the cumbersome parachute. Having spotted fresh footprints in the snow, Hogan quickened his pace and soon came upon a limping Corporal Butt.[56] Leaving Goose Bay, the corporal had worn fur-lined regulation flying boots over a pair of low-cut shoes, but the boots had slipped off as he descended by parachute. His feet had since become wet and numb and were in a bad way. To make matters worse, he had sprained his ankle on landing.[57] Together the two men headed for the coast; and so began their fifty-day ordeal.

The spring run-off had left streams and rivers swollen, forcing the pair to make wide detours or wade through waist-deep water, which made the journey longer and more exhausting. As luck or perhaps providence should have it, Hogan had the means to light a fire. Although a smoker, he rarely carried matches and instead used a lighter. However, just before boarding the Ventura, "I had occasion to rush to my room for something I had forgotten. On the table I had an extra large box of matches ... of the strike anywhere type. On rushing out of the room I grabbed a handful and put them in my tunic pocket ... It was those matches which contributed so much to our remaining alive." His only equipment was a pocketknife, given to him by a survivor of the USS *Truxton* disaster near St. Lawrence in February 1942. Adding to their woes, Butt's feet had become severely swollen, and "I had to slit his shoes to give him some relief." Come nighttime, Hogan had the corporal keep his feet as close to the fire as possible.[58]

For the first week, they bunked down nightly in a lean-to shelter made of boughs, subsisting on birch tree buds, marsh berries, and a frozen rabbit they were fortunate to find. A plane passed overhead one day but failed to see them or the smoke from their fire.

On 15 May, they came upon a trapper's shack at the end of West Lake but pushed onward towards the coast until striking the Torrent River. Following the river and nearing the head of Hawke's Bay, another old trapper's cabin appeared. Inside was a stale loaf of bread, some salt fish, a piece of soap, and perhaps more importantly, rabbit-snare wire. By boiling the soap in a broken saucepan, Hogan made an antiseptic solution for Butt's feet, which had now given out completely, and bandaged them with shreds of his own undergarments. The pair agreed that Hogan should carry on alone. The Ranger gathered a supply of water, buds, and leaves for himself and Butt and set out. Again, the river waters were too high and rapid to cross, "and I came to the conclusion that if anything happened to me ... Butt's chances would be jeopardized also." He returned to the cabin and spent the next few days making a raft, but the wood was too waterlogged to hold his weight (lacking dry firewood, they had burned the trapper's boats when they first arrived). From 23 May until late June, "life in our cabin settled down to routine," said Hogan, gathering leaves, buds, and firewood, and attending to Butt's feet. Each morning, he checked his snares and caught ten rabbits during their nearly five weeks at the cabin.

The Ranger was in a bad way too. His eyesight was blurring and he struggled to stand. When he did stand, he found his knees difficult to control. Then one day, Butt drew "my attention to what he thought was the sound of a movement of oars." Rushing riverside, Hogan hailed a pair of boats carrying Frank Perry, William Lawrence, and John Parsons, members of a geodetic survey party. "It was the end of fifty days of arduous isolation," said a relieved Hogan.[59]

Hogan and Butt's survival renewed hope for the two remaining men. Anderson carried out further aerial searches in the Norseman during July and hired a man from Port Saunders to do a ten-day ground search of areas not practicable to check by aircraft. Anderson engaged a second Port Saunders man that month to accompany Ferry Command security guard Arthur Howse on another search. The Norseman deplaned the pair in the mountains at a lake called Red Rod Feeder, east of where they believed the missing parachutists had landed. Howse and his colleague worked their way westward, and on arriving at Port Saunders two weeks later, sent word to Gander that they had found possible traces of the missing men. August opened with Anderson flying the area around Red Rod Feeder with Howse and another security guard as observers and with instructions to prepare for another ground search. The next day, Anderson dropped the guards at the lake and continued his aerial reconnaissance, alighting on Eastern Blue Pond and at two camps on the River of Ponds but finding no signs of the missing parachutists. What became of the guards' search went unrecorded in the unit diary. Anderson and Gilmore made several more flights to Port Saunders in September pursuing the search, but thirty-year-old Corporal Michael Maley of Glasgow, Scotland, and twenty-one-year-old Englishman Leading Aircraftsman Francis A. Moore, were never found.[60]

The following year, Governor Walwyn presented Hogan with the King's Police and Fire Service Medal for his "gallantry and devotion to duty."[61] A stanza in a poem published in a 1943 Ranger bulletin and entitled "Courtesy is the Best Policy," perhaps best sums up Hogan's character:

To be a real policeman
Be big and strong by heck
But let the strength be always found
Just above the neck.[62]

And that he did.

Special Visitors

Late in May 1943, 45 Group's new boss, Air Vice-Marshal Marix, arrived at Gander from Dorval aboard a Hudson bomber and then flew post haste to Botwood in a Catalina piloted by Captain Lowell Thompson. The purpose of his fleeting visit, as later revealed, was to greet Prime Minister Winston Churchill, on a brief stopover aboard the Boeing 314A Clipper *Bristol* following the Anglo-American strategic conference, codenamed Trident, held in Washington from 12 to 25 May. Accompanying Churchill was his chief military assistant General Hastings Ismay, Sir Allan Brooke, Chief of the Imperial General Staff (the professional head of the British Army), and General George C. Marshall, US Army Chief of Staff. Other conference attendees on the British side included Air Chief Marshal Sir Charles Portal, Chief of the Air Staff, Admiral of the Fleet Sir Dudley Pound, and Field Marshal Sir Archibald Wavell. Their return trip, simultaneous but separate from that of Churchill's, took them to Gander aboard a Return Ferry Service Liberator, where Group Captain Anderson dined and entertained the trio at "The Barn" before they continued their journey eastward.[63]

Some Lucky Airmen

Although not a Ferry Command flight, on one June day, American operations at Gander dispatched twenty-four of their B-17 Flying Fortresses overseas. Six returned because of the Prestwick weather forecast, while another ditched in the ocean 150 miles out after both starboard engines failed within minutes of each other.[64] It was nearing darkness at the time when 1st Lieutenant Kelmer Hall, pilot of the stricken bomber, "landed across the swells, into the wind as near as possible, ducking icebergs." Hall and his co-pilot exited "their windows and helped men out of the radio room which was filling up with water." The ocean landing broke off the fuselage at the ball turret and the main section quickly sank, while the tail remained afloat for about three minutes. Fortunately, Gander obtained a direction-finding bearing from the radio operator's SOS messages and transmitted the location to a convoy operating in the area. The ten-man crew had meantime escaped their sinking craft and taken to rubber life rafts. They floated around all night in heavy fog, dodging icebergs.[65] The Canadian navy minesweeper HMCS *Georgian* happened to be doing convoy escort duty in the area when around five in the morning the ship's commanding officer was "called to the bridge when flares were reported off our port bow."

The *Georgian* headed in that direction, wary that an enemy U-boat might have fired the flares to draw the escort ship out of position. The *Georgian* narrowly missed one iceberg and soon located the airmen's rafts "crowded between two huge bergs." The ship's scramble nets were lashed over the side and the airmen, cold and numb from exposure, were helped aboard by the *Georgian's* crew.[66] The ship then steered a course for the port town of Lewisporte. The bombardier had sustained head injuries, so Group Captain Anderson flew an American medical officer to the town in the unit's Norseman, returning to Gander with the injured airman and three of his crewmates.[67]

In July, Captain Lowell Thompson had a narrow escape when he test-flew Atlantic delivery B-25 FR145. As he was coming in to land, a connecting rod in the starboard engine failed, leaving a large hole in the cylinder wall and wrecking the engine. At the time, Thompson was flying low at three hundred feet with flaps down, "and only with the greatest difficulty," recorded the unit diary, did he avoid stalling and spinning down. Thompson "managed to retract the flaps and do a circuit on one engine and landed without damage." After some repair work, he left for BW-1 in the same aircraft a few days later, but thirty minutes into the flight, similar problems with the starboard engine forced him to return to Gander on one engine, losing altitude in the process from seven thousand to one thousand feet.[68]

Not one to sit idle, Thompson returned to Montréal where he picked up and then delivered a Liberator to the UK, stopping en route at Gander and Reykjavik. He then caught a Return Ferry Service flight by Liberator direct to Gander, where the now repaired B-25 awaited. Thompson wasted no time, and the next day, 8 August, finally made his way safely to BW-1 in FR145. Two days later, after an overnight stop at Reykjavik, he arrived in the UK. A busy man, that Captain Lowell Thompson![69]

October to December

October saw Gilmore busily engaged on mercy flights. Early that month he took FR405 to Westport in White Bay and returned with a seriously ill female for admission at the RCAF hospital. He revisited White Bay a few days later, this time going to Jackson's Arm, and flew back another woman who was admitted to hospital and operated on immediately. Gilmore flew her home later that month and returned with another patient.

October witnessed the arrival of American-born women pilots Roberta Leveaux and Katherine Van Doozer, both serving members of the British Air Transport Auxiliary, which delivered aircraft from the factories in Britain to the RAF squadrons. The pair, temporarily attached to Ferry Command, arrived at Gander Lake from Boucherville, Quebec, as supernumerary crewmembers aboard Catalina flying boats and were accommodated at "The Barn," there being "no other female accommodation here." The unit posted guards on the south side of Gander Lake to watch over their aircraft, which were successfully delivered to the seaplane base at Largs on the Firth of Clyde in North Ayrshire, Scotland. Later that month, another visiting Air Transport Auxiliary pilot, Opal Anderson, likewise lodged at "The Barn," having arrived from Dartmouth, Nova Scotia, aboard Ferry Command Catalina JV935.[70]

The last serious aircraft incident in 1943 occurred two days after Christmas when Captain Viruly's return ferry LB-30 Liberator AL512 crashed on the runway on take-off, sending the six crew to hospital. Four were discharged with minor injuries and two admitted, both with lacerations and one with possible fractures in the foot. Using a crane from the US Army and some of their personnel, Gilmore brought the wrecked aircraft to the RAF hangars.[71]

A New Endeavour

The year 1943 closed with the arrival of a man who, postwar, would alter Newfoundland's political future. His business then, however, was pigs; more specifically, the unit's RAF piggery, an ambitious, and for a time, contentious undertaking. Group Captain Anderson had earlier proposed the scheme to the Newfoundland government with the idea, initially at least, to supply the cafeteria and hotel operations with fresh pork. Newfoundland air representative Pattison saw its value as it put waste food from the cookhouses to good use. Medical authorities had already inspected and sanctioned the site, located adjacent to the RAF root (vegetable) stores in a wooded area three hundred yards east of Hangar 22.[72] The Newfoundland government approved the scheme and the unit's bulldozer broke ground as soon as the weather permitted. Meantime, Anderson had one of the temporary buildings converted for use as a sty until the contractor erected a permanent structure. Surely one of the unit's more unusual delivery flights occurred in April 1943 when Anderson arrived at Gander in a Catalina carrying a boar and twelve weaners. That was just the beginning. Before year's end, the operation increased by some 265 RAF porkers, and one civilian manager in the form of Joseph R. Smallwood.[73]

Smallwood, a former journalist and host of the popular radio program "The Barrelman," had recently operated his own small piggery near St. John's. The enterprise, says his biographer, Richard Gwyn, "failed miserably" when an epidemic wiped out the herd. Undaunted, Smallwood explored the idea of a super-piggery, founded on the availability of food scraps from all the military installations in Newfoundland. He pitched the idea to one of the US Army base commanders. The officer was receptive, but before they could enter into negotiations, Smallwood was off to Gander.[74] Anderson was persistent "and put a lot of pressure on Joey to come," remembered John Murphy, the group captain's private secretary. "I think it was only because he was promised accommodations for his family that he finally capitulated," although initially he lived in the same building as the RAF staff.[75] Either way, after a productive discussion over a meal at "The Barn," Smallwood and Anderson came up with a rather "unusual scheme of operation." The RAF provided the building, financed to the tune of about thirty thousand dollars, and Smallwood and his backers provided the pigs, hundreds of them, and covered the expenses, including staff. Payments were made on the building from the profits, and the remaining balance was then shared equally between Smallwood and the RAF, which turned over its share to the Welfare Fund.[76]

The operation was soon up and running. At feeding time, wrote Smallwood, the noise as the hungry pigs "squealed an impatient protest could be heard, when the wind was in the right direction, all the way across the airport!" Anderson, he added, rarely failed to show off the piggery to "hundreds" of visiting guests, among them British statesman Anthony Eden, Norwegian-American flier Bernt Balchen, and Field Marshal Jan Smuts.[77]

All was well and good until businessman and project benefactor Chesley Crosbie arrived at Gander and announced to Pattison "that he had come to look at his pigs."[78] A surprised Pattison immediately met with Anderson and explained that the Newfoundland government was interested in any arrangement that the RAF might make. After all, Newfoundland did own the land, and in this instance, Anderson had involved a third party.[79] Such a move, the government argued, could potentially establish Smallwood in the piggery business permanently and grant him rights to the air base even after they re-established control at war's end. Newfoundland wished to avoid any such embarrassment. In communication with the Dominions Office, a displeased Commissioner Woods suggested that the RAF at Gander "do not appreciate the position of the Newfoundland Government in relation to the Newfoundland-owned Air Bases ... operated by Canada for the period of the war." Anderson had not consulted with them beforehand, he added, "and probably thinks that everything is all right provided the Canadians agree."[80] The Dominions Office put the matter to rest, for the time being at least, when they assured Woods that the agreement allowed the RAF to buy out Smallwood at short notice or dispense of his services "without cause or compensation once he had recouped his capital."[81] The piggery operation continued under Smallwood's direction and eventually included an offshoot enterprise with the manufacturing of sausages, in charge of the unit's hotel department.[82] Smallwood used the opportunity to fly to Ontario, where the former superintendent of Canada Packers taught him curing techniques. Later, the piggery building was enlarged (with government permission) to include a smokehouse, and the product line expanded to include hams and bacon.[83]

Ultimately, the piggery incident revealed the informal nature of the RAF's relationship with the government as far as Gander was concerned. Unlike their Canadian counterparts, the RAF had no defined understanding with Newfoundland regarding operations there, especially as they pertained to buildings and developments. The site occupied by the RAF, explained Pattison, was generally agreed to during one of Bowhill's earlier visits. The "project was entirely on account of the Air Ministry," he said, so "we did not raise the question of any formalities, in fact, we assisted them with regard to selection of the site ... as at that time we ourselves were directly concerned in assisting the delivery of aircraft to the United Kingdom." The plan going forward obliged Ferry Command to obtain Newfoundland's formal permission for their projects in addition to RCAF approval.[84]

Year-End Switch

The year ended with some personnel changes within Gander's transatlantic control unit. McGrath, now promoted to senior flying control officer, got word from Dorval over teletype of a possible six-to-nine month posting to Bermuda as senior controller. His wife, Ruth, could go too, said Dorval, and when she agreed, he accepted. It had all transpired quickly and made for "rather shattering news," penned McGrath in his personal diary.[85] In December 1943, New Zealander Squadron Leader Leonard E. Clark arrived from Bermuda to replace the departing McGrath as senior controller for the upcoming year.[86]

Summation

Gilmore and his maintenance section's hallmark salvage successes had continued into 1943, as demonstrated in their determined and nearly year-long effort to recover Hudson AM844 near Deer Lake and their creative salvage of the Birchy Lake Ventura using skis. Fortunately, the number of accidents at the unit was fewer than in 1942, but no less tragic, as revealed in the loss of nineteen men aboard Return Ferry Service Liberator AL591. This vital ferry service nevertheless continued to operate unabated, with air traffic controllers, maintenance personnel, Shell Oil refuellers, and other ground support staff at the unit handling 166 east and westbound transatlantic Return Ferry Service flights during 1943. These same men and women likewise upheld the unit's primary objective and supported the safe delivery of 474 aircraft, with half that number Liberators and one quarter Catalinas and Mitchells. The remaining balance consisted of a mixed number of Fortresses, Dakotas, Hudsons, Venturas, Avro Lancasters, de Havilland Mosquitos, and Consolidated Coronado and Martin PBM-3 Mariner flying boats. [87] Although the delivery total for 1943 represented a thirty percent decrease over the previous year's figure of 670, the downturn was no indicator of things to come, as the year 1944 would turn out to be the unit's busiest since ferrying operations began in November 1940.

Joe Gilmore with parachute pack prepares for another jump over his native Ireland. He made upwards of fifteen such parachute descents. Courtesy Guy Warner.

Trucks load asphalt delivered by railway tank cars at Hattie's Camp, ca. 1937. The person sitting in the cargo bed of truck 106 (bottom left) wears a respirator. DND Image Library, PMR74-982.

Left. Levelling ground for the runways. DND Image Library, PMR74-977.

Civil hangar (later numbered 20) under construction, August 1938. DND Image Library, PMR74-980.

Hudson bombers from the second delivery group at Gander, November 1940. This flight took off from snow-compacted runways.

Top. Shell Oil truck refuels Captain Humphrey Page's lead Hudson T9427.

Bottom. Captain H.A. Sweet's snow-covered Hudson T9428, under guard by The Queen's Own Rifles of Canada. The Queen's Own Rifles of Canada Regimental Museum and Archive.

The crew was fortunate to escape the inferno that destroyed Hudson T9446, Gander's first mishap during the transatlantic flight experiment of November–December 1940. The Rooms Provincial Archives, GN 4/5, box 2, file AG/57/2.

Hudson T9449 rests on the shores of later named Banting Lake, 1941. The Rooms Provincial Archives, A6-147.

Members of The Royal Rifles of Canada on guard duty at Hudson T9449. The man in the centre is likely United Church minister Reverend Francis W. Mitchinson who accompanied Constable Gilbert Hiscock of the Newfoundland Constabulary to the crash by dog team. The Rooms Provincial Archives, GN 4/5, box 2, file AG/57/2.

Joe Gilmore, centre wearing white scarf, with a salvage crew near Codroy at downed Hudson FH235, March 1942. Courtesy John Murphy.

Top and bottom. Using ropes, wooden poles, and brute strength, a community effort allows for the salvage of Hudson FH235, March 1942. Author's collection.

Top and bottom. Unspecified crash and salvage, but likely Ventura AE689 on Belle Isle. North Atlantic Aviation Museum.

Left and right. Boston BZ277 that force-landed at Conche in November 1942. Built under lend-lease, the Boston still sports its US serial number, 42-33032. North Atlantic Aviation Museum.

Local men and boys help salvage an engine at an unspecified location. North Atlantic Aviation Museum.

Burial of Captains Fortune A. Dugan and Thomas R. Harmes at Gander cemetery following the crash of Return Ferry Service Liberator AL591. Author's collection.

Typical salvage team camp in the snowy wilds of Newfoundland. North Atlantic Aviation Museum.

Left. Damaged Norseman 2486 at Seal Cove, White Bay, February 1943.

Right. Norseman 2486's stranded crew at Seal Cove, February–March 1943 (L-R): presumably pilot Elwood Walmsley, Frank Corbett (without hat), and radio operator Thomas Gavriloff of Perdue, Saskatchewan. Behind them is Seal Cove resident Harris Rideout. Both courtesy Gary Rideout.

Left. Leading Aircraftsman Francis A. Moore in his mother's back garden on Alexander Road, Bearwood, Smethwick, Sandwell, UK. Moore went missing after he parachuted from Ventura AJ164 in May 1943. Courtesy David Moore.

Ranger John Hogan (left) and Corporal Eric Butt, his feet bandaged after their fifty-day wilderness ordeal, at Port Saunders, June 1943. Group Captain Anderson far right and in the background Norseman FR405. Thomas McGrath photographic coll., Library and Archives Canada, album #2, item 128.

Top. Extracting Norseman FR405 at Gander Bay using block and tackle, February 1944. Note the stencilled lettering "Flying Caribou" and caribou artwork (inset).

Left. Joe Gilmore, far right, supervises the salvage of Norseman FR405. Both courtesy Sean Gilmore.

Captain Vladimir Kabin, pilot of B-25 Mitchell KJ584 that crashed at Gander on 29 August 1944. Courtesy Rob Teteruck. Inset left, Sergeant Thomas T. Sheldrick, radio operator, and inset right, Flight Sergeant David Flood, navigator. Department of National Defence, Directorate of History and Heritage.

Gander's salvage experts raise downed Hudson EW896 in southern Newfoundland using block and tackle and spruce poles, January–February 1945. A portable heater dries out the engines. North Atlantic Aviation Museum.

Ski-equipped Hudson EW896 back at Gander safe and sound, February 1945. Another successful salvage for Gilmore's maintenance team. Courtesy Sean Gilmore.

Flight Lieutenant Maxwell Hutchings with his mother and daughters Hanna Gail and Phyllise (right), ca. 1944. Hutchings later became Bell Island's first mayor, serving from 1950 to 1955. He also operated a tavern called "The Broken Wheel," which took its name from his wartime RAF squadron insignia depicting a broken wheel. Courtesy Phyllise Stickel.

Funeral service for Joe Gilmore at the American chapel at Gander. Pat Gilmore stands left of chaplain. Courtesy Sean Gilmore.

Procession with Gilmore family prepares to depart the American chapel at Gander. Courtesy Sean Gilmore.

Firing party at attention as the Ratcliffe family leaves the RCAF chapel at Gander following the service for Squadron Leader Frank Ratcliffe. Thomas McGrath photographic coll., Library and Archives Canada, album #2, item 158.

Interment of Joe Gilmore and Squadron Leader Frank Ratcliffe, May 1945. Gilmore is the only civilian buried in Gander's present-day Commonwealth War Graves Commission Cemetery. Courtesy Sean Gilmore.

"The Barn," residence of the RAF Gander unit's commanding officer. Postwar, the building became home to airport manager H.A.L. Pattison. North Atlantic Aviation Museum.

Group Captain Anderson (centre) with his wife, Alma, and their dogs, surrounded by Ferry Command personnel. Gander Lake in the background. Thomas McGrath photographic coll., Library and Archives Canada, album #2, item 147.

Gander Ferry Command personnel pose alongside air-sea rescue Canso FT999, subsequently lost off Belle Isle in October 1945. Squadron Leader Tom McGrath is seated first row, third from right. Thomas McGrath photographic coll., Library and Archives Canada, PA-210752.

Shell Oil Company staff at Gander, winter 1945–46. Shell refuellers worked around the clock to keep the Ferry Command flights moving. Archives and Special Collections, Memorial University of Newfoundland.

Air-sea rescue Canso FT998 alongside Hangar 21 and the new control tower, winter 1945–46. Archives and Special Collections, Memorial University of Newfoundland.

Sitting on the aircraft tow tug beneath the Hudson bomber wing are civilian ground crew members Richard Gaul, John MacDonald, and Larry Mills. Unit Norseman (likely FR406) in the background, ca. 1945. Hazel B. Fausak coll., North Atlantic Aviation Museum.

The movements board, used in the joint RAF-USATC control room during wartime to track aircraft deliveries, is used in 1946 to track commercial flights for AOA, BOAC, PAA, and TCA. Gloria Lindsay coll., North Atlantic Aviation Museum.

Ron Reed uses the Morse key to work the southern route circuit, ca. 1945. Gloria Lindsay coll., North Atlantic Aviation Museum.

Hazel Fausak (née Bjornstad) at the front-office desk behind Marcel Auger, ca. 1945. Hazel B. Fausak coll., North Atlantic Aviation Museum.

John Murphy, secretary to the unit's commanding officers, in his office at the Ferry Command hangar, ca. 1945. Hazel B. Fausak coll., North Atlantic Aviation Museum.

Ferry Command radio operators Dorothea Trotter and Jeannie Menard enjoy some sun at the RAF marine base at Gander Lake, ca. 1945. Hazel B. Fausak coll., North Atlantic Aviation Museum.

Radio operators enjoy their downtime in Building A, December 1945. Top (L-R): Jeannie Menard and Agnes Watson. Bottom (L-R): Barbara Morey, Dorothea Trotter, Isabel MacKenzie, and Audrey Hall. Hazel B. Fausak coll., North Atlantic Aviation Museum.

John J. Gilmore's revised marker at Gander's Commonwealth War Graves Commission Cemetery, properly identifying his MBE (Member of the Civilian Division of the Order of the British Empire). Author's photo.

The Gilmore family at Gander. Top (L-R): Sean, Mary, Carrol, Joe, and Patrick. Bottom (L-R): Margo and Josie. Courtesy Sean Gilmore.

Commissioner Neill raises the flag and officially opens the new Gander terminal in September 1946. The hostesses (from left): Loretta Mackenzie, BOAC, Marjorie Hoopes, AOA, Jane Bray, PAA, Eleanor Hyland, TCA, Brita Booge, SAS, and Doris Johnston, TWA. Courtesy Robert Pelley.

TWA Constellations dwarf a civilian Beechcraft Model 18 as Gander opens its doors and runways to commercial transatlantic air travel, ca. 1946. Hazel B. Fausak coll., North Atlantic Aviation Museum.

Another successful parachute jump for Joe Gilmore. Courtesy Guy Warner.

CHAPTER 7 | THE COMMANDING OFFICER HAS GONE MISSING

The year 1944 opened with heavy blizzards that kept aerial activity at a standstill, and ended with a major rescue effort following the forced landing of a Hudson bomber carrying the unit's commanding officer. In between, the unit had to contend with mishaps to its Norseman and Fox Moth, another fatal crash near the airfield, several troubling de Havilland Mosquito losses, and a case of suspected sabotage to a ferry flight. There were some tense moments during another mercy flight and some lighter moments with the arrival of Russian aircrews on Gander Lake. The unit's primary role, of course, was to brief departing aircrews and service and ready their aircraft for the long flight eastwards. With no let-up in ferrying operations, 1944 would prove to be the busiest year for ground staff as delivery numbers reached their wartime peak.

When the weather finally cleared that January, a UK-bound delivery aircraft landed carrying a special passenger and occasional visitor, His Royal Highness Prince Bernhard of the Netherlands, whose family had taken refuge in Canada after Germany invaded their country. Before continuing his journey that evening, the prince was entertained by Group Captain Anderson at "The Barn."

North Atlantic Ice-up

An unfortunate incident befell the crew of Ventura JS920 when they encountered fuel feed and icing troubles four hours out from

Gander while en route to the UK. Following receipt of their SOS, Gander sent messages to the crew giving advice to remedy the problem. Gander received a second SOS and then lost radio contact and heard nothing further from the aircraft. Operations assumed it had gone down in the sea and took immediate search action. Happily, Captain Leslie A. Dickens landed the Ventura at Gander nine hours after take-off, still carrying heavy ice and with its wireless inoperable because of a broken lead.[1]

Gander Bay Troubles

Two minor mishaps in January and February 1944 involving the unit's Norseman and Fox Moth again demanded the expertise of the maintenance department. On 14 January, a mercy call had Anderson airborne for Clarke's Head, Gander Bay, in Norseman FR405, carrying Squadron Leader S.J. Navin, RCAF medical officer, and unit mechanic Angus Steele.[2] Before the war, aircraft were a rare sight over Gander Bay, but not anymore. Occasionally, writes Gander Bay native Gary Saunders, two or three yellow Harvard trainers "might roar past at nearly rooftop level, rattling the windowpanes and shivering the cups and saucers," with the noise inadvertently "sending the horses and sheep racing off the roads and into the woods." Today it was Anderson in the Norseman, but he was unfamiliar with the local geography and landed on the ice at George's Point on the south side of the bay instead of Clarke's Head, a mile away on the north side. A local pointed him in the right direction and Anderson decided to taxi the short distance, unaware that the channel was last to freeze because of the currents in the Gander River.[3] Suddenly, the skis broke through the thin ice. The nose sank, leaving the wings resting just above the unbroken ice. Anderson and Navin escaped through the rear door while Steele used the emergency exit in the roof. Locals took medical officer Navin to check on his patient, Susie Gillingham, while Anderson organized salvage operations. Back at Gander, maintenance foreman Jack Fennell left for nearby Glenwood with salvage equipment but found on arrival that no dog team was available for transport to Gander Bay. The next day, Gilmore took the Fox Moth and flew in a block and tackle and other equipment. He returned with Anderson and later flew in Fennell and returned with Navin.[4] Gilmore also flew patient Gillingham to Gander in the Fox Moth, said Saunders, and eventually she recovered in hospital.

To help with the salvage, Gilmore hired local trapper and storekeeper Brett Saunders under contract for one thousand dollars. Aircraft salvage work was not new to Saunders. The RCAF had previously hired him to recover a downed Hurricane fighter on a bog near the Gander River. Saunders floated the fighter to Gander Bay using two canoes lashed together "catamaran-style." From Gander Bay, the S.S. *Glencoe* took the Hurricane to Lewisporte where it was returned to Gander by rail.[5] The Norseman salvage would be altogether different, as Saunders explained:

> I hired Roland Gillingham to help me. We cut two thirty-foot poles for uprights. Chopping holes in the ice on either side of the fuselage, we set them firmly in the bottom mud. Across the top we laid a twenty-foot spruce stringer and notched and bolted it into place. This gave us fifteen feet clearance above the ice, enough for the skis to swing free so we could shove planks underneath when the time came. The last thing to do when everything was ready was to take up the strain of her weight on the chain block and chop her out of the new ice that had formed around the fuselage. Slowly, chopping very carefully with our axes for fear of gashing her fuselage or wings, we went all around the hole until she was clear and there was room for the skis to come up through. A crowd was watching as we hoisted her out; I made them stand back in case the ice collapsed. It proved easier than we thought. But what a sad sight, a fine plane like that with water streaming out of her engine and ice candles hanging from her struts! In a few minutes we had the planks in place. The ice held. She was safe and sound.[6]

"Joe was delighted," said Gary Saunders, but anxious to get the waterlogged engine dried out. With local help, they hauled the Norseman close to shore and made a shelter over the forward half with a tarpaulin. Using gasoline heaters and a blower, they forced the moisture from the engine. For several days and nights, Saunders and Gillingham lived in a canvas tent on the ice in temperature lows of minus ten degrees Celsius, guarding the aircraft and keeping the heaters going. Then one day Anderson arrived to bring the Norseman back to Gander. He looked the aircraft over and "climbed into the cockpit … He pressed the starting button. Nothing happened. The battery was dead," and Saunders knew why. "Several times, after the mechanic and Joe had fixed her up, they started the engine," explained Saunders. "And when they weren't around I started it myself, showing different people how. One time I did it and the tarp got tangled up in the propeller and rolled up in a big ball." Saunders's curiosity and the tarp incident had presumably drained the battery, and Anderson, likely unaware of these transgressions, was none too pleased about having to return without the Norseman. The unit flew in a generator, and on 25 January, eleven days after Anderson's mishap at Gander Bay, Gilmore piloted the now airworthy aircraft back to Gander. The operation had taken ten days, and made Saunders and Gillingham a thousand dollars richer.[7]

Gander Bay brought little luck for the unit, it seems. Gilmore, having befriended the Saunders family, would occasionally drop in for a visit. Such was the case late in February when he arrived from Gander and parked the Fox Moth on the ice just off the wharf. Gilmore stayed for dinner, and when it was time to leave, "as usual, a crowd had gathered to watch the takeoff." Gilmore completed the engine start-up sequence, hand cranking the prop, when the throttle control failed and the aircraft lurched forward, pilotless. "Joe ran and jumped onto the lower wing to try to climb into the cockpit and hit the switch," described Saunders, "but she was already moving too fast." Gilmore fell to the ice, got back on his feet, and resumed the chase, but it was too late. The Fox Moth, "this little plane gone berserk," picked up speed and crashed into a rock-filled pier, damaging its undercarriage, engine mount, and airscrew. Gilmore was rescued and returned to Gander when salvage operations began a few days later. Captain Patterson with the USAAF unit carried Gilmore by Piper Cub back to Gander Bay, and the RCAF's Flying Officer Westaway flew in two maintenance men, Sam Blandford and Harry Young. Twice in March, a Dakota appeared over Gander Bay and dropped equipment and tools. "The youngsters were tickled" with all the activity, said Saunders, and "dogged Joe's footsteps" as he and his crew went about their work, installing a new prop and shaping pieces of wood at the local sawmill for the damaged spruce framework in the wings. Finally, mid-month, Gilmore took the now flyable Fox Moth back to Gander, accompanied by one member of the salvage party. An RCAF Harvard collected the other man. "Again the youngsters were watching. When the Harvard's pilot stepped down from the cockpit in his helmet and goggles and leather jacket, with his "Mae West" life preserver on and a .45 automatic pistol in a holster on his side, their eyes were as big as saucers." Back at the unit workshop, maintenance removed the Moth's wings and engine and completely overhauled the aircraft. Both the Fox Moth and Norseman were out of commission until May when spare parts arrived from Dorval and work began to get the aircraft back to proper airworthiness condition.[8]

Lost Over Grand Lake

Neither aircraft was search-ready when Mosquito KB230 disappeared en route to Gander from Dorval on 20 May. At no time did the aircraft make direct wireless communication with Gander, although several intercepted bearings given by stations elsewhere suggested that the twenty-five-year-old civilian pilot, Californian Captain Robert Adkison, was on course and in no trouble. A married man with one year's ferrying experience under his belt, including trips to Gander, Adkison had recently returned from delivering a Dakota to the UK. His next assignment was Mosquito KB230, and initial reports had the aircraft down somewhere in western Newfoundland. Gander staff believed that Adkison and his Canadian radio operator, Paul F. Zyvitski, had force-landed north of Stephenville.[9]

At the Newfoundland Ranger detachment in Deer Lake, word reached none other than Ranger hero John Hogan that an aircraft was heard flying low near the logging camps in the Glide Brook area. "Shortly afterwards," Hogan reported, "her engines were heard to cut," followed by "a noise like an explosion." A concentrated search of the area by aircraft from Gander and Dorval revealed nothing. Wing Commander J.A.H. Tuck and Corporal Kelly of the security detail took the westbound train to investigate and met up with Hogan at Deer Lake. The trio then proceeded to the town of Howley, where someone had found a cap and a glove on Grand Lake. Spread along the shoreline for a distance of some seven miles, they found pieces of the missing aircraft, an RAF Transport Command hat, parts of a battle dress, and other evidence that neither crewmember had survived.[10]

Also in May

Civilian employee Bill Locke of the marine base staff was standing on the slipway that May when he heard an outcry from across Gander Lake. Locke spotted an overturned boat and hurriedly made his way to the scene in a marine launch. He found a Canadian padre, the only one wearing a lifejacket, holding up a Canadian army soldier. A second soldier had disappeared from view. Searchers found no trace of his body. The men had been pleasure cruising on the lake when their boat capsized.

May closed with the unit having dispatched 156 aircraft (no delivery figures appear in the unit's official monthly reports for January–April 1944), and another unfortunate loss. On the morning of the twenty-fourth, Pilot Officer Piotz Glydziak of the Polish Air Force, his Polish navigator, Flight Lieutenant Josef Rojek, and RCAF radio operator, Warrant Officer Second Class George S. Streisel, left for Lagens in the Azores in Mitchell HD352. Gander maintained wireless communications until Lagens accepted control. Three hours into the flight, all communications ceased and nothing further was ever heard: no distress signal or indication of trouble.[11]

James Reid Remembers

Early in June, Liberator KG847, one of several aircraft being ferried that day by Polish crews, was warming for its flight to the Azores. Maintenance worker James Reid was watching as he had looked after this aircraft prior to its engine run-up. For some reason,

Flying Officer Wojciech J. Dolewski, the crew's flight engineer, stepped off the aircraft to look around. He then turned to go back aboard, deciding to take a shortcut between the two running engines, but he misjudged the distance and the propeller blades struck him. "For a moment I was paralyzed," recalled Reid, and "then frantically tried to get the attention of the pilot to shut down, which he finally did." The crew aborted the flight and the other Polish crews shut down as well. The injured airman was rushed to hospital but shortly succumbed to his injuries. "It put a feeling of gloom over all of us that day," lamented Reid. Fellow crewmembers and personnel from the unit attended a short funeral service at the RCAF chapel, but his remains were not interred locally.[12]

Early in 1944, the Canadians and British had discontinued using the nearby cemetery, deciding instead to hold future burials in St. John's, where they were considering transferring all military remains at Gander after the war. So a train took the remains of Flying Officer Dolewski to St. John's for interment at the Joint Services Cemetery (later amalgamated with Mount Pleasant Cemetery). Pattison, having shed his "air representative" title and assumed the position of Newfoundland Director of Civil Aviation, recommended against relocating the remains to St. John's after the war, arguing that it "might cause distress to relatives." Besides, he added, "the site is pleasantly situated and with care in maintenance we need not fear any adverse feelings of relatives."[13] Canadian authorities ultimately shared Pattison's view but continued to send burials to St. John's, as did the British. The Americans, on the other hand, used Gander cemetery until war's end.

James Reid also recalled a less serious but memorable incident involving a supervisor, answerable to Gilmore and his polar opposite in demeanour. The man was impatient, loud, and constantly swearing, and this particular day directed Reid to tow three B-17s into the hangar bay. This was routine work for Reid, but the man kept "swearing at me to go faster and faster, waving me onward. I could see clearly that I was on a collision course with the steel girder, but he was the boss!" The wing tip struck and the man went into a swearing rant, "but Gilmore laid no blame upon me when I talked to him." Reid usually took directions from his crew chief and mentor, Sam Blandford, and figured Gilmore had already learned the truth from him about the mishap. Reid recalled another incident involving a commanding officer subsequent to Anderson. "Fellows at my level" typically had no contact with the unit commander, he said, but this one day, he chose Reid and Richard Gaul to accompany him in the Norseman he was piloting to the marine base at Botwood. "We took off and the first thing he did was pull out a flask" and tip back a good guzzle. Reid glanced at Gaul, rolling his eyes in disbelief. "Meanwhile, he had some friends fishing the Gander River just above Glenwood," Reid recalled, and was soon buzzing them in low-flying, tight circles. His passengers were terrified. "However, we survived it!"[14]

The Russians Are Coming

The crew of Liberator KG852 had a close call in June when Gander received an SOS that two engines were cutting out and the aircraft had lost altitude. The aircraft continued onward, landing safely at Prestwick thirty minutes after its ETA. The month ended with a record 219 aircraft ferried through Gander, including a group of twenty-one Russian Naval Air Service PBN-1 Nomad aircraft, an improved version of the PBY, but these were painted dark blue and sported Soviet red stars on the fuselage and wing tips. The Nomads, en route to Murmansk under the ferry movement code name "Pitch," landed on Gander Lake carrying 126 officers and men.[15] Flight plans, weather briefings, and radio traffic along the route were given in English, which the Russians could not speak, so Ferry Command assisted with the movement by assigning an experienced pilot and radio operator/navigator, or "safety crew," to each aircraft to handle the flight as far as Reykjavik. From there, the Russians would continue on their own to Murmansk.[16]

Shell Oil employee Calvin Pelley was working on the *Leapin' Lena* refuelling barge at Gander Lake when they landed. In their native tongue, the Russians asked for oil and gas. That much he could understand. With a man on each wing and a lead watching to ensure that everything was done safely and according to procedure, the process of getting the barge underway and completing the refuelling took an hour and a half.[17] Their visit gave the unit "its first opportunity of getting to know our Russian allies." Lieutenant Colonel Khrolenko, Assistant Naval Attaché for Air at the Soviet embassy in Washington and passenger aboard one of the aircraft, was Anderson's guest at "The Barn." Officials placed all recreational facilities at the disposal of their Russian visitors, who showed a particular interest in swimming, bowling, cinema shows, and their nation's favourite pastime, chess.[18]

A second "Pitch" movement of Russian PBN-1s commenced early in July using Gander Lake. Ferry Command personnel again accompanied the Russians as twenty-three aircraft were delivered to Reykjavik.[19] To assist with onboard communication on the Atlantic flight, the RAF provided both the Russians and the Ferry Command "safety crews" with duplicate lists of words and phrases. "The English sheets started with the English word, then its translation into phonetic Russian, then in Cyrillic Russian," said ferry pilot Flying Officer John W. Narburgh, who helped deliver two PBN-1s during the "Pitch" movement. "The Russian sheets had the same words and phrases, but in reverse order starting with Cyrillic Russian." Despite these verbal challenges, Ferry Command helped safely deliver all the PBN-1s to Iceland. "Our job was to fly with the Russians," said Narburgh, "but beyond that there was to be no fraternizing" with their Communist counterparts.[20] Unfortunately, the Russians did not manage too well on the leg to Murmansk and had several accidents, including one in which they lost their senior officer.[21]

A minor incident on the lake at the unit marine base in July saw the ever-reliable Norseman FR405, now sporting floats and a new engine, struck by an arriving Catalina as Captain Robert E. Perlick taxied up to the refuelling barge. The Norseman sustained minor damage. The bad luck continued when several days later, the recently rebuilt and likewise float-equipped Fox Moth sank at its mooring. The machine was raised and beached and back flying in a couple of weeks. The month closed with a drop in deliveries to ninety but an increase in the unit's home-based aircraft as Catalina FP530, nicknamed the "Galloping Goose," joined the Norseman and Fox Moth for air-sea rescue and communications work.[22]

Overseas deliveries picked up in August and came in at 120, with seventy of that number Liberators and Dakotas. Locally, Gilmore and newly arrived air-sea rescue pilot Flying Officer John Narburgh, not long finished his Russian PBN-1 delivery flights, made a number of mercy flights to rural communities. Regrettably, August also marked the unit's first fatal crash since February 1943.

Mitchell Down

Captain Vladimir J. Kabin, a thirty-one-year-old Canadian of Ukrainian descent, arrived at Gander from Dorval on 27 August 1944. This would be his fourteenth trip overseas since joining Ferry Command more than a year earlier and his third flying B-25 Mitchells. His cheerful disposition and "reputation for carefulness and efficiency made him very popular and crews were always desirous of making ocean flights under his captaincy," praised the *Ukrainian Weekly* newspaper. It helped too, that he had gained considerable flying experience before the war. Although born in Winnipeg, Kabin spent much of his life in Toronto and in the mid-1930s obtained his flying license with the Toronto Flying Club. "He continued his study," reported the *Weekly*, "until he had first-class papers in all branches of aviation – pilotage, navigation, radiology, and meteorology." For a time, he carried out high-altitude flying to gather temperatures for the Toronto Observatory, and next moved into commercial flying as a pilot with TCA. Kabin spent part of the war at Malton airport (now Toronto Pearson International) as an instructor and airfield control officer with the BCATP. He arrived at Ferry Command headquarters in Montréal with twenty-six hundred hours of flight time logged. He completed a flight check in May 1943 and six days later was bound overseas as first officer aboard a Hudson bomber. His first flight as captain came in September with the delivery of a Ventura on the South Atlantic route. Another delivery early in 1944 would establish a record as the first-ever Ventura to land at Lagens. Kabin then delivered a Dakota and a Ventura in February and March, and four Bostons and one B-25 Mitchell during the four-month period April to July, before arriving at Gander in August. This voyage, in Mitchell KJ584, was scheduled to be his last as he was afterwards due to return to TCA.[23]

Kabin's navigator on this flight was RAFVR (Volunteer Reserve) Flight Sergeant David Flood of Glasgow, Scotland. The twenty-one-year-old's only previous ferry trip was in July aboard a Dakota from Montréal to the UK via Goose Bay and Reykjavik. Early in August, Flood took a return flight to Montréal aboard a Consolidated Coronado flying boat. A few weeks later, he was crewed up with Captain Kabin. Assigned as KJ584's radio operator was twenty-four-year-old Sergeant Thomas T. Sheldrick, also RAFVR. A native of Greenwich, London, Sheldrick was no stranger to North and South Atlantic ferry operations, or Gander for that matter. He had one year with Ferry Command, helping deliver three Dakotas and two Venturas. Three of those flights he made direct from Gander to Lagens. His last ferry assignment, in Dakota KG738, terminated in the UK with stops at Goose Bay, Greenland, and Iceland. On 8 August, a Coronado flew him direct to Montréal where the present assignment awaited.[24]

For Flood and Sheldrick, this would be their first crossing in a B-25 Mitchell. The first leg of their flight on 29 August would take them to BW-1 in Greenland. It would be a nighttime departure. Refueller Calvin Pelley remembered speaking with the crew and refuelling the aircraft that summer night. During the run-up, he recalled, one of the engines was running rough and popping loudly, and he thought the pilot might abort the take-off and return to the hangar. Pelley watched as Kabin instead continued his take-off run, passing the Ferry Command hangars to his right as the Mitchell slowly gained altitude.[25] The aircraft was only seconds airborne when the starboard engine suddenly failed, putting the aircraft in a spin. Kabin regained control, but his lack of height and forced rate of descent left him helpless. The B-25 continued downward, crashed into heavy timber, and exploded in a ball of fire.[26]

The crew was killed instantly. Their remains were laid to rest at the Joint Services Cemetery in St. John's. At the graveside service, the RCAF provided a firing and mourning party and the Canadian navy, a band and naval buglers to sound the last post. St. John's mayor Andrew Carnell attended the funeral and placed a wreath on Kabin's grave at the request of Toronto mayor Frederick Conboy. Captain Vladimir Kabin left behind a wife and young daughter.[27]

Mercy Flights and Mosquitos

The Gander unit dispatched 149 aircraft in September but also had a couple of mishaps on the airfield with arriving Ferry Command aircraft. Liberator KH145 belly-landed after its undercarriage collapsed, and Avro Lancaster KB828 ground-looped and piled into a ditch off the runway. There was no loss of life in either case.[28]

September saw the air-sea rescue unit again respond to an emergency medical request, this one from the Newfoundland government. Word came that an epidemic had broken out among the children in Wild Cove, White Bay, and had caused one death. Gander expected a complete weather shutdown the next day, so Anderson left immediately in the Norseman and dropped off a nurse and doctor. "The epidemic," later wrote Anderson's secretary, "is now reported to be under control and there have been no further deaths." The month closed with the air-sea rescue unit strengthened when Ventura AE698 arrived from Dorval at the hands of pilot Narburgh.[29]

October marked the return of Flight Lieutenant McGrath from Bermuda as senior control officer for what was largely a routine month with deliveries numbering 115, including the first direct flight from Gander to the UK by a Mosquito. Captain Ernest M. Gill made the flight in KB492 in a record time of six hours and forty-four minutes. Another mercy flight saw Gilmore fly a doctor 110 miles to Westport, White Bay. The request came at short notice and Gilmore took off an hour before sunset. Battling a strong headwind, he landed in near darkness, but the winds prevented him from turning around and taxiing to sheltered water. "Seas broke continually over the aircraft and nothing could be done but repeatedly to shut off the engine and drift back, then restart the engine and crab toward what appeared to be the entrance to a narrow inlet. Signal flares were fired at intervals and after about two hours a motor boat came out and with some difficulty tied up alongside a float and managed, with the assistance of the Norseman engine, to get the aircraft turned around and headed for the shelter and safety of the harbour. It was a rather shaken young doctor who landed there to attend his first emergency call in Newfoundland. The following day the doctor and patient were flown back to Gander."[30]

On the heels of Captain Gill's record-setting flight in KB492 in October came some troublesome Mosquito deliveries. Mosquito KB504 was one of a pair dispatched five minutes apart to BW-1 on 12 November. American civilian Thomas F. Campbell occupied the pilot's seat, accompanied by Pilot Officer George D. Boyd, RCAF, radio operator/navigator. Campbell's counterpart, Captain John G. Teas in Mosquito KB505, was unable to clear the weather front even at twenty-seven thousand feet and returned to Gander. Campbell presumably encountered the same daunting weather system. The flight had clearly taken a turn for the worse when, at an estimated position halfway between Newfoundland and Greenland, the SOS went out. When nothing further was heard from KB504, two US Coast Guard weather boats and a PBY from BW-1 commenced a search. Rescue aircraft at Gander could do nothing as the weather closed in and light faded in the search area. The next day dawned with no news as aircraft from BW-1 and Coast Guard boats started a square search pattern. An American B-17 managed to leave Gander before the weather again shut down the field. The crew searched until dark in a one-thousand-foot ceiling over rough seas and later landed at Moncton, New Brunswick. More bad weather on the fourteenth meant no flying and no organized search from Newfoundland. The Coast Guard's effort nevertheless continued. Back at Gander, a frustrated senior control officer, dissatisfied with the information they were receiving on the search effort, especially from the Coast Guard ships, complained to Dorval. The results eventually trickled in, but on the very day that Dorval sent word to abandon the search.[31] A second incident at month's end saw Mosquito KB535 leave Goose Bay for BW-1 and likewise disappear.[32]

Overall, reported Anderson, the month of November had been disappointing in terms of aircraft movements, with only eighty-eight deliveries because of poor weather that shut down the field for more than half the month.[33] April and November months generally brought many fogged-in days, recalled maintenance worker James Reid. With no planes to service, "5 and 10 cent poker games abounded, and many, many hours were passed playing poker, or watching it being played."[34] Along with increased gambling and slow-moving deliveries, November brought worrisome news of possible sabotage to a B-25 Mitchell that arrived from Dorval.

Put a Cork in It

On 4 November, Gander operations dispatched eleven Mitchells overseas via BW-1. Nine of that number landed safely at BW-1, while one returned to Gander due to inclement weather and another because of radio trouble. Pilot Officer Glen C. Acheson's Mitchell KJ680, on the other hand, never got off the ground. A terse entry in the control officer's diary stated simply, "Case of suspected sabotage in KJ680. CO [commanding officer] dealing with it."[35] On 16 December 1944, Royal Canadian Mounted Police (RCMP) Assistant Commissioner V.A.M. Kemp, Director, Criminal Investigation, notified the chief of the Newfoundland Constabulary in St. John's that their Canadian counterparts had been requested (presumably by Ferry Command headquarters in Dorval) to investigate the matter. "Information received," added Kemp, "indicates that the gas line of this plane was tampered with and this could not have been committed except at Gander where refuelling was taking place prior to the aircraft being flown overseas." Investigators were then at Dorval but expected to continue their inquiries at Gander.[36] Ultimately, Kemp's was essentially a courtesy letter, intended to explain his officers' anticipated presence at Gander while welcoming the cooperation of Newfoundland authorities.

On the morning of 22 December, RCMP constables Sein Marel and J.J. MacDonald arrived at Gander from Dorval aboard a Ferry Command aircraft and shortly afterwards called on Newfoundland Constabulary Constable Charles Whitten. The RCMP investigators revealed to Whitten that "there was a small piece of cork discovered in the gas line of one of the tanks," and asked that he have the Shell Oil Company summon the men who refuelled the aircraft that day. Whitten contacted Shell manager Ron Hayden and soon, two presumably nervous and bewildered young men, Leonard Miller of Trouty, Trinity Bay, and Pearcey Bartlett of Goose Cove near Trinity, arrived at the Gander police detachment. The RCMP questioned the pair inside the magistrate's office in the presence of Whitten and RAF security officer Flight Lieutenant Frank Godson, and concluded that Miller and Bartlett knew nothing about the cork. Indeed, they could remember little about the aircraft in question, having refuelled ten or twelve planes that day. The RCMP constables left Gander the following morning and what became of their investigation is unclear. However, in conversation with Godson, Constable Whitten discovered that the pilot and co-pilot had conflicting accounts about whether they had used the fuel tank in question coming from Dorval. If they had not used it, then the cork could have been there before they arrived at Gander.[37] Maintenance carried out the necessary repairs and Gander dispatched KJ680 overseas two weeks after it had initially landed and five weeks before the RCMP investigators arrived, so re-examination of the aircraft was not an option.[38]

Interestingly, both Constable Whitten's report and the RCMP's correspondence with the Newfoundland government suggest that the Mitchell flew to Gander direct from Dorval. However, Acheson's Ferry Command crew assignment card reveals that the crew stopped en route at Sept-Îles (Seven Islands), Quebec, on the north shore of the St. Lawrence River. For reasons that are unclear, they remained there for several days before proceeding to Gander. The flying control officer's landing log indicates that there was no let-up in arrivals at Gander from Dorval during that time, so presumably it was not weather-related. Nor is it clear if ground personnel carried out maintenance or refuelling on the aircraft at Sept-Îles.[39]

Postwar, stories of the suspected sabotage circulated around Gander. In an interview published in the Gander *Beacon* in 1977, former Shell employee Cecil Edison told how Ferry Command "had been losing a lot of B-25's in mid-flight and no one seemed to know why. After the plane had flown for a while, the fuel in the wing tanks would be all used and the captain would then switch to the bomb bay or cabin tanks for the last leg home. This usually occurred in mid-ocean." At this point, goes the sabotage theory, the blocked line would starve the engines of fuel, sending the aircraft into the ocean.[40]

Published research into Ferry Command fatal accidents, especially the work of author Carl Christie, suggests that the total number of mid-flight B-25 Mitchell losses during overseas ferrying operations was not abnormally high in comparison to other aircraft types.[41] In any event, on "this particular day," Edison continued, ground staff "had to leave the cabin because the fumes were coming back from the fuel pipe instead of going out the vent pipe and found that a cork plug had been inserted into it. The plane showed no signs of trouble until the auxiliary tanks were switched on then this cork plug would cause a vapor lock and the plane would go down before the crew had time to find out what was wrong." Edison also claimed that authorities found the culprit at Dorval responsible for plugging the fuel lines of KJ680 and other aircraft, but this is unconfirmed and likely attributable to common wartime rumour.[42]

Censorship and Security

Gander's succession of commanding officers were nevertheless mindful of the potential for sabotage, and when the need arose, they introduced counteractive security measures. The Canadian Army provided external security, manning guard posts and Bofors antiaircraft guns around the unit and guarding the outer entrances to the hangars. For internal security, the unit later organized a Ferry Command warden section to, among other things, guard downed aircraft, check people entering the hangars, and ensure that no unauthorized persons tampered with hangar equipment or the aircraft stored inside. In mid-1943, the Canadian Army guards provided by The Pictou Highlanders were withdrawn permanently from Beaver Centre and the unit's security guards took over.[43] The guards, mostly Newfoundland ex-servicemen, came recommended by the chief of the Newfoundland Constabulary and were distinguishable from other uniformed personnel by their bright red berets.[44] The chief warden handled any disturbances that might arise at the Gander Inn or Eastbound Inn. Access to the marine base at Gander Lake was likewise subject to security protocol. The dirt road leading to the base passed adjacent to the cemetery and the transmitter site, which also had a security detail. "In order to prevent careless sabotage of government property," guards at the transmitting station allowed access to the marine base only if personnel presented a signed Ferry Command pass.[45] An incident late in 1944 saw the guards take up arms when the RCAF commanding officer notified the unit of a possible enemy craft near Fogo Island carrying a landing party. Nothing came of it, but authorities stopped and searched the trains and a unit Hudson flew reconnaissance over Fogo.[46]

The commanding officer's routine orders occasionally warned staff about careless talk over the radio or teletype. Such offences, he emphasized after receiving reports of "unauthorized chit-chat by W/T and Teletype operators," will involve "not only instant dismissal, if civilian, but will render the offending persons liable for prosecution or court martial."[47] Indeed, radio operator Hazel Fausak told of an incident, possibly at Dorval, when a member of their signals group sent an un-coded, one-word greeting to friends at another station. "This was a very serious breach of security," she said, "since it may have given the enemy a clue this was a British station and they would then monitor it extremely closely. He was gone within hours."[48] These concerns also extended to the leakage of information in letters. The Newfoundland government had initially allowed Ferry Command to send private east and westbound mail by their own aircraft, but they withdrew part of that privilege in mid-1942. All westbound mail went instead to the Gander post office to be censored and sent forward by TCA. Eastbound mail was likewise censored at the local level. Postal authorities then returned the mail to the unit for dispatch to the UK by Ferry Command or BOAC aircraft. The privilege previously accorded commissioned officers to censor their own mail and sign their name and rank on the envelope was permitted to continue.[49]

In addition to handling Gander's westbound mail, TCA operated the Canadian Government Trans-Atlantic Air Service, a non-commercial initiative that began delivering mail and VIPs overseas in July 1943. The service "maintained a schedule of three round trips a week" using nine modified long-distance transport versions of the Canadian-built Avro Lancaster X.[50] The RAF transatlantic flight log, kept by Gander's senior control officer at the joint control centre, indicates that roughly seventy percent of these TCA-operated wartime crossings to the UK were made non-stop from either Dorval or Goose Bay, with the remaining balance using Gander.[51]

The Search for Commander Anderson

The last major salvage operation of the year by Gander's maintenance staff began with another wintertime forced landing, this one several days before Christmas 1944. Hudson EW896, sent to the unit in November as a staff transport aircraft, departed Gander that December on a routine flight to Dorval, piloted by air-sea rescue specialist and newly promoted Flight Lieutenant John Narburgh, an Englishman from Carshalton Beeches, a neighbourhood in south London. With him was navigator and fellow countryman Flying Officer Derrick W. "Bill" Caddick, and local boy, radio operator Flight Lieutenant Maxwell D. Hutchings of Bell Island. His friends called him "Hutch." Twenty-one-year-old

Narburgh had been two years with the Ferry Command, making his first delivery in a PBY out of Bermuda in November 1942. His flying destinations during 1943 were mixed, with landings at Gander, Goose Bay, Elizabeth City (North Carolina), Miami, Nassau in the Bahamas, and Accra on the Gold Coast. The first half of 1944 would be little different, aside from several flights into Reykjavik, and perhaps more importantly, his marriage to Miss Alice Elizabeth "Georgie" Blue of Montréal.[52]

In mid-1944, rumours of postings to England circulated around Dorval. Hopeful of getting one, a disappointed Narburgh instead received a six-month posting to Gander as captain of the unit's air-sea rescue unit with crewmen Hutch and Caddick. "There was some interesting and exciting flying, interspersed with long periods of boredom," he admitted, "and of course I was living away from Georgie, which was the biggest negative of all." At Gander, Narburgh had four aircraft at his disposal: the PBY "Galloping Goose"; a Ventura that he used both for trips to Montréal and to run a weekly mail and passenger service to Harmon Field and RCAF Station Torbay near St. John's in eastern Newfoundland; and Norseman FR405 and Fox Moth VO-ADE, which he described as his "fun" aircraft "as they were a delight to fly." The Norseman he used as a recreation aircraft, to fish the nearby lakes and streams, and "to pick up patients in outlying villages, and bring them in to the hospital at Gander." The Fox Moth likewise became invaluable for transporting patients, "particularly after it started to snow. I'd put the skis on, land in the snow outside the village, and taxi right up to the house where the patient lived." Passenger space was limited, but once the patient was aboard, a few locals "would grab a wing, swing the plane around, and off we'd go back to Gander." Group Captain Anderson, "a very easy going father figure type of man," he lauded, never interfered with Narburgh's flying. "I was a free agent," and the Norseman seemingly his personal aircraft.[53]

As December approached, Narburgh anticipated getting a few days' leave at Christmas, intending to spend them in Montréal with his wife. Instead, he was scheduled to fly to Dorval and return to

Gander for Christmas, stopping along the way to pick up Group Captain Anderson's son, William, from boarding school in Bangor, Maine. Narburgh's Christmas hopes were dashed – or were they? "Suddenly I had an idea, a brilliant flash of genius. If the Group Captain could fly his son to Gander for the holidays maybe I could fly Georgie up as well!" Anderson supported the idea, and eventually so too did the air commodore at Ferry Command headquarters in Montréal. The only dissenting voice was Narburgh's father-in-law, averse to risk his daughter's life flying to Newfoundland in winter. He lost the argument.[54]

Hudson EW896, airborne from Gander on 21 December, also carried as passengers Group Captain Anderson and a Mrs. Parry. The intended direct flight to Dorval did not materialize as bad weather forced Narburgh to divert to Goose Bay. Conditions shortly improved and EW896 continued its journey, albeit briefly, as mechanical trouble forced the crew and passengers to return and overnight at the Labrador base. The flight resumed the following day and arrived at Dorval where passenger Parry deplaned.[55] Georgie was there, awaiting the arrival of her pilot husband. Another passenger, Flying Officer Clarke, also joined the flight. The plane was unheated, so both crew and passengers wore RAF-issued padded flying suits and winter boots. On 23 December, the Narburgh crew and passengers crossed the American border into the state of Maine. "It was Georgie's first flight, and I had her up in the cockpit most of the time," said Narburgh. "She loved it, although she felt a bit sick just before we landed at Bangor," where Anderson's son joined the flight. The weather looked fine from Bangor on, so Narburgh set course for Gander more than seven hundred miles to the northeast. Several hours later, however, snow and poor visibility greeted the pilot, "but operations brought us on" until about forty miles out when they suddenly announced that the field was unfit. Everything had closed in except Goose Bay. Spotting a break in the overcast, Narburgh descended. Below the clouds and with the ground barely visible through the snow, he circled in near darkness as navigator Caddick did his calculations. They would arrive at Goose Bay well after dark and with fifteen minutes of fuel to spare. "Too close for comfort," Narburgh figured, "especially with the weather playing tricks."

A useful guiding landmark for lost pilots was the Newfoundland rail line, running east–west across the island and adjacent to Gander airfield. After a brief and unsuccessful search for the narrow-gauge railway, Narburgh prepared to exercise his remaining option and belly-land in the snowy wilds of Newfoundland. Caddick took the co-pilot's seat while Anderson took charge in the back, getting everyone "to take up crash positions with knees up to the chest and hands clasped at the back of the neck." Anderson "wanted me to land on a lake, but I wasn't taking any chances on the thickness of the ice." After the pilot spotted a suitable snow-covered bog, Hutch started sending out mayday signals. Narburgh flew two low-level circuits to find a good spot and check for obstructions, and then "down we came, wheels up."[56] Narburgh described the landing:

> I had full flap down and stalled the aircraft a few feet above the snow and had her touch down tail first. As we touched I yelled for Bill [Caddick] to cut all the switches in the hope that this would reduce the risk of fire. Actually the landing was so smooth that the gas tanks were not even ruptured. The plane skidded for about 200 yards and slithered to a stop. Total silence, the only sound came from the nose of the plane, where the plexiglass had smashed and water was seeping in. This didn't amount to much, except it soaked some of the luggage that had been stowed in the nose – luckily it wasn't ours. We all breathed a sigh of relief; we were on terra firma, no one was hurt not even a scratch, and even the plane was not badly damaged. The tips of the props were bent, the flaps were ruined, but that was about all.[57]

The radio was still operable, so Hutch notified Gander of their landing. The crew and passengers exited the aircraft into the bitter cold and pushed through two feet of snow to a clump of trees two hundred yards away where they started a fire. A forced landing in the wilderness was not something to rattle Hutch. Exposure to danger had become routine while on operations overseas with RAF Coastal Command's No. 59 Squadron. Little could surpass the day in August 1943 when his Liberator crew attacked a U-boat in the Bay of Biscay. Despite heavy flak from the U-boat, the pilot pressed on and managed to release two depth charges.[58] A year later, Hutch was in Montréal, attached to the RAF Ferry Command.[59] After this flight, he was scheduled on leave and homeward bound to Bell Island for Christmas and a Boxing Day family wedding, but that was unlikely to happen now. Knowing that rescue in his native Newfoundland was measurable in days or weeks, he immediately drew upon his well-honed survival skills.[60] "We were really thankful for this," Narburgh admitted. Hutch could take down a tree with a few hard shots, whereas "Bill and I would chop for what seemed like hours."[61] Using an axe carried aboard the Hudson, Hutch cut poles for a lean-to shelter.[62] The men covered the top and sides with branches and over that spread several parachutes, making it snow and windproof. They also removed the Hudson's aluminum engine cowlings and placed them around the fire to reflect heat towards the shelter.[63] The winter boots and padded flying suits helped too.

Food supplies consisted of packages of K-rations, "nutritious but very boring," admitted Georgie, and a few sandwiches from packed lunches taken on at Dorval, so to supplement their meagre rations, Hutch set rabbit slips in the woods.[64] It happened too, that the Hudson carried bags of Christmas mail for the personnel at Gander. Some of the parcels contained fruitcakes, "easily identified as the bakeries had prepared them for mailing by sewing them into canvas bags," said Narburgh. Georgie fondly recalled Group Captain Anderson, sitting legs crossed in the shelter, going through the parcels and grinning each time he found a Christmas cake or cookies, which he passed to her for safekeeping.[65]

An organized search that night by American and Canadian aircraft quickly yielded results when light from the campfire below attracted the attention of a USATC B-17 Flying Fortress piloted by Captain Behrens. An Aldis lamp signalled from below in Morse code that all hands were unhurt. Behrens then flew back and forth over the area several times and returned to Gander, reporting that the downed aircraft was 12–15 miles north of the town of St. Alban's in southern Newfoundland.[66] Rescue would not be forthcoming this day, so everyone settled in for a night in the bush.

Dawn the next day, Christmas Eve, found Joe Gilmore searching the crash area in Norseman FR405, but the effort was in vain. Poor visibility and a malfunctioning radio compelled him to return to Gander, where heavy snow soon closed the field. Meantime, the RCAF was arranging to have a ground rescue party leave from St. Alban's. In St. John's, radio station VONF broadcast the Hudson's position and appealed to listeners in the area to aid the rescuers. Word also came from Montréal that an American air-sea rescue unit out of Manchester, New Hampshire, was taking over and assuming responsibility for the rescue. "Are we to do nothing for our own a/c [aircraft]!!??," questioned someone in disbelief in the margins of the control officer's diary. Ferry Command personnel at Gander were not content to stand idly by, and after consultation with Group Captain Anderson by radio, he instructed the senior control officer to "continue rescue operations."[67]

The absence of rescue aircraft that day was worrisome to those on the ground. Perhaps the B-17 had incorrectly marked their position. They decided it best to send out another signal but discovered that the Hudson's radio had since become water-damaged and inoperable. Hutch then remembered that the aircraft carried a "Gibson Girl" emergency transmitter, powered by a hand-crank generator that emitted a distress signal as the crank handle was turned. A fold-up metal frame box kite also came with the transmitter. Its flying line served as an aerial wire, but getting the kite airborne in the deep snow was no easy task. One man held the line while another walked off with the kite, playing out the line. Despite "their best efforts and using up all their energy trying to run in the snow, it would not take off." During their last attempt, the runner unceremoniously tripped over a snow-covered USAAF duffle bag that the B-17 had dropped the night before. A search of the area revealed several more bags containing rations, sleeping bags, clothing, flashlights, matches, axes, coffee, a stove, cooking utensils, chocolates, and a rifle. "That night we all ate and slept well," said Narburgh.[68] Indeed, the married couple took up residence in the Hudson, where they found a dry place on the floor and squeezed into a single sleeping bag.[69]

Search crews were on deck at 0500 hours Christmas morning, briefed and standing by for take-off. The Americans lent a hand with their C-47 Dakota and Beech C-45 Expeditor. At 0810 local time, the search was on. Gilmore still had trouble finding the downed Hudson and was about to give up when he spotted the seven cheering and waving castaways. He landed his ski-equipped Norseman next to EW896 and in the early afternoon flew to Gander with passengers Clarke, Georgie, and Anderson's son. Gilmore got in another trip that day, bringing in the group captain and Narburgh, who spotted Georgie, "standing on the tarmac in her fur coat waving." Poor weather the next two days prevented further rescue flights, but an American C-47 did get through and dropped supplies. On the twenty-eighth, Anderson got involved and flew Fox Moth VO-ADE in to retrieve the Christmas mail. Later that day, Gilmore dropped off two security guards in the Norseman and returned with the balance of the crew, Caddick and Hutch, and not a moment too soon, as a blizzard came on, shutting down all the runways.[70]

Georgie stayed in Gander almost two weeks, "and we had the most wonderful Christmas and New Year's imaginable," her husband fondly recalled. Everyone fussed over her, but "the anti-climax was when I got home," she lamented, as "no one had even heard that we had crash landed in the wilderness!"[71] Maxwell Hutchings missed the Boxing Day wedding, but his safe arrival home sparked a huge party and a re-enactment of the nuptials. His daughter Phyllise, then nine years old, was told years later "that it took seven strong men to lift my father's trunk up onto the porch because he had picked up quite a few bottles of booze for the celebration." And Max Hutchings had every reason to celebrate after the adventure with Hudson EW896.[72]

A Record-Setting Year

While the number of east and westbound transatlantic Return Ferry Service flights serviced by the Gander unit remained consistent with 1943's figure of 166, any similar comparison with delivery figures painted a very different picture. The year 1944, it turned out, brought little downtime for the unit's air traffic controllers, refuellers, signals staff, and ground crew, or "Erks," as the RAF fondly nicknamed them. The senior flying control officer's transatlantic flight log shows a year-end tally of approximately 1,375 deliveries, almost triple that of 1943. Liberator bombers represented the largest number of crossings at roughly 430, followed by some 365 C-47 Dakota transports. Combined, these two aircraft types accounted for fifty-eight percent of the deliveries in 1944, with the remaining percentage, or 580 aircraft, made up of Bostons (146), Catalinas (120), Mitchells (100), Lancasters (95), Fortresses (58), Mosquitos (30), Venturas (16), fourteen C-87s (Liberators modified for transport work), and one B-26 Marauder.[73]

Notwithstanding the successes that saw the war effort tilted in favour of Allied forces, there would be little slack in transatlantic ferrying operations through Gander during the first half of 1945. Regrettably, more losses of both aircraft and people lay in store for the unit. Among the latter was a man key to Ferry Command's delivery achievements at Gander.

CHAPTER 8 | A SAD DAY FOR GANDER

The year 1945 opened with a change in command as the popular and long-serving Group Captain Anderson concluded his tour of duty at Gander and left with his wife for a posting in Australia. Anderson, praised Air Commodore Griffith "Taffy" Powell, who headed up preparations at Gander for the inaugural flights in late 1940, "was one of the pillars of our delivery programme through those difficult winters and for that he would have merited even more rings and scrambled eggs on his cap."[1] Anderson's final "Order of the Day" was a letter addressed to everyone in the unit, conveying his appreciation for their loyalty and cooperation, and the "many happy memories of Newfoundland and many valued friendships made during my 2½ years amongst you." Squadron Leader A.W. Mack, DFC, assumed command on an interim basis pending the arrival of Group Captain J.A.S. Brown later in January.[2]

Brown was Anderson's complete opposite, recalled Flight Lieutenant Narburgh, taking a more disciplined approach to his command. Casual dress became a no-no. It was regulation only. Parades and drill became more frequent, as did barracks and kitchen inspections. Airmen improperly dressed, or "who failed to salute an officer, or who didn't have their beds made up according to regulations, were put on charge ... Everyone was grumbling as morale slumped." Most people, said Narburgh, just "tried to keep out of his way." His flying abilities were questionable too, and the pair soon butted heads during a flight in the unit Catalina. Narburgh was practicing "touch and go" water landings at the time when Brown, having tagged along for the flight, demanded to take the controls. Narburgh, unsure if the commander had ever done one or was even qualified on the type, suggested that he take the co-pilot's seat until he got the hang of things. Besides, the crew's safety was also Narburgh's responsibility. Brown reacted furiously, called out Narburgh and ordered him out of his seat and out of the cockpit. Narburgh refused and Brown ordered him back to Gander to face possible disciplinary action.[3]

Piggery manager Smallwood related another startling episode on a flight to Buchans to deliver two dachshunds that Group Captain Anderson had left in his care to sell. Brown was piloting the Norseman with Gilmore as co-pilot. Smallwood, his son Ramsay, and the dogs sat behind. Along the shores of Red Indian Lake, Brown spotted the small logging settlement of Millertown and dropped the Norseman's nose down to get a closer look. The aircraft gathered speed. Smallwood was uneasy and Gilmore, by the look on his face, was "clearly alarmed. He looked at Brown, and then down again, and back, and suddenly he seized the wheel with a shout at Brown and pulled back, at first gently and then quickly with all his strength." The aircraft levelled off, nearing the ground. Brown resumed control, and when he landed at Buchans, "gave Gilmore a mild perfunctory reprimand." Once in private with Smallwood, Gilmore let loose, describing the group captain as a "madman." When Gilmore seized control, he told Smallwood, the Norseman was in a power dive and "we were in danger of tearing the wings off."[4]

EW896 Takes Flight

In addition to a change in command, January marked a shift in focus from rescue to salvage at Hudson EW896 near St. Alban's. During the first week of January, Gilmore's men set up camp at the site, established radio communication with Gander and arranged regular supply schedules. The work took six weeks, but by mid-February, they had repaired EW896 and fitted its undercarriage with skis. The flying expertise of Captain Lowell Thompson was once again highlighted by another "perfect" landing at Gander as the repaired Hudson came in, marking "yet another successful salvage to Gilmore's credit," praised senior control officer McGrath.[5] Gilmore, too, had performed yeoman's work, making no less than twenty flights to EW896 in Norseman FR405 during salvage operations. He made a further half-dozen trips after the recovery, presumably to gather supplies and equipment left behind.[6]

As for Flight Lieutenant Narburgh, his six-month tour at Gander ended in March and he returned to Dorval, expecting to go back on deliveries; but it was not to be. Word came that he was to be posted back to England. This might have been his preferred choice six months earlier, but circumstances had changed. Georgie was now pregnant and could not travel in her current condition. Besides, "I want to be with her when our little one is born," he told his parents. "I pulled all the strings I knew but to no avail. Then the idea suddenly struck me, why not volunteer to go back to Gander for another six months?" The strategy worked, and he was soon back with the unit, and considering himself "lucky to be here."[7]

Mosquito Misfortunes

The changing situation in Europe and the winter weather that often delayed operations on the North Atlantic did not interrupt Ferry Command aircraft movements through Gander during the opening months of 1945. The unit serviced a total of 150 deliveries in January and February, with half of the aircraft being non-combat C-47 Dakota transports and the rest a mix of Lancasters, Liberators, Bostons, Fortresses, and Mosquitos. March was busier still, with operations dispatching nearly two hundred aircraft, sixty-five of them Mosquitos. Sixteen aircraft returned safely because of poor weather or mechanical problems,[8] but Captain Woodrow Walden's Mosquito KB593 disappeared en route to the Azores carrying British civilian radio operator/navigator Thomas Scotland.[9]

Narburgh, only days returned, searched for twelve hours, which "was more flying than we used to put in in a month."[10] Dorval suggested a very large probable search area, to which an unimpressed McGrath retorted, "They are not very helpful really." The uncertainties surrounding the loss of KB593 also left the RCAF reluctant to take its aircraft off operations to assist. The US Navy alerted its weather ships in the region and Lagens dispatched a search aircraft, but it crashed on take-off. An American B-17 tried to reach the search area but engine trouble thwarted their efforts. Three days after the disappearance of KB593, Dorval cancelled the search. The Mosquito captains at Gander were now concerned enough to want to cross by the southern route, but Dorval had ruled otherwise, explained McGrath.[11] The recent run of missing Mosquitos, including one each out of Goose Bay and Gander in November 1944, two more on the South Atlantic route in December, and one out of BW-1 in February 1945, was not lost on officials with the manufacturer, de Havilland Canada in Downsview, Ontario. Indeed, a Mr. Reginald V. Corlett represented the company when the accident investigation convened at Gander "to specially inquire into the circumstances leading up [to] and resulting in the loss" of Walden's aircraft.[12]

Mosquito problems continued to dog North Atlantic ferry operations. On 16 April, KA968 disappeared between Gander and Prestwick with its two Polish crew, Flying Officers Jerzy Wielondek and Marian Zajac. Things could have gotten worse that day when Mosquito KA959, flying through cloud and ice at eight thousand feet, sent an emergency signal that their oxygen was gone. The crew descended to four thousand feet and shortly reported that everything was fine. A presumably relieved Captain Sandison eventually made landfall and set down safely at his destination in the Azores.[13]

A Welcoming Gesture

Around this time too, some seventy returning Newfoundland troops arrived at Gander aboard the eastbound train. Waiting to greet them at the station were fellow Newfoundlanders and Ferry Command unit members McGrath, Hutch, Flying Officer Frank Corbett (he was granted a CC commission as pilot officer in May 1944 and promoted to flying officer in October 1944), and Flight Lieutenant Frank Stirling, who started in operations in April 1942 as a CC commissioned pilot officer and became a flying control officer in March 1945. Each man brought with him a bottle of rum to share around. The Newfoundland Airport Club, a social organization formed before the war, provided each man with beer and cigarettes. The troops were "very appreciative," wrote McGrath, who had reason to celebrate too. That same day came word from Dorval of his promotion to squadron leader (with effect from December 1943). The next day, after some alterations at the tailor's, he appeared in his squadron leader "stripes for [the] first time."[14]

A Beloved and Respected Man Is Lost

Joe Gilmore, the seemingly ubiquitous head of maintenance, had by 1945 become widely known and respected in central Newfoundland, especially in rural outport communities where he flew in medical aid or evacuated patients. With the war effort clearly tilted in the Allies' favour and a subsequent slackening of censorship restrictions, local newspapers the *Western Star* and the *Daily News* featured a story on the work of the Gander unit in serving "the fleets of bombers being delivered to the war fronts." The writer, unit piggery manager Smallwood, applauded both the Newfoundland labour component among the aircraft maintenance staff, and the domestic flying activities and exceptional work of Gilmore and the recently departed Group Captain Anderson, "both of them men with deep interest in and liking for Newfoundland and Newfoundlanders." The maintenance department, praised Smallwood, "is one of the most skilfully efficient operating anywhere," and the local flying, although incidental to the unit's primary job, from "Newfoundland's standpoint ... had been of the utmost value." Smallwood further elaborated:

> That flying has been done mainly in single-engined Moths and Norseman planes, and twin-engined Cansos. It has been done with wheels, floats and skis, in all seasons of the year, under almost all conceivable types of Newfoundland weather. The ships are based at Gander for RAFTC's air-sea rescue work, and some of the flying has been done in connection with that work. Some has been done as mercy flights to bring patients to Gander or elsewhere for hospitalization. Many flights have been made in connection with searches, with repairs to stricken aircraft, with routine calls to outlying depots associated with RAFTC, and a variety of other purposes falling under no particular classification.
>
> Of the 500 or more flights made in Newfoundland by RAFTC Gander-based planes in the past two years, these veteran fliers have piloted well over half. Group Captain Anderson himself has flown over 100 hours, while Chief Engineer Gilmore has flown even more – 241 hours. These have almost without exception been flights made by both pilots apart from their onerous normal duties at the airport. Again, from a Newfoundland standpoint it is a lucky thing that Group Captain Anderson and Chief Engineer Gilmore made so many flights, for each of them almost invariably took a Newfoundland-born member of the Aircraft Maintenance staff with him as aircraft engineer.[15]

"Joe was quiet, competent, and informed," praised James Reid years later. "He got things done, played no favourites, and was well respected by the whole department."[16] John Murphy described him as "a surrogate father to us young guys away from home," and Smallwood further added that a case could be made to "support the claim of numerous transatlantic pilots who say that he is the greatest airplane mechanic in the world today."[17]

Sadly, the next newspaper headline on Joe Gilmore was to announce his loss. The oft-flown and previously submerged Norseman FR405 was due for an overhaul, and it fell to Gilmore to get the aircraft to Montréal for servicing. April closed with Gilmore and signals section boss Squadron Leader Frank Ratcliffe en route to Dorval, escorted by a Catalina piloted by Flight Lieutenant Narburgh. The two aircraft overnighted at Harmon Field and resumed the journey the next day, 1 May. Narburgh was to guide Gilmore to Prince Edward Island where he would refuel, he explained, "because on his own it would be difficult to navigate across the roughly 200 miles of sea" between Newfoundland and Canada. Having reached the coast of Prince Edward Island, the Catalina radioed Gilmore, wished him well, and continued on.

"That was the last we heard of him," said Narburgh. Some fifteen miles east of Charlottetown near Peakes Station, the Norseman inexplicably dove into a farmer's field and burst into flames, killing "two of the most deeply respected and admired men of the station." Narburgh heard the news only after he reached Dorval. Details were skimpy, and he never did learn what happened.[18] A Ferry Command aircraft flew their remains to Gander, where separate funeral services were held on 4 May at the RCAF and the American Roman Catholic chapels, followed by a combined procession. It was "a sad afternoon for Gander," wrote Squadron Leader McGrath, who took part as a pallbearer.[19]

Notwithstanding any previous pronouncements that saw deceased service personnel sent to St. John's, Gilmore and Ratcliffe were buried at Gander. Ratcliffe left behind a wife, Margaret, and a young son, Michael, and Gilmore a pregnant wife and five young children. "For the thousands of aircrews who have been flying the Atlantic these past years," eulogized the *Evening Telegram*, Gilmore "was something of a tradition for cool-headed efficiency. A large number of Newfoundlanders have been trained as aircraft maintenance mechanics by Mr. Gilmore, and it is simple truth to say that to them his death is almost like that of a beloved parent. Throughout the great airports of the North Atlantic the news of Mr. Gilmore's tragically untimely death will be heard with personal sorrow, for he was universally as fondly liked as he was deeply respected." The paper praised Ratcliffe too, as the man principally responsible for training a large number of Newfoundlanders as radio operators and "for the fine world-wide reputation which the great Gander radio organization enjoys today."[20]

Reflecting on the loss, Narburgh was more prosaic. In those days, fatal plane crashes were "not unusual … so people quickly got over the shock and went on with their lives."[21] So it was then that days after the funeral, the somber mood turned celebratory throughout much of the airfield with word of Germany's unconditional surrender. Not so at the RAF unit. Group Captain Brown warned against any undue celebrations, so it was business as usual, although it "all seems a bit unnecessary," admitted McGrath, and

Brown's orders left hard feelings among the staff. McGrath celebrated nonetheless that evening with a bottle of champagne at Flight Lieutenant Stirling's place.[22] Naturally, the unit's important work had to continue, so soon after the funeral, Brown's routine orders saw maintenance foreman Jack Fennell assume superintendent Joe Gilmore's duties, at least temporarily until John Neidy was appointed to the position.[23]

Summer Events

In May 1945, joint RAF-USATC transatlantic air traffic control at the control room in Hangar 21 ceased after two years in operation, and the US section moved to Hangar 9 in the American sector.[24] During this two-year period, the busy control staff handled a total of 7,500 USAAF and RAF Ferry Command aircraft on overseas delivery flights.[25] The departure of the Americans left the control room solely in the hands of the RAF, whose air traffic controllers and senior control officer were called upon in June to handle a major movement of RCAF Lancasters returning from overseas via the Azores. Some 150 Lancasters landed at the field that month without incident, although a couple came in with an engine out. In one case, the aircraft was more than three hundred miles out, so as a precaution, Gander alerted the unit's air-sea rescue Canso and an RCAF Hudson from Torbay, equipped with a droppable airborne lifeboat. There were some tense moments nearing the coast after Gander lost radar and radio contact, but the Lancaster came in safely.[26] The bombers were bound for Canada and service with Tiger Force, a long-range heavy bomber force scheduled for deployment to the Pacific theatre of war. (The deployment would become unnecessary when Japan capitulated in August following the bombing of Hiroshima and Nagasaki.)[27]

Early in July, Dorval-based RY-3 Liberator JT982 with 45 Group's 231 (Transport) Squadron disappeared over the Atlantic carrying six crew and nine passengers from the UK civil service (six of them women), returning home following the United Nations Conference in San Francisco. Liberators carrying droppable

Lindholme rescue gear (cylinder-shaped floating containers that housed a dinghy and other survival equipment) took up the search, as did a B-17 equipped with a droppable airborne lifeboat. One Liberator picked up something on the distress frequency, but it turned out to be a boat. Then, on the third day, a search aircraft spotted two dinghies with six people. The sighting caused a "great flap," with aircraft converging from all directions, dropping Lindholme gear and a lifeboat. In dramatic fashion, Canso FT998, sent from Dorval and staged out of Gander on the search, alighted on the water and picked up the survivors. Only after the Canso got airborne did Gander discover that they were not from the RY-3 but a Liberator out of Torbay that had run into trouble searching for the RY-3 and ditched in the ocean. Regrettably, the pilot was killed in the forced landing. The rescue earned accolades from the RCAF and senior control officer McGrath, who believed the Canso pilot, Flying Officer Jack R. Revill, deserved a medal for his efforts, although it was "a great anti-climax for us," he added. Two more days of searching turned up nothing. For his actions, Revill, having "exercised considerable skill and coolness," subsequently received a King's Commendation for Valuable Service in the Air. Efforts to find the missing RY-3 had meanwhile brought no results and the search was abandoned.[28]

The month of July also saw American forces at Gander begin trials with an aircraft blind-landing radar system called Ground Control Approach (GCA). A trailer housing the radar gear and operators was towed by truck to the active runway. The following year, the commercial airlines operating through Gander cost-shared their own GCA system. It would become a standard airport feature, guiding aircraft to safe landing in adverse weather, but in 1945 it was new and ground-breaking technology.[29] On invitation to the American side, Ferry Command controllers and the unit's air-sea rescue Canso crew watched a movie on GCA and afterwards witnessed from the tower as the system "worked very well" bringing in a B-17. Senior control officer McGrath made some trial flights aboard a US B-17 and watched several approaches on the equipment from the GCA trailer. Although the new apparatus left one arriving BOAC pilot sceptical and he refused to try it initially, other arriving Ferry Command pilots tried the system with generally positive reviews.[30]

V-J Day in August brought celebrations, speeches by the US, RCAF, and RAF commanding officers, and thanksgiving services throughout the airfield. The Canadians hosted a fireworks display and a few pistol flares were fired off on the RAF side.[31] A week later, the unit welcomed France's General Charles de Gaulle on his first visit to Gander. Group Captain Brown met the general and his party, introducing them to the commanding officers of the RCAF station and USAAF base unit. After inspecting the RCAF honour guard, de Gaulle was entertained at "The Barn," where he spent the night before leaving for Washington in the morning.[32]

That same evening, after several difficult months, Mary Gilmore and her five children boarded an RAF B-24 Liberator and left Gander for good. With no flight clothing, the family huddled together for warmth in the freezing bomb-bay. Battling a headwind, "the trip seemed to last forever," recalled Sean Gilmore, then eleven years old. They arrived at Dorval in the early morning hours to find the airfield empty. The family had to wait until sunrise to get a ride to Verdun. Of that day, said Sean more than seventy years later, "I do recall feeling as sad as I have ever felt in my life. It was a physically painful sadness."[33]

Final Delivery Numbers

Ferry flights through Gander had slacked little from January 1945 to V-J Day in August. During this eight-month period, the unit's hard-working ground staff handled in excess of eight hundred deliveries. As in 1944, Liberators and Dakotas were the dominant aircraft types on this transatlantic route, at nearly seventy percent of the delivery total. Some 150 Lancasters and one hundred Mosquitos also made the crossing, along with a handful of Fortresses, RY-3s, and Douglas C-54 Skymaster transports.[34] After Japan signed the Japanese Instrument of Surrender early in September, formalizing its surrender, all deliveries stopped. Contracts with ferry personnel were terminated, a process that had been ongoing for some months, and "many pilots found positions with airlines or fledgling aviation companies hoping to take advantage of a postwar flying boom."[35] The BOAC-operated Return Ferry Service, which continued to function for the time being, had likewise showed no slowdown during the first eight months of 1945, with overseas arrivals and departures of its Liberator transports totalling 125.[36]

Sunk off Belle Isle

October marked the unit's last ever major mishap, and fittingly, the rescuers this time were the same rural Newfoundlanders for whom the Gander unit had so often rendered airborne medical aid. Early that month came word that a lighthouse keeper on Belle Isle had sustained a serious hand injury that required immediate medical attention, so the unit sent out recently arrived air-sea rescue Canso FT999. Among its five-man crew was St. John's native Flying Officer John D. Sinnott, assigned to Gander two months prior as FT999's radio operator. Overseas with the RAF, Sinnott had completed twenty-nine operational sorties over enemy territory, including six to Berlin. His "coolness under fire ... outstanding ability and strong sense of duty" earned him the DFC.[37] Now he was home, only this day facing howling winds and rough seas rather than German searchlights and flak. After two attempts, Flying Officer Henry L. Buxton landed the Canso off Belle Isle and took aboard the injured man and two passengers, employees of a weather station on the island. Assistant light keeper Spoffard Earle and his associate, Hedley Buckle, had rowed the men out in a dory and now stood by as the Canso prepared to leave. Battling a fierce wind, Buxton opened the throttle wide, but each take-off attempt was in vain. A heavily laden Canso could struggle for three minutes just to gain enough airspeed to "get on the step" and get airborne. For Buxton, however, just as it seemed that the Canso would unglue itself from the ocean, it fell back heavily. "After being tossed about helplessly for some time," reported the St. John's *Evening*

Telegram, "the violent waves smashed holes in the craft, and it began to settle in the sea as water poured in." Passengers and crew scrambled from the stricken Canso and perched on the wings and other parts of the rapidly submerging aircraft.[38]

Buckle and Earle, witnessing this from their dory, dropped their oars in the water and began to row. Their boat was small, but Earle got six rescued men to sit in the stern "and lie back in one another's arms ... We figured the rest must have drowned." Suddenly, another man emerged from the cockpit, ran across the wing, and got aboard the boat. The last man, Earle recalled, came up from beneath the water, looked right at him and said, "I'm goin' to drown." He went down again, and the next time he surfaced by the stern of the dory, Earle grabbed him. Eight minutes later, the Canso slipped beneath the waves, but they had rescued all eight men. Their combined weight, plus that of Earle and Buckle, left the dory some six inches above the water. One man started singing the hymn "Pull for the shore, sailor, pull for the shore," and "we pulled and pulled and pulled on the paddles," said Earle. With the sea breaking all around and an easterly gale threatening to push them past the island and into the strong tidal currents of the Strait of Belle Isle, the exhausted rescuers finally made it ashore and to the wharf. "That was a hard day," reflected Earle years later. "I don't believe I ever told that story without cryin', without breakin' down. This day and age we would have got a medal; all I got was sore feet."[39] The Canso crew overnighted on the island and an RCN Corvette brought them to St. John's. A few days later, an RCAF Norseman collected the five airmen and returned them to Gander. Two weeks after the mishap, with the unit's air-sea rescue Canso submerged off Belle Isle, Dorval sent replacement Canso FT998 and a new crew with Flying Officer Jack Revill as pilot. The delivery of Norseman FR406 that month also met the need for a replacement utility aircraft.[40]

A New Commander Arrives

Also in October, Gander bade farewell to Group Captain Brown and welcomed in his stead Wing Commander Leonard E.

Botting, DFC, and recipient of the Polish Médaille Militaire and French Croix de Guerre. Botting arrived at a watershed period for the unit as the RAF was slowly releasing service personnel from active duty. Others could apply to a newly created review board for compassionate postings or leave to the UK. The unit nevertheless continued to function and settled into a more "normalized" peace-time work week routine with all staff, except watchkeepers and other essential personnel, working a half-day Saturday and observing Sunday as a full day of rest. Unit members continued to form new sports, entertainment, and welfare committees, while the signals section's social-oriented Sparklub regularly sponsored dances and symphonic concerts. Having issued a three-game challenge to their Canadian counterparts, service and civilian members formed a basketball team, and later a hockey team called the Atomics. "The general morale of the unit has improved considerably," recorded the unit diary, "due, no doubt, to the efforts to provide adequate entertainment for the coming winter months and to improve the tenor of life here."[41]

Concurrent with Botting's arrival and the winding down of operations at the Ferry Command unit, commercial airline companies were pressing Newfoundland to begin scheduled transatlantic passenger services through Gander, which was still under RCAF control. No date had yet been set for Newfoundland to resume control; nor had anyone carried out a detailed postwar assessment on the availability and suitability of airport infrastructure for commercial operations. To address the latter, Newfoundland would turn to commander Botting as Gander prepared to transition from a military base to a civil airport and position itself to become a key player in transatlantic commercial aviation.

CHAPTER 9 | CROSSROADS: A NEW BEGINNING

Peace in 1945 signalled the beginning of a new era for Gander. The US slowly phased out its operations, reducing personnel strength and sending equipment and surplus supplies to its other Newfoundland bases at Fort Pepperrell and Harmon Field. This gradual process saw infrastructure in the American sector – hangars, barracks, mess halls, maintenance, sporting and recreation facilities, and other buildings – returned to Canada on a piecemeal basis. Concurrently, three American airlines prepared for the introduction of the transatlantic landplane services that war had delayed, and for which the airfield was originally intended. Pan American Airways was quick out of the gate, and soon after V-J Day on 15 August, had a Douglas DC-4 Clipper complete the airline's first route check of the northern airway via Gander, which, for the time being at least, remained under RCAF control. Next came representatives of both AEA, soon to merge with American Airlines to become American Overseas Airlines (AOA), and TWA to survey the airfield and its maintenance facilities.[1]

In October 1945, under the International Air Services Transit Agreement, or "Two Freedoms Agreement," Newfoundland authorized the three American carriers to operate their scheduled routes through Gander. The "Two Freedoms Agreement," signed in December 1944 at the Chicago Convention on International Civil Aviation, gave civil air carriers (1) overflight privileges, or the right of transit over another country without landing, and (2) "the right to land in another country 'for non-traffic purposes.' " The latter freedom allowed aircraft to land at Gander for technical reasons, such as refuelling, maintenance, and emergencies, but not for commercial or traffic purposes, such as embarking or disembarking passengers.[2] Having said that, attending nations at the Chicago convention had also ratified additional freedoms that would permit commercial traffic rights, but Newfoundland would not immediately grant them until the "general use of all airports in Newfoundland territory for commercial use has been decided," reported the St. John's *Daily News*.[3]

The first American use of Gander airport under the transit only arrangement created some quiet controversy, explains historian Peter Neary, when on 23 October 1945 an AEA flight, bound overseas from the US, disembarked one passenger and sixteen hundred pounds of mail, thus violating its transit privileges. A dismayed Pattison "immediately telephoned [Newfoundland government Commissioner Sir John C.] Puddester in St. John's ... and was told that both passenger and mail would have to be taken back on board and carried on to England. The commissioner changed his mind about the passenger, however, when Pattison explained that it was none other than His Excellency James F. O'Neill, the Roman Catholic Bishop of Harbour Grace. He could hardly be sent winging out over the Atlantic in order to maintain the letter of the law, and his unorthodox arrival was excused by the government because of his 'high position in the church.' " The Americans, however, refused to take the mail back aboard, so it was "held by Newfoundland customs pending the return journey of the plane, when it would be picked up and carried back to the United States." Newfoundland issued no written grievance on the matter, although "an indignant Puddester saw Robert J. Cavanaugh, the United States vice consul in St. John's, and through him called on the State Department to remonstrate with the offending airline."[4]

Other problems soon arose at Gander. The arrangement that saw Canada control the airfield also left Newfoundland hamstrung and unable to move forward with a permanent set-up for commercial operations. With some airlines now routing traffic through Gander and planning to centralize their Newfoundland operations there using Goose Bay and Stephenville as poor-weather alternates, civil aviation director Pattison warned the Commission of Government that there were no terminal facilities or staff of any kind. This was Newfoundland's responsibility, he reminded them, and unlikely to change with the airfield still under active occupation by military forces.[5] Deplaning passengers, held over for technical reasons, were ushered into an ad hoc waiting room in one of the airfield's vacant hangars. "Passengers arriving late at night," reported *Collier's* magazine, "were forced to sit up in the drafty hangar huddled in blankets."[6] The airlines were understandably unhappy with this arrangement, so Pattison found what he described as a temporary solution. Fortunately, the commanding officers of the various units were sympathetic and cooperative and desired to assist with the opening of commercial operations. The Americans, in particular, were rapidly shutting down their sector, leaving vacant a number of buildings. Once the US declared the buildings surplus, Pattison proposed that Newfoundland obtain the release of a select number of them from the Canadian government, the rightful owners, and develop a hotel complex.[7] Meantime, at Newfoundland's request, the US Army agreed to provide short-term accommodations. The US expected this arrangement to last a few weeks, but nothing had changed when the airlines met with Pattison two months later. "Tangible progress" on Pattison's suggested hotel arrangement, complained one PAA official, "has been almost imperceptible."[8] Newfoundland soon got moving on the matter and converted building 64 into a hotel, and eventually added barracks buildings 61, 62, and 63 to form an Airlines Hotel complex. The hotel operated "on the so-called European plan, under which meals and accommodation are charged separately," reported Newfoundland government auditor F.G. Smallwood. During the first year of operation in 1946, permanent employees of the airlines and oil companies occupied three buildings within the complex, while the fourth accommodated transient guests of all kinds, but mostly "affluent transients," he added. Nearby, a former US noncommissioned officers' mess was converted into a lounge, bar, and airlines dining area that operated around the clock and could accommodate 250 patrons. Guests registered at the main office, located in the dining building, but were checked in and out at their respective quarters by a steward or stewardess, assigned to each quarters building to supervise cleaning and maintenance work. "In terms of total numbers of guests and meals served," wrote auditor Smallwood, "the Airlines Hotel is as large as, if not larger than the Newfoundland Hotel" in St. John's.[9]

Late in 1945, the St. John's *Daily News* reported that "statements [were] heard that the Newfoundland government had taken over Gander airport." This was untrue, corrected the Honourable James S. Neill, Newfoundland Commissioner for Public Utilities, as the matter was "still in a state of flux" and depended on the international situation regarding aviation. With the military withdrawing from Gander, explained the commissioner, "someone had to look after things," so the government appointed Robert A. Bradley as chief engineer (the same Bradley who was assistant engineer during Gander's construction), while Pattison continued as civil aviation director.[10] There were also important administrative matters to address, reported the public utilities commissioner, like the financial arrangements surrounding the return of airport control to Newfoundland, management of staff, a possible housing scheme, and business relations with the operating airlines. For the position of airport business manager, the government turned to Newfoundlander Eric Winsor, a qualified accountant with four years' experience as the Atlas Construction Company's office manager at Gander.[11] These appointments may have stimulated rumours that Newfoundland had taken control of the airport. Gander's wartime occupation "had produced a very complicated setup owing to the combined presence" of the RCAF, RAF Ferry Command, and US forces, added Commissioner Neill.[12] Indeed, a caveat in the 1941 agreement threatened to complicate matters further for Newfoundland, as the signatory governments had agreed to consult beforehand on Canada's continued postwar use of the airfield. Pattison was concerned that if Canada insisted on leasing all the areas entitled to them under the agreement, it would leave insufficient space for civil air operations.[13] Such matters would be addressed early in 1946 at a conference in St. John's.

By the end of 1945, AOA and PAA were operating scheduled transoceanic passenger services through Gander, making one flight daily each way, east and west, using the Douglas DC-4, a four-engine, prop-driven airliner.[14] Swedish Intercontinental Airlines (SILA) was making six round trips monthly between Stockholm and New York using modified B-17 Flying Fortresses, while TCA had two round trips daily between Moncton and St. John's using Lockheed Lodestars, and four round trips weekly between Montréal and Prestwick using Avro Lancastrians.[15] Transcontinental and Western Airlines was carrying out preparatory survey flights and in February 1946 commenced a scheduled transatlantic service using the fast, sleek, and pressurized Lockheed L-049 Constellation, which AOA and PAA soon added to their inventories.

Negotiating the Return of Gander

With wartime operations ended, the time had come for officials to hammer out matters regarding the disposition of Canadian defence installations in Newfoundland and Labrador. From 29 January to 6 February 1946, delegates from Newfoundland, Canada, and the UK gathered in St. John's to discuss a myriad of issues, among them the handover of Gander airfield and the RAF area at Gander. The conference concluded with Canada agreeing to transfer control of the airport back to Newfoundland on 31 March 1946. The UK would follow suit on the same date. To maintain continuous operation of the airfield, certain RCAF personnel would remain and be withdrawn progressively from that date to 31 May. Canada also agreed to forego its right to the fifty-year lease as established under the terms of the April 1941 transfer agreement, and to sell to Newfoundland its buildings, hangars, works, and certain equipment and supplies for the bargain sum of one million dollars. The hangars and buildings were of no "particular use to Canada," admitted the Canadian delegation, which also recognized that any insistence on a long-term lease "would certainly create a good deal of antagonism in Newfoundland, whose people strongly resent the idea of granting" such leases to other countries.

The British delegation announced at the conference that their government would transfer Hangars 21 and 22 and all buildings in the RAF sector "without consideration." This decision, claimed the Canadian delegation, also influenced the low price set by the Canadian government.[16] However, historian Peter Neary points out that the UK subsequently sold its buildings and assets, valued at $2,500,000, to Newfoundland for $200,000.[17] To assist with the post-handover transition, the RAF agreed to provide one signals officer for six weeks and four Atlantic control officers for three months. All other RAF personnel would be withdrawn as soon as possible, while the Newfoundland government agreed to take over any civilian personnel on the RAF payroll remaining on the transfer date. Still, the transfer date notwithstanding, it was neither possible nor practical for Newfoundland to take over the unit in one move. At a meeting between Wing Commander Botting and his subordinates, the decided order of handover, a piecemeal approach, identified first the transport section (except the commanding officer's car and one station wagon for the remaining RAF officers), then the cafeteria and wholesale store, followed by the signals section, furniture and other equipment, and lastly the works and buildings section.[18]

Botting's Plan

Botting was also directed to advise on matters regarding Gander's post-handover terminal and housing facilities and had just put the finishing touches on a detailed airport plan for Commissioner Neill. In it, Botting identified the RAF side of the field as the most compact compared to the USAAF, RCAF, and Canadian Army sectors. All the buildings were within a few yards of one another and the concrete apron outside the hangars "laid out in a manner which can only be described as ideal for the handling of civilian passenger aircraft." The RAF area, he stressed, should be regarded as the operational side, handling the aircraft and control in flight, and providing maintenance, signals, and meteorological services, and housing for airline aircrew layover personnel and transient passengers. The other areas, he suggested, were better suited to house Newfoundland government and airline company employees. With some alterations, mostly partitions and eight-foot-high doors, the four hangar bays could be allotted to eight major airlines, two per bay, and any overflow taken to hangars on the USAAF and RCAF sides. By removing three walls, said Botting, a passenger-handling section was possible with airline counters, a customs and excise counter, cloakrooms, washrooms, and a snack bar. The RAF cafeteria could continue to offer twenty-four-hour service, "providing meals for transient passengers ... held over for periods in excess of one hour." He identified one barracks building as a potential transient hotel and another for overflow. The third barracks, he proposed, could be converted into a suite of administrative offices for each airline company. Other buildings allowed for housing for aircrew members, stewards, VIPs, and "female passengers who are accompanied by men folk." Botting then made recommendations on the organization of the American and Canadian sides of the field to house each airline company's single and married employees and to provide dining, recreation, and general welfare services. Buildings were plentiful and included a gymnasium with a swimming pool and two theatres/cinemas, which Botting pointed to as "a most necessary adjunct to the general welfare of all personnel based at Gander." Besides, he hinted, American authorities were said to be prepared to sell their projectors and lighting to the Newfoundland government.[19] As things turned out, Botting's report looks to have made a favourable impression on Commissioner Neill and the airline executives.

The RAF Withdraws

The RAF unit meantime continued to wind down operations. The majority of east and westbound flight arrivals in the early months of 1946 were now commercial, mostly DC-4s from AOA and PAA, and lots of them. In January alone, the two airlines accounted for more than 130 landings.[20] Occasionally, a BOAC Return Ferry Service Liberator dropped in. Despite the cessation of hostilities, there was still a military requirement for the service to carry passengers, and diplomatic and official mail.[21] On one January day, a TCA-operated Lancaster landed carrying English war brides, "the first to arrive in Gander en route to the States and Canada," recorded the unit diary. Also that month, the Gander Inn closed its doors and a new hotel opened in the south wing of Building C. During February and March, Newfoundland took over the RAF cafeteria, Building A, and Hangars 21 and 22, but allowed the RAF to continue using their offices and parking their vehicles in the hangars until the withdrawal was complete. Flying activity within the unit amounted to infrequent local flights in the Norseman and Canso, so both aircraft were returned to Dorval, while the ever-reliable search and rescue Fox Moth VO-ADE, idle for some months in the hangar, was dismantled.[22]

As the transfer date neared, departing Newfoundland civilian staff at the unit turned in their security button badges and on resigning their posts, signed a waiver absolving the RAF of any claims, responsibilities, demands or obligations that the employee had or might have or enforce against the RAF. Air transports flew their Canadian counterparts to Dorval, although some preferred to return by train and boat or had arranged to remain and work for the Newfoundland government. As March came to a close, a BOAC Liberator flew six remaining female radio operators to Dorval, and an RAF Dakota also flew to Montréal carrying nine passengers, among them maintenance crew chief Norm Linington and unit plant engineer Durand, his wife and four children.[23]

By agreement, Canada and the UK then formally returned all sectors of the airfield to the Newfoundland Department of Civil Aviation at midnight on 31 March 1946. On the Canadian sector of the field, the padres held their last services in the station chapel, and the final Ensign lowering took place in the presence of Group Captain F.J. Ewart, station commanding officer, and a flight of airmen.[24] There were still loose ends to tie up at the former RAF unit that ran into April as a two-person Board of Survey examined files and all unregistered documents, destroying some and crating others for air delivery to Dorval or the Air Ministry. The remaining RAF civilians, except a small maintenance staff, were discharged on 1 April. The majority took positions with the Newfoundland government, including Squadron Leader Brant, now civilian in charge of signals, and Squadron Leader McGrath, who became airport operations manager, although AOA tried to recruit him as a dispatcher. Early in April, John Murphy, confidential secretary to every commanding officer since the unit's inception, signed and sent one final signal to Dorval, reporting the departure of two unit clerks aboard a BOAC Liberator. He then cleaned out his office inside Hangar 21 and immediately went to work for TWA.[25] As agreed, a small contingent of RCAF personnel stayed until 31 May to assist with the transition, among them several flying officers at the control tower at Hangar 21. The tower log for May records the arrival of civilian controllers, who worked alongside their RCAF counterparts. During June, the tower became a completely civilian operation in the capable hands of Robert Raymond, Rex Tilley, Maxwell Butler, Robert Banfield, Herbert Chafe, Clement Elms, and others who would shortly follow.[26]

If You Build It, They Will Come

The burgeoning postwar market for transatlantic commercial air travel now included European carriers Air France, KLM Royal Dutch Airlines, and BOAC, and with air traffic intensifying, the need for improved and expanded facilities became more acute. At meetings held in Gander and St. John's in January and February 1946, the managers of the US airlines complained to Commissioner Neill that Newfoundland was acting too slowly on certain housing infrastructure projects for airlines personnel. The problem, countered Neill, was supply, and besides, he added, the handover "of the airfield had come upon us suddenly," and such "criticism that we should have planned ahead was not soundly founded." He then suggested that the airlines themselves attempt to secure the necessary construction materials. In other words, he reported to the government, "I gave them the ball and if they cannot get these supplies they will realize that they have no grounds for 'grouse.' "[27]

A week of productive meetings held in Gander in March brought together officials from TWA, AOA, PAA, BOAC, SILA, and TCA, along with an architect from New York and government representatives Pattison, Neill, airport engineer Bradley, and business manager Eric Winsor. Botting sat in on some meetings as well. Their discussions covered a number of airport operational issues, including runway maintenance, hospital facilities, and public transportation. Airline officials identified fifteen existing buildings in the American sector for conversion to permanent married quarters and agreed to assume the initial costs, recoverable through rents. For recreation purposes, they requested the use of a log cabin on Deadman's Pond, two buildings for a club and bowling alley, as well as Hangar 3 for tennis and Hangar 4 for a skating rink. (The RCAF had taken over Hangar 4 from the US in 1945 and converted it into a rink.) Finally, the airline companies and Commissioner Neill jointly agreed to construct a proper terminal building and air passenger hotel. In keeping with Botting's recommendations, they settled on adjoining Hangars 21 and 22 for conversion to a terminal, and adjacent barracks Buildings A, B, and C for conversion to a hotel complex for in-transit guests of the operating airlines.[28]

The airlines were anxious to get the terminal-hotel project moving. Commissioner Neill suggested that they lease the required buildings and "make alterations for their own account." The airlines were reluctant to do this but were willing to "pay a reasonable rent for facilities completed and ready for occupation." Neill was unreceptive and claimed that Newfoundland had no funds for any such project, although he "believed" that the UK had approved funds to construct a "modest terminal facility." The airlines, preferring expediency to Neill's ambiguity, and doubtful that incoming airport management could secure the capital quickly, agreed "to advance the necessary money, and contract" for the work. Newfoundland, in turn, would offer a rent credit for an agreed-upon amortization period "until the initial capital expenditure is liquidated." It happened too, that the airlines were unprepared at that time to make any long-term commitment to use Gander. No specific rate for landing fees had been set, and uncertainty still surrounded whether or not Newfoundland was capable of providing proper runway maintenance and the "efficient operation of communications, navigational and radio aid requirements." Consequently, the airlines suggested a three-to-five-year plan or trial period, which they could extend if the airfield and management proved suitable.[29]

In May, with the airport officially back in Newfoundland's hands, representatives of the three American and four European carriers, along with TCA, reassembled at Gander. Led in their negotiations by James M. Eaton, AOA Vice President of properties and facilities, who would also coordinate the "modernization" project, the eight "Lessee Airlines" ratified a five-year lease agreement with Newfoundland that included provisions on the capital cost of converting the former RAF hangars and barracks into a terminal and hotel. Both the government and the airlines agreed to share the cost of the work, but with the latter given credit for "the work so done against future rentals payable by them." The airlines agreed to advance to AOA, their representative agent, the total sum of $71,500 to construct office facilities in Hangar 22 and to convert the barracks into hotel buildings, collectively referred to as the Skyways Club. The airlines had "free hand in the choice of contractor," with materials, equipment, and furnishings allowed entry duty-free. Newfoundland agreed to cover the cost associated with remodelling the public space of Hangar 22 into a passenger lounge with a bar and other amenities, "at a cost of not less than $20,000," and to furnish and equip the Skyways Club hotel buildings. "By exclusion," reported auditor Smallwood, "the cost of improving Hangar 21 (the administrative half of the Terminal Building) would presumably be met by the Government direct."[30]

The agreement also included provisions on the use of both the terminal and Skyways Club. The terms held that Newfoundland would operate the hotel as it desired to accommodate passengers and flight crews, and would assume financial responsibility for its operation. The airlines agreed to cover all expenses of their passengers and crews accommodated therein. Terms for the terminal were decidedly more complicated. Each airline agreed to pay rent per square foot for hangar and office space, to be "offset by our construction advances." Common storage space for aircraft of all lessee airlines was available free for the first twenty-four hours. After that, a fee applied. The government agreed to maintain the terminal itself, providing heat, light, water and sewerage, janitors, etc., but with expenditures incurred for such services recovered monthly from the lessee airlines. The agreed formula for determining the amount each airline paid, calculated by the resident government agent (a duty subsequently assumed by Pattison), was as follows: one-third of the total in equal shares per month, one-third pro-rated to the scheduled monthly landings of each airline, and one-third pro-rated to the number of seats scheduled monthly for each airline.[31]

At a press conference in July, Commissioner Neill announced that the third and fourth freedoms of the air under the International Air Transport Agreement, which also derived from the 1944 Chicago convention, would take effect immediately at Gander. These traffic rights allowed aircraft to disembark mail, passengers, and cargo taken on in the carrier's country of origin, and to embark mail, passengers, and cargo destined for the carrier's country of origin. The fifth freedom, the "unrestricted right of planes of any nationality to pick up or set down passengers in any country," added Neill, would shortly take effect.[32]

By the summer of 1946, carpenters from the Horwood Lumber Company were making good progress at Gander, assured Neill in communication with a concerned James Eaton. "Things do not move with arithmetic precision in all lands!" added the commissioner.[33] An incident that July in the US validated the work underway, especially at the future Skyways Club hotel, which would provide much-needed additional airline passenger accommodations. Following a TWA crash in Pennsylvanian, US officials grounded all Lockheed Constellations, fearing a serious technical defect in the aircraft type. As a result, "passengers of all nations were stranded" at Gander's "famed airport," reported the *Daily News.* The Airlines Hotel complex, the previously converted barracks buildings on the former American side, "was crowded to capacity" with "members of South Africa's Military and Civil Delegation to Washington, French actresses, Jewish Rabbis, and wives of American soldiers."[34]

Meanwhile in New York, Eaton, having consulted with his airline representative in Gander, set out to acquire furniture for the terminal and hotel bedrooms, at the Newfoundland government's expense. For the terminal, Eaton got an option on leather-covered wall bench seats and settees, red for the lounge and reptile for the bar, red round tables for the bar and black for the lounge, leather-covered chairs, ash stands, and counter stools for the snack bar. For the hotel bedrooms, he selected 160 dressing table shelves (in lieu of bureaus) and a like number of mirrors, and 236 bedside shelves (in lieu of bedside tables) and a matching number of chairs. The option came with a tight timeframe, so Eaton closed the deal, $12,263 with delivery shipside at New York, and arranged shipment direct to St. John's through the Furness-Withy Steamship Company. Additional purchases by Eaton for the hotel, likewise scheduled for ocean shipment, included 236 box springs and mattresses, a matching number of pillows and bedspreads, 472 blankets, and 20 chaise lounges for the pilots' restroom.[35] On 21 August, business manager Eric Winsor reported that he had received the furniture imported by Eaton and "that it is now the property of the Newfoundland Government."[36]

Collectively, Hangars 21 and 22 comprised the terminal building. Once renovations were completed, half the original floor area remained for aircraft hangar space. The remaining section in Hangar 22, a "building within a building," as Smallwood described it, housed the passenger lounge or waiting area, and the airlines' offices and red-coloured ticket counters. The spacious passenger lounge with its light yellow ceiling, blue endwalls, and gray sidewalls, boasted comfortable seating for 250 people. Passenger amenities included a lunch counter, postal telegraph office, novelty booth with gifts, souvenirs, and newspapers, and the soon-to-be-famous Big Dipper bar, intended solely for the use of the travelling public. Outside the terminal entrance, the Skyways Club's celestial-themed and former RAF buildings included the Saturn and Jupiter hotels for passengers, Mercury with its crews' lounge and sleeping quarters, and Venus, the stewardesses' lounge and sleeping quarters. Mars contained resident apartments, and North Star housed a restaurant with seating for two hundred, two passenger lounges, and the Little Dipper bar.[37]

Saturday, 14 September 1946, marked a red-letter day for Gander as airline representatives, government officials, and members of the press and public gathered for the official opening of the new terminal building. Commissioner Neill's welcoming address touched on Gander's early history and wartime significance, and the magnitude of the task involved in building up a civil airport in less than six months from the date of resuming control from the RCAF. "We had to arrange for the many and varied ancillaries of a great airport," he said, including "radio, meteorology, fuelling, housing of staff, government and private, administrative offices, catering, accommodation of transients, and so forth." He expressed gratitude for the work of Pattison and airport chief engineer Bradley. To James Eaton, he gave credit as a skilled negotiator. "His broad vision was never blunted. He was generous in his appreciation of our viewpoint and it has been a pleasure to work with him," praised Neill. In closing, the commissioner declared the terminal building open, saying, "May God grant safe passage to those who pass through its portals."[38]

Outside the terminal entrance below a sign reading "Gander Airport," Commissioner Neill raised Newfoundland's red ensign flag and posed for a photograph together with six hostess representatives of the American, Swedish, Canadian, and British airlines. Gander was ready for business, and on its way to becoming the "Crossroads of the World."

CHAPTER 10 | GANDER'S HELPING HANDS

Success at the Gander Ferry Command unit was built upon a solid foundation of hardworking civilian and RAF service personnel. Whereas some civilians continued careers in aviation after the war, others chose different paths, while remembering fondly their Gander experience. Indeed, in an unexpected, if not unusual twist, the RAF Welfare Fund, to which many civilian ground support staff contributed, would benefit the growing town of Gander years after the benevolent services fund was dissolved upon the closure of the unit in 1946.

A New Airport Manager

With Gander now a major layover for commercial transatlantic carriers, the Newfoundland government looked to secure an airport manager. Eric Winsor had been handling certain managerial duties since October 1945, but under the job title "Business Manager." Some of his duties did parallel those of an airport manager, but the government had hired him mostly for his business acumen. Newfoundland reached out to the British Air Ministry for a suitable candidate. In July 1946, the ministry came back with two names, Wing Commander G.D. Middleton and Group Captain A.H. Owen. Both were willing to accept the appointment for two years as proposed by Newfoundland. Owen was then commanding officer of RAF Station Uxbridge in Middlesex, and Middleton second airport manager at London Airport (now Heathrow). After some deliberation between Commissioner Neill and Pattison, they settled on forty-two-year-old Wing Commander Middleton.[1]

Middleton attended prep school in England, Switzerland, and France. From 1919 to 1923, he served in the merchant service, and during 1924–25 qualified as a land and seaplane pilot in the RAF. He next spent several years in Malta as a seaplane pilot. Following Malta, he became a flight commander at a flight training school in the UK and then relinquished his commission to accept an appointment as chief seaplane instructor with a private outfit. His duties included initiation courses for the conversion of Imperial Airways pilots to flying boats. In 1939, he accepted a post as manager of Ipswich airport, where he oversaw a flight training and observer school, the Aero Club, the local civil air guard, and a restaurant and workshops. With the outbreak of the Second World War, he returned to uniform as commander of an advanced training squadron and then as chief ground instructor for an operational training unit. From 1942 until war's end, Middleton served with the Air Ministry in the Directorate of Operational Training. Early in 1946, he completed airport management training and was assigned to London Airport. Several months later, he was bound for Gander as its first official postwar airport manager.[2] He had hardly settled in when the matter of the former RAF piggery and its manager, Joseph Smallwood, crossed his desk.

Piggeries and Politics

During the war, Smallwood, a rousing and effective public speaker, occasionally strayed from the piggery business to host or attend organized debates and discussions around the airfield, and to the annoyance of some, broadened his venue to include the RAF cafeteria during mealtime.[3] The American counter-intelligence section at Gander was aware of his activities and in January 1945 told how Smallwood had been "appealing to Newfoundlanders to boldly launch a political party that will claim the right to govern the country."[4] Secretary John Murphy got to know him well, living in the same building for a time. Indeed, when Smallwood published his memoirs in the early 1970s, he recalled how he invited Murphy to a scheduled discussion club meeting with Captain Laurence J. Lynch, the American chaplain. "Actually," corrected Murphy, "Joey took a little poetic license with that incident since we were the ones who invited him."[5] He also became a thorn in the government's side, organizing unions and encouraging civilian employees to demand higher wages under threat of strike action. James Eaton was aware of his activities, having received notice only weeks before the terminal officially opened that Smallwood had been frequenting the TWA maintenance shop. Rumour had it, warned Eaton's Gander contact, "that Smallwood intends to organize Newfoundland employees working in Maintenance Departments for the airlines."[6] On another occasion, while standing in the queue outside the movie theatre, writes biographer Richard Gwyn, Smallwood voiced his displeasure with the pecking order process. Unlike his fellow countrymen, American servicemen went in without waiting. Smallwood stirred up the crowd "and a riot threatened until the manager emerged to restore order. He pointed out that the Americans had built the theatre."[7]

Postwar, Smallwood headed efforts to create the Gander Mutual Benefit Society, which opened a co-operative grocery store, first located in the American commissary building. Securing the building took some maneuvering on Smallwood's part. Pattison turned down society members when they first expressed interest in the commissary. Smallwood thanked him "and said we would take up the matter with the Commission of Government," recalled society secretary Charles Warren. Pattison relented, and at the next meeting, offered them the commissary but set the rent too high. Smallwood repeated his threat. Pattison again relented and they got their building at an affordable rate. "We later learned," said Warren, "that the director [Pattison] was a shareholder in the business we were competing against."[8] More than seventy years later, the co-op continues to serve Gander residents.

A few years after the war, having bought out the RAF's holdings on the piggery, Smallwood abandoned the project. He knew early on that he was in a precarious position, given that Newfoundland would eventually take over the land. Still, he hoped to recover his investment and planned to continue the operation until late 1945. Officials did not discuss the piggery during airfield transfer negotiations. Only when the RAF unit closed did commander Botting tell Pattison that he had sold the buildings to Smallwood. The government had no immediate use for the land and therefore did nothing to terminate the enterprise, which was then in operation. Such an action, cautioned Pattison, would have given Smallwood "justifiable complaint that for no reason we were curtailing an enterprise" that was providing food "at a time of world shortage."

The year 1946 closed with the sties all empty, but Smallwood's name soon surfaced at airport manager Middleton's office in a request for a lease. The area now sported a passenger terminal and accommodations, and it was impossible to foresee future developments. Nearby, Imperial Oil had installed a petrol distribution system, with Shell and Texaco likely to follow suit. It made sense to keep the oil companies grouped together, but the piggery occupied the best site. In a calculated move, Pattison suggested a one-year lease with a renewal option, "which might have the effect of causing Mr. Smallwood to hesitate to re-open the piggery."[9] The public utilities commissioner concurred but wanted caveats in the lease agreement covering payment of water and electricity, snow and garbage removal, and the cleanliness of the premises. In April 1947, the government notified Smallwood of the conditions of the lease proposal, but he never responded.[10]

While others expressed interest in re-opening the enterprise, the government was now reluctant to grant anyone a lease on the property. Apart from its undesirable location within view of hotel guests, health concerns had arisen because the land sloped towards the winter water supply at Deadman's Pond. The airport engineer feared that the piggery was too near the pond to avoid contamination.[11] Meantime, while officials debated the land lease, Smallwood was debating his country's future as an elected member of the National Convention, a forum established to recommend constitutional options for Newfoundland. Smallwood aimed at bringing

Newfoundland into confederation with Canada, and in 1949, after two polarizing referendums, the RAF's former piggery manager did just that, becoming the new province's first premier. He even tried to recruit John Murphy to come work for him. Murphy declined. He was happy with his job at TWA. So much so that his career with the airline lasted forty years.

As for the piggery, Newfoundlander Cyrus Oates took over the operation after the war, albeit on a smaller scale, and continued the enterprise into the mid-1950s with the co-operative grocery store as his main client.[12] The location thereafter went undeveloped for other purposes. Today, remnants of the original elongated piggery building remain among the overgrowth of birch trees and alders.

In 1984, Smallwood suffered a stroke that left him unable to speak. Murphy later went to visit him at his home on Roaches Line near St. John's. "It was sad to see a man who loved to talk so much not being able to say a single word," said Murphy. "He showed us all the awards he had received and all he could do was to point them out."[13]

Funding the Future

In February 1946, with the closure of the RAF unit looming, questions arose about the unit's non-public funds. The monies service members had contributed to the unit's Officers Club Fund and the Airmen's Club Fund could easily revert to the RAF Central Reserve Fund, which provided support towards the formation of messes and canteens on new RAF bases. It was not so simple with the Welfare Fund, to which many civilians had contributed. With the transfer of control of the airport to Newfoundland in March, those employees who stayed on now fell under the Newfoundland Department of Civil Aviation, so RAF officials gave a proportion of the Welfare Fund, a cheque for three thousand dollars, to Commissioner Neill, suggesting that they use the money for benevolent and recreational purposes as originally intended.[14] Neill, in turn, sought the advice of Pattison, who worried that a decision on the matter might prove difficult. Many former RAF civilian employees were now members of the Newfoundland Airport Club (similarly mandated to provide social and recreational amenities), but before giving them the full sum, Pattison proposed that they break down the figures of those workers who contributed to the original fund and remained in Gander, together with the members and non-members of the Airport Club.[15] His analysis revealed that one hundred employees at Gander were former members of the RAF unit and that one-half were members of the Airport Club. Consequently, Pattison recommended that the sum be held in trust by the Department of Public Utilities, "and we could make recommendations in the future should any need become apparent from which payments from this fund would be suitable." Neill concurred, forwarding the cheque to Pattison in September 1946 for deposit, with instructions that he make no withdrawals without the government's approval and a proposal explaining the need for the withdrawal.[16] The funds sat untouched in the Royal Bank, Gander branch, for the next five years.

Following confederation with Canada in 1949, Pattison became airport manager at Gander under the federal Department of Transport. In a February 1951 intra-departmental memo to the Newfoundland provincial government, he revealed that to date, he had neither made a withdrawal from the fund nor received a proposal that met the criteria, which held that projects benefit the community as a whole. However, a Gander film council had recently formed under the National Film Board of Canada, supported, Pattison pointed out, by the Gander Consumers' Co-operative Society, local schools, churches, Boy Scouts, Elks Club, Lions Club, and unions. The film council proposed to control and operate a film projector, with the parent organization and the provincial Department of Education supplying films at no charge. The film council had raised $100 of the $600 needed to purchase the projector equipment, so Pattison requested $500 from the unused fund.[17] The Newfoundland government was receptive but now desired to dispose of the fund in its entirety.

With confederation, control of Gander had changed hands, leaving the Department of Public Utilities "diffident about accepting authority for the disposal of this money," which now amounted to $3126. Nevertheless, the department agreed, "somewhat reluctantly," wrote the assistant deputy minister, to share in the responsibility for its distribution. The minister approved the $500 for the film council and suggested that they allocate the balance to the Amalgamated School Board and the Roman Catholic School Board on a per capita basis.[18] In June 1951, Pattison and Eric Winsor proposed a broader arrangement. Besides the film council, which had received its cheque for $500, they asked that the Gander public library receive $250, the Lions Club $200 for a public playground, the Gander community centre $800, the amalgamated school $1103 (422 students), and the Roman Catholic school $363 (139 students).[19] Newfoundland approved all but the community centre funds, arguing that "the activities of the centre are not sufficiently broad in their scope" to qualify as beneficial to Gander as a whole. Instead, the government suggested that the $800 be allocated to the schools using the existing formula.[20] Pattison and Winsor were disappointed with this decision, explaining to Newfoundland government assistant deputy minister J.F. O'Neill that the centre had been operating successfully for a year with a voluntary management and paid-up membership of five hundred single and family members, representing a total membership of one thousand or more. The Canadian Department of Transport had provided the centre with furnishings and a building rent-free and was "anxious to see this project continued."[21] The Newfoundland government recognized the community centre as a worthwhile activity but "felt that it is not fully representative of the persons who subscribed to the fund." The government, anxious to close the fund, held firm that allocating the $800 to schools would ensure the widest range of application for the benefit of Gander as a whole.[22] Correspondence in the archival files ends there, leaving the writer to speculate that the community centre was not among the beneficiaries. In any event, thanks to its contributors, Gander residents benefited from the RAF Welfare Fund well beyond the war years.

Of Lives Lived, And Lost

While many former RAF civilian personnel stayed on at Gander after the war to work in the commercial aviation industry, aircraft maintenance worker James Reid determined that "there must be more to life than barbed wires." After some deliberation, he left Ferry Command in the fall of 1945 and went home to Codroy to finish high school. In January 1946, with some urging from his former crew chief Sam Blandford, Reid returned to Gander and took a job with American Airlines. "All my old friends were with one or the other of the several civilian airlines using Gander at the time." Still, the changed postwar working environment left him unsettled, so he quit, "after just one payday!" He never regretted his decision.[23] Sometimes, life takes us full circle, and so it was for Reid. He later studied theology and began his ministry in Mary's Harbour and Battle Harbour in Labrador. In 1970, he returned to Gander and ministered at St. Martin's Anglican Cathedral for more than two decades.[24]

Radio operators Hazel Fausak and Gloria Lindsay returned to their Canadian hometowns in Alberta and Ontario, respectively. In 1946, Gloria boarded a train and visited Hazel for a week at the Fausak family farm. Seventy years would pass before their next encounter. In November 2015, on the seventy-fifth anniversary of the ferry service's inaugural transatlantic flights, the pair met in a surprise reunion, organized by their families, at the North Atlantic Aviation Museum in Gander. They reminisced, held hands, and even tested their skills on the Morse key.[25]

Just as secretary Manning predicted of the young operations officer back in 1940, Tom McGrath proved capable of bigger things in the aviation industry. After confederation, he transferred to the civil aviation branch of the Canadian Department of Transport and became airport manager at St. John's airport, the former RCAF Station Torbay. Other subsequent jobs included airways inspector, superintendent of property management for all Canadian airports, and numerous director-level positions within the department. He had a lifelong passion for Newfoundland and transatlantic aviation history, researching, writing, and lecturing on the topic. He contributed articles to the Canadian Aviation Historical Society's journal and in 1984 published *History of Canadian Airports*. He died in Ottawa in 1994.[26]

For the Gilmore children, their father's work at Saint-Hubert in 1940–41 meant that he "was absent more than present in our lives," recalled Sean Gilmore. Still, "we always understood the importance of his work and were proud of him … While at St. Hubert he was more often at the hangar than at home or traveling to Gander or elsewhere ... We looked forward to his return and being with him with far more eagerness and excitement. Going to and living in Gander was the longest spell that we lived as a family, unfortunately far too short."[27]

In July 1946, a year after his death, His Majesty the King appointed Gilmore "a Member of the Civilian Division of the Order of the British Empire for meritorious service with the ground staff in Canada of the R.A.F. Transport Command." Regrettably, for many years after, his headstone did not reflect this posthumous distinction. The Commonwealth War Graves Commission corrected the omission in 2005 with a new granite marker.[28] Today, Gander has memorialized Gilmore in a street name, Gilmore Place. A fitting tribute to a man whose actions, be they salvage, search and rescue, or humanitarian, deserve lasting recognition. Indeed, Gilmore's work with Ferry Command, from its formative days at Saint-Hubert under the CPR to his untimely death in May 1945, makes him a worthy candidate for national recognition and a place in the Canadian Aviation Hall of Fame.

CHAPTER 11 | MISSION ACCOMPLISHED

Ferry Command's transatlantic air bridge, a constantly moving supply line connecting Gander on one end and Prestwick on the other, proved vital to the Allied aerial bombing campaign over Western Europe and elsewhere, aided in no small part to ultimate victory by Gander's dedicated ground support staff. By war's end, the brave crews of Ferry Command had delivered more than nine thousand aircraft across the North Atlantic, South Atlantic, and Pacific oceans. Of that number, about five thousand used the North Atlantic route by way of Gander or Goose Bay, while a handful used Harmon Field at Stephenville. Thousands more were serviced in Gander's American sector in connection with US overseas ferrying operations under the Air Transport Command.

An analysis of select sources offers a reasonable estimate on the number of Ferry Command aircraft serviced by Gander's RAF unit. Although landing registers specific to the airfield are incomplete, surviving RAF movement logs cover the period November 1940 to December 1941, and another invaluable series, presumably kept by Tom McGrath and other flying control officers, cover the period May 1943 until war's end and beyond. The existing unit diary, which begins in mid-September 1942, also recorded arrivals and departures, but this practice ended in October 1943 and was not always precise. Operations and control were likewise keeping records, and the commanding officer considered the duplication unnecessary. As well, Air Chief Marshal Sir Frederick Bowhill began submitting monthly operational activity reports to the Air Ministry in August 1941. For the first fourteen months, each report gave only a sum total of deliveries to the UK via the North and South Atlantic routes. Not until October 1942 did Bowhill identify specific delivery numbers for Gander and other airfields and marine bases. Consequently, the only gap in the Ferry Command records specific to Gander is the nine-month period from January 1942 to mid-September 1942. Here, the work of British aviation historian the late Peter Berry proved helpful. Using mostly operations record books maintained on the UK side, he compiled a record of delivery and return ferry flights across the North Atlantic. However, except for direct flights, the flight legs for most arriving aircraft are not given. Therefore, it remains unclear if an aircraft arriving in the UK from Greenland or Iceland originated at Gander or Goose Bay. Using these sources collectively puts the number of Ferry Command aircraft delivered through Gander from November 1940 to V-J Day in August 1945 at about four thousand, in addition to layovers of more than seven hundred east and westbound transatlantic Return Ferry Service flights. But it came at a cost.

Today, twenty-four Ferry Command and Return Ferry Service personnel from five accidents rest at the Commonwealth War Graves Commission Cemetery in Gander, and four more from two mishaps rest at the Joint Services Cemetery in St. John's, which became the RAF burial location in 1944 when they discontinued using Gander cemetery. The number of airmen missing after departing Gander for overseas, their chances of survival at the time clearly remote in the event of a forced water landing on the stormy North Atlantic, stands at sixty-four. This puts the aggregate number of Gander-related casualties at about one hundred, including non-Ferry Command passengers and aircrew buried elsewhere before the Gander cemetery opened, specifically the Hudson crew that carried Sir Frederick Banting.

The United States, which shared the cemetery at Gander with the RAF and RCAF, accounted for more than fifty wartime burials, the majority victims of ferrying accidents involving US Air Transport

Command aircraft. In November 1945, in an effort to centralize its war dead to a "more suitable site where constant care of the grave[s] can be assured," US graves registration personnel disinterred the remains of these American servicemen and moved them to the American Post cemetery at Fort Pepperrell army base near St. John's. Included in the relocation effort were three American-born Ferry Command pilots, Texan Captain Jack "Buster" Stagner, Captain Fortune A. Dugan of New Orleans, and Californian Captain Robert M. Lloyd, casualties from the February 1943 crash of Return Ferry Service Liberator AL591. Late in 1947, under a US War Department repatriation program, their remains were again disinterred and then trucked some eighty miles over gravel road to the American naval base at Argentia. Their bodies, and those of several hundred American service personnel lost on active duty in Newfoundland and Labrador, were taken to New York Harbour aboard the US Army Transport ship *Joseph V. Connolly*. From New York, the military sent the remains to distribution centers country-wide for shipment to next of kin and final burial.[1]

Related to US casualties and likewise deserving of mention are the circumstances surrounding the loss of Ferry Command Liberator BZ935 on 1 March 1944. This incident stands out as an anomaly among ferry service mishaps in Newfoundland and Labrador due to its flight crew origins. The aircraft, occasionally documented as still missing out of Harmon Field, was actually discovered by hunters in 1947 in the Gaff Topsails, a barren plateau in western Newfoundland. Although pieces of wreckage bore RAF roundels, identification cards found at the scene suggested that the aircraft carried an American crew, so US officials handled the matter. While many Americans flew with Ferry Command, this crew arrangement turned out to be rather atypical. A ground search team from Pepperrell Air Force Base (formerly Fort Pepperrell and renamed in 1946) recovered the remains, which they identified as a US Air Transport Command crew from the 2nd Ferry Group, 63rd Squadron, out of Wilmington, Delaware. It happened that the five-man crew had been loaned to RAF Ferry Command and assigned to deliver BZ935. The flight plan from Harmon Field called for the pilot, 1st Lieutenant Cecil M. Dorsett, to overfly Gander and proceed direct to Reykjavik, Iceland, but the Liberator never reached Gander and inexplicably crashed one hundred miles from Harmon Field. Aircraft from Gander and Harmon Field, including a PBY-5A sent from Presque Isle, Maine, searched for a week but found nothing.[2] Today, the crewmembers of BZ935 rest in a common grave at Zachary Taylor National Cemetery in Louisville, Kentucky.

Ultimately, success at the Gander Ferry Command unit became a multi-national effort involving three armed forces, British, Canadian, and American, and a complement of civilian staff likewise diverse in its nationality. Collaboration and cooperation at the airfield was paramount, as evidenced in the opening of the joint RAF-USATC air traffic control room in May 1943, which dispatched and guided thousands of aircraft overseas with Gander's signals staff in support. Cooperation also came from the resident population, who helped downed airmen or lent a hand salvaging aircraft with Joe Gilmore's expert maintenance section. Conversely, the unit came to assist these same residents by providing much-needed mercy flights to rural Newfoundland.

Ferry Command aircrews, like their counterparts with the US Air Transport Command, routinely risked their lives on delivery fights, often in unforgiving and unpredictable North Atlantic weather, and with few navigational aids. Their heroic efforts, and those of the civilian and service personnel operating under the RAF banner on the ground at Gander, helped open the North Atlantic skyways, and in so doing, accelerated the growth of postwar commercial transatlantic aviation. Indeed, the Ferry Command experience allowed many from Newfoundland and Labrador and elsewhere to learn trades and continue careers in aviation immediately when commercial passenger carriers began to descend on Gander in earnest in 1946.

More than eighty years after Captain Bennett led his ragtag group of airmen across the North Atlantic in November 1940, the town of Gander still proudly remembers and celebrates its triumphant place in transatlantic aviation history as the genesis of Ferry

Command. This history is on display at the North Atlantic Aviation Museum, located on the Trans-Canada Highway. The museum is presently fundraising to build a Ferry Command Memorial Hall and to house its most prized possession, a rare Lockheed Hudson bomber that a group of Gander volunteers acquired for the town in 1967. After many years mounted on a pedestal near the airport, the aircraft was relocated to the museum when it opened in 1996.

On the former Ferry Command side, Hangars 21 and 22, reoccupied over the years, most notably by Eastern Provincial Airways and for provincial government air ambulance and water bomber services, still stand as the only remaining structural reminders of Gander's busy wartime Beaver Centre. The control tower that stood alongside Hangar 21, overlooking the rows of delivery bombers and transports, long since dismantled, was resituated inside a new passenger terminal, officially opened by Her Majesty Queen Elizabeth II in June 1959.

Inside NAV Canada's Gander Area Control Centre, a modern-day version of the wartime joint control centre, located on Memorial Drive in the town itself near the long-abandoned wireless radio receiving station, air traffic controllers continue to direct air traffic over the western half of the North Atlantic oceanic airspace. Prestwick still takes care of the eastern half. The International Flight Service Station, also located at the Area Control Centre, provides long-range voice communications with pilots, relaying clearances, instructions, position reports, and meteorological information. On average, Gander oceanic control handles a staggering one thousand flights daily, although only a fraction of these land at Gander International Airport. In striking contrast, on one cold November night in 1940, seven aircraft and twenty-two airmen owned the entire airspace over the North Atlantic ocean, on a historic crossing that took them each more than eleven nerve-wracking hours. Today, air travellers can safely and comfortably criss-cross the North Atlantic in a fraction of that time. And for that, we owe thanks to the men and women of Ferry Command and to Gander, the North Atlantic Crossroads.

POSTSCRIPT: FROM A CHILD'S PERSPECTIVE

The wartime arrangement that allowed the families of RAF civilian personnel to live on base meant that children would be present. The hustle and bustle of a multinational Allied airfield with ground defence troops manning antiaircraft guns and streams of bombers coming and going carrying thousands of airmen, created a world of wonderment and curiosity for children, even if the magnitude and significance of events was lost on them. Eileen Elms lived on the Canadian side of the airfield and befriended her neighbour, Mickey Ratcliffe, son of signals section boss Frank Ratcliffe. She recalled when the RAF built the apartment building for civilian employees, which meant more families, and better yet, more friends. When the Durands, a French-Canadian family, arrived from Quebec, Eileen was "thrilled to meet the daughters Renée and Lise at the usual RAF Christmas party given for children." At first, the girls said nothing; they only smiled. Eileen was perplexed but soon discovered that they spoke no English. "I had never met French-speaking people before," she said. "They quickly learned English in school and we were friends till they left." The Durands lived in Building B on the RAF side and Eileen and her friends would often visit, taking a bus that ran a scheduled service throughout the airfield. While there, "our sometime fun was to visit the piggery."

Eileen recalled a worrying incident, at least for adults it turned out, when "there was an air-raid scare one night and we were all told to dress and be ready to leave our homes. I remember sitting up for some hours in my winter clothes, till we heard the all-clear." The next day, the RAF kids told her "that they had been moved somewhere away from the hangars to the woods … We didn't get scared about things like that; it was rather exciting." The RAF hosted social events for all the kids too, she recalled, "sometimes on Bonfire night [Guy Fawkes Night], and skating on Deadman's Pond or an outdoor rink," followed by refreshments. It was triple the fun for kids at Christmastime with the RAF, USAAF, and RCAF hosting parties, with gifts! More than seventy years later, and "I still have a gold cross and chain from the RAF."[1]

The fun could sometimes be of a practical nature. The commanding officer's routine orders occasionally warned adults against throwing empty bottles out of windows. Besides littering, he was concerned that children might break them. "We did not break bottles," insisted Sean Gilmore, son of Joe Gilmore, and not for fear of scolding by his father or the commanding officer. His reasons were strictly entrepreneurial. "Coke bottles were worth five cents each," he explained, and a great source of spending money for a kid. The American forces kept a log cabin at Deadman's Pond for rest and relaxation, and this too, provided a supply of empty coke bottles. "It would not surprise me to hear that the bottom of the pond is still littered with empties," Gilmore speculated. "We abandoned the idea of retrieving them at night after we were shot at by sentries on our last sortie. Thankfully, they shot at us with .45s [Colt pistols]. The range and darkness helped too."[2]

Then there was the time that a group of visiting Russian airmen stopped young Sean on a roadway near the Eastbound Inn. Laughing and singing, they formed a circle around the boy. One man picked him up and tossed him to the next, and then the next, and so on, until he had completed the circle. They then set him down, gave him several Russian coins impressed with a star and a hammer and sickle, and, with roars of laughter, sent the confused boy on his way.

Eight-year-old Luke Lush moved from Pinchard's Island in Bonavista Bay to Gander in December 1942. He was awestruck, having never had "electricity, running water or toilets before." His family's apartment was steam-heated, so there was no fire to light or wood to fetch. "Trucks and cars were going everywhere. Airplanes were always taking off." Some mornings, Luke awoke to the sight of rows of bombers parked wingtip to wingtip. If one crashed, Luke and his friends were often "first on the scene." No one stopped them. One morning while boarding the bus for school, they spotted a crashed Liberator resting on the bog. They quickly exited the bus and were soon inside, exploring. "The guns on the fuselage were still in position and some bullets were still there. It hadn't been cleaned up yet. We didn't touch anything. We just went in to look at it."

Wartime Gander offered a host of conveniences, and everything was free for children, including bus rides and USO shows. Service people at the canteen gave them anything they wanted, candy bars or soft drinks, and at the movies, "the armed forces took us right to the front seat." Luke happened to be at the American theatre when the projectionist suddenly stopped the movie to announce that the war was over. "The military boys were cheering, everybody was happy and saying, 'We're going home.' It was a good feeling."[3]

Long-time Gander resident, Dr. Peter Blackie, son of wartime signals supervisor Charles Blackie and "arguably, the first native Ganderite," he affirms, remembers riding on the bus with his father to the RAF sector. Soon after the war, his father's workplace changed when VOAC radio and air traffic control (ATC) moved from Hangar 21 to Fleet Street on the former Army side. Conveniently, Peter lived within walking distance of Fleet Street. Sometimes, on sunny summer afternoons, he would walk from his house on Chestnut Street to the VOAC building, using a back trail to the Army side, and then drive home with his father, a VOAC shift supervisor. Peter's attire on arrival was perhaps not unusual for a young boy at that time. "Cowboy movies were a Saturday afternoon indulgence," he recalled, and "we played cowboys and Indians in our back woods. I had a set of cap guns with Roy Rogers' name in large letters on the back of the belt. So I would proudly wear this gear into the building and up to the supervisor's desk, and no one ever raised an eyebrow." The ATC control centre was on the second floor, he said, and in those days the "initial communication between Signals and ATC was a clothesline that ran from the second floor to the supervisor's desk with messages clipped onto the line with teletype or handwritten flight information."[4]

Sean Gilmore remembers hearing the men in Building C listening to their Bing Crosby, Hoagy Carmichael, Andrews Sisters, and Glenn Miller records.[5] Adjacent to Building B, and serving a dual purpose, was a playground and children's wading pool. Firstly, it allowed for exercise, but it also kept the junior curiosity seekers out of the hangars, which in any event were off-limits to youngsters.[6] Gilmore recalled only twice entering them. Once was with his father when a crane brought in a damaged Lancaster. The second time was by force. It started when "the usual suspects" began rocking the bus on the way to school. The driver threatened to report them, and sure enough, on the return trip that afternoon, he bypassed their usual stop at the pumphouse and instead "drove around the tarmac to the hangar entrance. There we were told to line up and march into the CO's office." One of the boys, innocent of that morning's misdeeds, took the matter seriously and paraded in "stiff as a Grenadier" and "as if we were about to be awarded the Victoria Cross." Gilmore found the whole thing funny and began to laugh. The commanding officer was unimpressed, pointed at the young man before him and bellowed, demanding to know his father's name. "Capt. Joe Gilmore," he proudly replied. "The Group Captain looked as if I had kicked him somewhere below the belt, his face flushed a vivid red and he sat back down, speechless. The whole thing went downhill for him from then on and relatively well for us."[7]

"It was wartime rules, and by and large we followed them," said Gilmore. Still, it was his curiosity and that of his friend Tommy Fennell in the first place that highlighted a need for some alternate form of distraction. One winter during a snowstorm, the pair salvaged a cockpit coaming from a nearby aircraft crash. It became their personal "fighter aircraft," until someone took it away and decided that an actual playground would be more appropriate. "Ask yourself," Gilmore reflected years later, "who needs a playground when there is a scrapped B-25, an abandoned tar tank 'submarine,' and discarded fuel tank 'rafts' to play in, on, and with." There were rabbits to hunt in the nearby bush, "frozen Butterfinger chocolate bar targets to shoot at with our .22," and boats to sail on Deadman's Pond. For a young boy or girl, wartime Gander *was* a playground, and in Gilmore's estimation, "the best of places to be during what was for most the worst of times."[8]

NOTES

Notes to pages 1–4

Chapter One | Gander: Genesis

[1] Don Jamieson, *No Place for Fools: The Political Memoirs of Don Jamieson* (St. John's: Breakwater Books, 1989), p. 30.
[2] Peter Neary, *Newfoundland in the North Atlantic World, 1929–1949* (Kingston and Montreal: McGill-Queens University Press, 1988), pp. 11–15; and Gene Long, *Suspended State: Newfoundland Before Canada* (St. John's: Breakwater Books Ltd., 1999), pp. 66–7 and 72–5.
[3] "Newfoundland Royal Commission, 1933, Report. Presented by the Secretary of State for Dominion Affairs to Parliament by Command of His Majesty, November 1933" (London: His Majesty's Stationery Office, 1934), pp. 1–2 and 223–4.
[4] Neary, *Newfoundland*, p. 47.
[5] Ottawa Conference Report, 1935–1936, GN 4/5, Public Works and Services (hereafter PW), Civil Aviation, box 1, file AG/2, The Rooms Provincial Archives of Newfoundland and Labrador (hereafter Rooms).
[6] "Trans-Atlantic Air Service," Ottawa, 2 December 1935. Addendum to "Discussions on Transatlantic Air Services, Ottawa, November–December 1935, Minutes of Final Meeting," prepared by Squadron Leader A.T. Cowley, secretary, ibid.; and Neary, *Newfoundland*, p. 111.
[7] Carl Christie, *Ocean Bridge: The History of RAF Ferry Command* (Toronto: University of Toronto Press, 1995), p. 13.
[8] Ottawa Conference Report, 1935–1936, Rooms; and "Report of United Kingdom Air Mission to North America, November–December, 1935," pp. 6–8, AVIA 2/1957, The National Archives of the United Kingdom and Northern Ireland (hereafter TNA).
[9] Neary, *Newfoundland*, p. 110; Christie, *Ocean Bridge*, p. 18; and "Survey of

Notes to pages 5–8

Newfoundland for Suitable Air Base for Trans-Atlantic Service," extract of minutes of 23rd meeting of IACC, 25 March 1936, AVIA 2/1943, part 1, TNA.

10 Ivor McClure, "Report on the Selection of Bases in Newfoundland for the Ireland–Newfoundland Air Route, 23 August 1935," GN 4/5, box 5, file NA/2, Rooms.

11 Lt.-Col. H. Burchall, Imperial Airways, to Lt.-Col. F.C. Shelmerdine, Air Ministry, 23 July 1935, AVIA 2/1943, part 1, TNA.

12 McClure, "Report on the Selection of Bases," Rooms.

13 Bert Riggs, "Early Aviator Was Pioneer," *The Telegram* (St. John's), 4 March 2002.

14 McClure, "Report on the Selection of Bases," Rooms.

15 A.B. Butt to secretary for PW, 24 August 1935, and "Reports of T.A. Hall and A. Vatcher on Proposed Site for Transatlantic Airport in Newfoundland," 15 November 1935, GN 4/5, box 5, file NA/2, Rooms.

16 Neary, *Newfoundland*, p. 111.

17 Batterbee to Lodge, 6 August 1936, T 161/1031/2, TNA.

18 Lodge to Batterbee, 23 July and 20 August 1936, AVIA 2/1946, TNA.

19 Batterbee to J.G. Gibson, 28 August 1936, ibid.

20 Lodge to Batterbee, 23 July 1936, ibid.

21 Hall to R. Manning, secretary for PW, 5 December 1936, and newspaper clipping "A Visit to the Nfld Airport," 8 January 1937, GN 4/5, box 5, file NA/5, vol. 1, Rooms.

22 Burchall to Col. Outerbridge, Harvey and Company, 28 May 1937, and Malcolm MacDonald, Secretary of State for Dominion Affairs (hereafter SSDA), to Sir Humphrey Walwyn, Governor of Newfoundland, 29 May 1937, GN 4/5, box 1, file AG/16, Rooms. Harvey and Company was the Newfoundland agent for Imperial Airways.

23 Batterbee to Lodge, 23 July 1936, GN 4/5, box 6, file NA/8, Rooms.

24 Meehan, Newfoundland Airport, to Manning, 12 June 1937, and Hall to Manning, 24 June 1937, GN 4/5, box 1, file AG/16, Rooms.

25 P.D. McTaggart-Cowan, "Transatlantic Aviation and Meteorology," *The Journal of the Royal Astronomical Society of Canada* XXXII, no. 5 (May–June 1938): p. 223; and Pattison to secretary for PW, 18 December 1946, GN 4/5, box 7, file NA/16, vol. 1, Rooms. In his correspondence of 18 December 1946, Pattison pointed out that so rarely did seaplanes divert to Gleneagles that it became impractical to maintain the staff house. Consequently, the government leased the building to Reid both for his own purposes and to accommodate any diverted crews. Reid gave up his complete tourist operation around 1940. The RCAF took over the property in April 1941 and used the staff house as a rest camp for their officers.

Notes to pages 9–12

[26] Minutes of Air Ministry conference, 25 November 1936, GN 4/5, box 5, file NA/3, Rooms.

[27] J.J.W. Herbertson, Secretary for UK, to Inter-Governmental Committee (Ad Hoc) on Transatlantic Air Services, 7 July 1937, GN 4/5, box 1, file AG/16, Rooms.

[28] Christie, *Ocean Bridge*, p. 23.

[29] SSDA to Walwyn, 22 January 1938, GN 38, Secretary of the Commission of Government, Public Utilities (hereafter PU), Airport, box S5-5-1, file 8, and Lewis-Dale to Sir Wilfrid W. Woods, Commissioner for PU, 11 June 1937, GN 4/5, box 5, file NA/4, vol. 1, Rooms.

[30] Hall to Manning, 25 August 1937, and Pattison to Air Ministry, 21 September 1937, GN 4/5, box 5, file NA/5, vol. 2, Rooms.

[31] Staff Sergeant Vernon Bobbitt, "A Brief History of an Airport in Newfoundland," *The Propagander*, United States Army Air Base Publication, Gander, Newfoundland, Fall 1944, p. 5.

[32] C.F. Warren, editor, *Life at the Crossroads of the World: A History of Gander, Newfoundland, 1936–1988* (Gander, Newfoundland: Gander Seniors Club, 1988), p. 6.

[33] Jewett to Manning, 30 April 1938, and High Commissioner, Ottawa, to Administrator, St. John's, 23 March 1938, GN 38, box S5-5-1, files 1 and 8, respectively, Rooms.

[34] SSDA to governor, 9 October 1937, GN 38, box S5-5-1, file 8, Rooms.

[35] Jewett to Manning, 30 September 1938, GN 38, box S5-5-1, file 1, and Herbertson, monthly progress report, 12 September 1938, GN 4/5, box 1, file AG/16, Rooms.

[36] Jewett to Manning, 31 July 1938 and 30 September 1938, GN 38, box S5-5-1, file 1, Rooms; and *Princeton Alumni Weekly*, 4 November 1938, p. 132.

[37] J.N. Johnson, Marconi engineer-in-charge, to secretary for PU, 29 October 1937, accompanying memorandum, GN 4/5, box 6, file NA/8, Rooms.

[38] Bobbitt, "A Brief History," p. 22.

[39] Air Officer Commanding (hereafter AOC), Eastern Air Command, to Secretary, Department of National Defence (hereafter DND), 19 May 1940, Paul Bridle, editor, *Documents on Relations Between Canada and Newfoundland,* Vol. 1, 1935–1949, Defence, Civil Aviation and Economic Affairs (Ottawa: Department of External Affairs, 1974), pp. 77–8. Newfoundland later issued a proclamation that from 22 August 1940, the area encompassing the settlement, railway station, and post office would be named Gander, while the airport itself would continue to be called Newfoundland Airport. Mail was to be addressed "Newfoundland Airport, Gander." See Dominions Office to secretary, Air Ministry, 8 October 1940, AVIA 2/1943, TNA.

Notes to pages 12–16

[40] Bobbitt, "A Brief History," p. 22.

[41] Ibid., pp. 22 and 33.

[42] Newfoundland Airport Landing Register, 79/1, vol. 1, Department of National Defence, Directorate of History and Heritage (hereafter DHH).

[43] "Trans-Atlantic Meteorology," *Evening Telegram* (St. John's) (hereafter *ET*), 26 May 1938, p. 5.

[44] "Address by Dr. P.D. McTaggart-Cowan on Early Trans-Atlantic Aviation in Newfoundland," 18 November 1975, pp. 6–7, DHH 80/350.

[45] Dominions secretary to Walwyn, 6 November 1939, Bridle, *Documents,* pp. 53–4.

[46] Bobbitt, "A Brief History," p. 22.

[47] Newfoundland Airport Landing Register, vol. 1, DHH; and Alex Dawydoff, "How Atlantic Aviation Serves Business Flying," *Flying,* October 1959, p. 56. The landing register records that an RCAF Norseman and British naval Walrus aircraft also visited that year but landed on Gander Lake.

[48] Christie, *Ocean Bridge*, p. 23.

[49] "Address by Dr. P.D. McTaggart-Cowan," p. 23, DHH 80/350.

[50] AOC to DND, 19 May 1940, Bridle, *Documents*, pp. 77–8.

[51] Dr. Patrick D. McTaggart-Cowan, interviewed by David W. Phillips, Bracebridge, Ontario, 5 October 1983.

[52] Walwyn to Dominions secretary, 26 May 1940, Bridle, *Documents*, p. 76.

[53] AOC to DND, 19 May 1940, ibid., pp. 77–8.

[54] John Pudney, *Atlantic Bridge: The Official Account of R.A.F. Transport Command's Ocean Ferry* (London: His Majesty's Stationery Office, 1945), pp. 6–7.

[55] Sholto Watt, *I'll Take the High Road: A History of the Beginning of the Atlantic Air Ferry in Wartime* (Fredericton: Brunswick Press, 1960), pp. 20–3.

[56] Air Vice-Marshal D.T.C. Bennett, *Pathfinder: A War Autobiography* (London and St. Albans: Goodall Publications Ltd., 1988), p. 82.

[57] Christie, *Ocean Bridge*, p. 41.

[58] Gilmore personal notebook, Gilmore family private collection, courtesy Robert Pelley; and Captain A.S. Wilcockson, "Report Covering Return Ferry Service," 22 September 1941, subsection "General Report," p. 1, AIR 38/2, TNA.

[59] Bennett, *Pathfinder*, p. 82.

[60] "Address by Dr. P.D. McTaggart-Cowan," p. 25, DHH 80/350.

[61] Air Commodore Griffith Powell, *Ferryman: From Ferry Command to Silver City* (Shrewsbury, England: Airlife Publishing Ltd., 1982), pp. 25–6.

[62] Warren, *Life at the Crossroads*, pp. 20–1. McGrath provided this information in a short autobiography and contribution to the noted publication.

[63] Woods, memo for the Commission of Government, 6 August 1943, GN

Notes to pages 17–24

38, box S5-5-2, file 1, Rooms. McGrath also obtained a pilot's license in England in 1934.

64 Manning, "Report on Visit to Airport, 14–18 May, 1940," p. 19, GN 4/5, box 6, no file number, Rooms.

65 Powell, *Ferryman*, p. 26.

66 Watt, *I'll Take the High Road*, p. 46.

67 Quoted in Pudney, *Atlantic Bridge,* pp. 12 and 16; 10 (Bomber Reconnaissance) Squadron, RCAF, Operations Record Book (ORB) daily diary, 29 October 1940, Library and Archives Canada (hereafter LAC); and RAF Watch Log, Newfoundland Airport, DHH 79/1, vol. 2.

68 Bennett, *Pathfinder*, p. 85.

69 Quoted in Pudney, *Atlantic Bridge*, p. 13.

70 Bennett, *Pathfinder*, p. 86; Powell, *Ferryman*, p. 27; Pudney, *Atlantic Bridge*, p. 13; and Lieutenant-Colonel William T. Bernard, "The Queen's Own Rifles of Canada, 1860–1960, One Hundred Years of Canada." Draft copy posted at *The Queen's Own Rifles of Canada Regimental Museum and Archive* website. Retrieved 26 November 2018, from https://qormuseum.org/history/timeline-1925-1949/the-second-world-war/newfoundland-and-new-brunswick-1940-1941/.

71 Bennett, *Pathfinder*, pp. 86–7.

72 Quoted in Pudney, *Atlantic Bridge*, pp. 13–14.

73 Bennett, *Pathfinder*, p. 87.

74 Quoted in Pudney, *Atlantic Bridge*, pp. 15–16.

75 Bennett, *Pathfinder*, p. 88.

76 Powell, *Ferryman*, pp. 28–9; and RAF Watch Log, vol. 2, DHH.

77 Watt, *I'll Take the High Road*, p. 45.

78 Pattison, report on accident to Hudson T9446, 31 December 1940, p. 1, and statements of Watt, Loughridge, and Smith, 29 December 1940, GN 4/5, box 2, file AG/57/2, Rooms.

79 Watt statement, ibid.

80 Statement of N. Stuart Knapp, medical officer, and Smith statement, ibid.

81 Pattison, accident report, pp. 2–3, ibid.

82 Statement of R.N. Wells, ibid.

83 Pattison to secretary for PW, 3 January 1940, and Pattison, accident report, pp. 2–5, ibid.

84 Ted Beaudoin, "Earth Angels Rising Chapter Four." *RAF Ferry Command.* Retrieved 2 December 2018, from http://www.ganderairporthistoricalsociety.org/_html_war/Lockheed.Vega/Earth%20Angels%20Rising%20Chapter%204%20%C2%BB%20RAF%20Ferry%20Command.htm.

85 RAF Watch Log, vol. 2, DHH; and extracts from McGrath's diaries, DHH 74/635. See also Darrell Hillier, "The 'Spirit of Lockheed-Vega

Notes to pages 24–8

Employees': A Counterargument." *Gander Airport Historical Society*. Retrieved 2 December 2018, from http://www.ganderairporthistorical society.org/_html_war/Hudson_vega.part2.htm.

86 RAF Watch Log, vol. 2, DHH.

Chapter Two | The First Full Year

1 Powell, *Ferryman*, p. 29.

2 Sampson, employment card, DHH 84/44.

3 "ATFERO: Report by Mr. W.P. Hildred July 1941," appendix II, summary of personnel as of 15 June 1941, p. 22, AIR 20/6154, TNA; "British Pilots Shuttle across Atlantic Regularly and Prove Land Plane Service Feasible," *Lethbridge Herald*, 10 January 1941, p. 17; and Frank Tibbo, "Reminiscing With John Murphy." *Gander Airport Historical Society*. Retrieved 27 November 2018, from http://www.ganderairporthistoricalsociety.org/_html_4658/JMreminiscing.htm.

4 Murphy, employment card, DHH 84/44; John Murphy, email message to author, 18 May 2010; and Tibbo, "Reminiscing."

5 Tom McGrath, professional diary, 11, 15, 18, and 20 January 1941, Thomas M. McGrath fonds, MG 31, A 23, vol. 1, file 14, LAC. McGrath does not disclose the nature of the required engine modifications; however, in his report on the Return Ferry Service prepared in September 1941, Captain Wilcockson spoke of the problems encountered during the initial months of ferrying operations. In addition to oil cooler issues, Wilcockson revealed that aluminum spacer washers or oil seal washers had been failing on the Hudsons and causing engine trouble. After maintenance crews at Saint-Hubert made several engine changes due to this problem, the UK grounded all the Hudsons until they were modified by replacing the aluminum washer with a steel washer. See Wilcockson, "Report Covering," AIR 38/2, TNA. CPR staff first moved into some bedrooms at the Eastbound Inn on 20 December 1940, allowing the release of two railway sleeping cars. See McGrath, airman's diary, 20 December 1940, vol. 1, file 13, LAC.

6 Bennett, *Pathfinder*, p. 90; and Powell, *Ferryman*, p. 29.

7 McGrath, professional diary, 8–10 and 14–15 February 1941, vol. 1, file 14, LAC; and RAF Watch Log, vol. 2, DHH.

8 Michael Bliss, *Banting: A Biography* (Toronto: McClelland and Stewart Ltd., 1985), p. 133.

9 Banting, personal notebook, Manuscript Coll. 76, Banting papers, University of Toronto, Thomas Fisher Rare Book Library.

10 Kelly Field Correspondent, "Lieutenant Mackey Completes Refresher Course," *Air Corps News Letter*, 1 January 1939, pp. 7–8.

Notes to pages 29–33

[11] Banting, personal notebook and daybook diary, 19 February 1941, Banting papers, University of Toronto.

[12] Deposition of Patrick McTaggart-Cowan, "Enquiry into Death of Sir Frederick Banting, Wireless Operator William Snailham and Navigator William Bird," GN 4/5, box 2, file AG/57/2, Rooms; Banting, daybook diary, 29 February 1941, and C.M. Tripp's account of Banting's last days at Gander, box 45, Banting papers, University of Toronto.

[13] RAF Watch Log, vol. 2, DHH.

[14] McGrath, professional diary, 20 February 1941, vol. 1, file 14, LAC. McGrath's diary clearly notes that six aircraft were scheduled for departure that night and he briefly described each take-off. Oddly, the RAF Watch Log does not record the Hudson that McGrath reports as having gone off the runway.

[15] Deposition of Joseph C. Mackey, Enquiry, Rooms.

[16] "Pilot Unfolds Tragic Story of Plane Crash," *ET*, 22 March 1941, p. 5.

[17] Mackey deposition, Enquiry, Rooms.

[18] Ibid.

[19] Bennett, *Pathfinder*, pp. 93–4.

[20] Mackey and Allison depositions, Enquiry, Rooms; and "Pilot Unfolds," *ET*, 24 March 1941, p. 5.

[21] Bennett, *Pathfinder*, pp. 94–5.

[22] Mackey deposition, Enquiry, Rooms; and Roland W. Abbott, "The Story of the Banting Plane Crash," unpublished manuscript, no date.

[23] McGrath, professional diary, 28 February and 1–2 March 1941, vol. 1, file 14, LAC.

[24] "Sir Frederick Did Duty as Doctor Before He Expired," and "Banting and Others All Wore Parachutes," *Ottawa Citizen*, 26 February 1941, p. 1.

[25] "Pilot Unfolds," *ET*, 22 and 27 March 1941, pp. 5 and 13, respectively.

[26] "N.Y. Story Says Banting Plane Was Sabotaged," *Hamilton Spectator*, 24 March 1941, p. 13.

[27] Bliss, *Banting*, p. 305.

[28] "Banting Killed on Only Plane Lost in Transit," *Hamilton Spectator*, 23 April 1941, p. 1.

[29] "Pilot of Banting Plane, Mackey One of Victims," *Globe and Mail* (Toronto), 15 August 1941, p. 1; "Capt. Joseph Mackey Not Aboard Ferry Plane in Which 22 Killed," *Gazette* (Montréal), p. 1; and "Pilot Mackey Back from Britain Reads of His 'Death' in Crash," *Globe and Mail*, 28 August 1941, p. 13.

[30] Magistrate Hollett to G.B. Summers, Secretary for Justice, 3 March 1941, Enquiry, Rooms.

Notes to pages 34–9

31 Rod Goff, "Another Side of Banting Debate," *Packet* (Clarenville), 16 July 2001, p. 11.

32 The Royal Rifles of Canada war diary, 7, 9, 18, and 20 February 1941, RG24-C-3, vol. 15229, file no. 1042, LAC.

33 Addendum to Royal Rifles war diary for March 1941. Experiences and duties of Sauson and rifleman R. Wilson at crash of T9449, 24 February to 4 March 1941, and Robertson, "A Special Guard Duty," ibid. The RCAF flew in two Fairchild FC-71 aircraft, numbers 644 and 645.

34 Three Sauson brothers, Edward, Lester, and Oliver, served with The Royal Rifles of Canada and fought at Hong Kong. Only Oliver made it home. Like Edward, Lester was taken prisoner and died in captivity. See *Hong Kong Veterans Commemorative Association* website. Retrieved 30 November 2018, from https://www.hkvca.ca/index.php. While at Gander, the regiment adopted a Newfoundland dog named Pal as their mascot and renamed him "Gander." The dog went with the regiment to Hong Kong. When a Japanese grenade fell among some wounded Canadian troops, Gander picked it up and rushed towards the enemy, dying in the ensuing explosion. In October 2000, Sergeant Gander was posthumously awarded the Dickin medal, the animal metaphorical equivalent of the Victoria Cross. See Robyn Walker, *Sergeant Gander: A Canadian Hero* (Toronto: Natural Heritage Books, 2009), pp. 65 and 78.

35 Hollett to Summers, 3 March 1941, and Coulombe deposition, Enquiry, Rooms.

36 Walwyn to King, 2 and 24 April 1941, and King to Walwyn, 10 April 1941, Enquiry, Rooms.

37 Report by Captain D.C.T. Bennett, Observer at Court of Inquiry into the accident of Hudson T9449, addendum to letter from Bennett to Woods, 25 March 1941, Enquiry, Rooms.

38 Walwyn to King, 2 April 1941, Enquiry, Rooms.

39 Bennett report, Enquiry, Rooms.

40 King to Walwyn, 28 February 1941, RG 25, External Affairs, series A-3-b, vol. 2692, file 6-AS-40, LAC.

41 Dickins to Air Commodore G.V. Walsh, 25 March 1941, Enquiry, Rooms.

42 Norman A. Robertson, Acting Under-Secretary of State for External Affairs, to C.J. Mackenzie, Acting President, National Research Council, 15 April 1941, RG 25, External Affairs, series A-3-b, vol. 2692, file 6-AS-40, LAC.

43 Dickins to Air Commodore G.V. Walsh, 25 March 1941, Enquiry, Rooms.

44 Bliss, *Banting*, p. 305.

45 Wilcockson, "Report Covering," subsection "General Report," p. 4, AIR 38/2, TNA.

Notes to pages 39–43

[46] Christie, *Ocean Bridge*, pp. 76–7.
[47] RAF Watch Log, vol. 2, DHH.
[48] Christie, *Ocean Bridge*, pp. 126–7; Powell, *Ferryman*, p. 40; and G/C F.V. Heakes for Chief of the Air Staff to Under-Secretary of State for External Affairs, Ottawa, 18 June 1941, Bridle, *Documents*, p. 347.
[49] Colonel Stanley W. Dziuban, *Military Relations Between the United States and Canada, 1939–1945* (Washington: Office of the Chief of Military History, Department of the Army, 1959), p. 183; and Eric Fry, "Report on an Investigation for Landing Areas near Northwest River, Labrador," 10 July 1941, Bridle, *Documents*, pp. 349–50.
[50] RAF Watch Log, vol. 2, DHH.
[51] Ibid.
[52] Watt, *I'll Take the High Road*, p. 138.
[53] Winston Bray, *The History of BOAC* (Surrey: The Wessex Press, 1975), p. 27.
[54] RAF Watch Log, vol. 2, DHH.
[55] Bennett, *Pathfinder*, p. 98.
[56] RAF Watch Log, vol. 2, DHH.
[57] Peter Berry, "Trans-Atlantic Air Deliveries, 1940–1946," unpublished document, no date.
[58] Dickins to Breadner, 15 March 1941, file S19-55-1, vol. 1, LAC; and Hildred, "ATFERO: Report," appendix II, p. 30, AIR 20/6154, TNA. A small motor launch at Botwood named *Rover* was given to ATFERO to use but sank on Gander Lake in a storm the day after it was launched in April 1941. A bigger launch from Gleneagles was then made available to the ferry organization. The sunken *Rover* was recovered, taken to the hangar for repairs, and back in commission by mid-May 1941.
[59] Murphy, email message to author, 21 May 2010.
[60] RAF Watch Log, vol. 2, DHH; Pudney, *Atlantic Bridge*, p. 24; and Case, crew assignment card, DHH 84/44. The Clipper carried Air Chief Marshal Bowhill, en route to Montréal to take up his post with RAF Ferry Command. The Clipper flew on to the US and Bowhill continued his journey from Gander to Montréal aboard a Ferry Command Hudson.
[61] RAF Watch Log, vol. 2, DHH; *Hamilton Spectator*, 20 June 1941; Christie, *Ocean Bridge*, pp. 215–16; and Watt, *I'll Take the High Road*, pp. 153–4.
[62] RCAF Station Gander ORB daily diary (hereafter RCAF Gander), 8 and 11 August 1941, C-12186, LAC.
[63] Melvin Baker and Peter Neary, "Governor Sir Humphrey Walwyn's Account of His Meetings with Churchill and Roosevelt, Placentia Bay, Newfoundland, August 1941," *Newfoundland and Labrador Studies* 31, no. 1 (2016). A radiogram handed to Churchill suggested that Beaverbrook's

Notes to pages 43–6

flight to Gander was eight hours overdue. Seconds later, another message told that Beaverbrook had arrived at Gander at the scheduled time. Churchill was relieved at the news but annoyed at being given the first message when the second message was in existence.

64 RAFFC Dorval ORB daily diary (hereafter RAFFC Dorval), 15 August 1941, AIR 24/505, TNA; Cleeve, crew assignment card, DHH 84/44; and RAF Watch Log, DHH 79/1, vol. 3. The RAF Watch Log for Gander records the arrival of Hudson V9181 on 8 August 1941, but for reasons that are unclear, does not refer to the accident on 15 August. Wing Commander Mulholland had previously sustained severe facial injuries in a crash overseas and was returning to duty following convalescence in Canada. He later commanded 458 Squadron, Royal Australian Air Force, and was lost on operations over the Mediterranean early in 1942. See "RAF Australians – Wing Commander Norman George Mulholland (DFC)." *Militarian: Military History Forum*. Retrieved 4 December 2018, from http://www.militarian.com/threads/raf-australians-wing-commander-norman-george-mulholland-dfc.5835/.

65 RAFFC Dorval, 21 and 27 September and 11 October 1941, TNA; and Christie, *Ocean Bridge*, p. 311.

66 RAF Watch Log, vol. 3, DHH.

67 RCAF Gander, 12 September 1941 and amendment to entry, LAC. In the interests of secrecy and security, presumably, the royal visitor's name went unrecorded in the passenger list in the RAF Watch Log.

68 Donald Jones, "The Mystery Surrounding Prince George's Death," *Toronto Star*, 19 January 1991, p. H2.

69 RAF Watch Log, vol. 3, DHH.

70 Ibid.

Chapter Three | The Birth of Beaver Centre

1 "Requirements of Canadian Pacific Air Services in Canada and Newfoundland to Cope with Trans-Atlantic Flight Deliveries of Aircraft," memorandum, 20 February 1941, Bridle, *Documents*, p. 335.

2 Wilson to Power, 25 February 1941, Bridle, *Documents*, pp. 334–5.

3 "Requirements of Canadian Pacific Air Services," 20 February 1941, Bridle, *Documents*, pp. 335–6.

4 Wilcockson, "Report Covering," subsection "Construction Programme and Facilities at Gander and Dorval," p. 1, AIR 38/2, TNA.

5 Memorandum of Agreement Between the Government of Canada and the Government of Newfoundland, 17 April 1941, GN 4/5, box 10, file NA/91, Rooms.

Notes to pages 46–52

6 Permanent Joint Board on Defence, Journal of Discussions and Decisions, New York, 17 December 1940, Bridle, *Documents*, pp. 409–10.

7 Minutes of Meeting of Cabinet War Committee, Ottawa, 18 December 1940, ibid., p. 411.

8 Secretary of State for External Affairs to Governor of Newfoundland, 25 January 1941, ibid., p. 417.

9 Memorandum of Agreement, 17 April 1941, Rooms.

10 McGrath, professional diary, 15 April 1941, vol. 1, file 14, LAC.

11 Memorandum of Agreement, 17 April 1941, Rooms.

12 L.E. Emerson, Acting Commissioner for PU, Memorandum for the Commission of Government, 30 January 1942, GN 38, box S5-5-2, file 1, Rooms.

13 Wilson to Moore-Brabazon, 3 June 1941, Bridle, *Documents*, p. 344.

14 Roosevelt to Churchill, Bridle, *Documents*, p. 342.

15 Quoted in Christie, *Ocean Bridge*, p. 92.

16 RCAF Gander, 15 June 1941, LAC.

17 Woods, Memorandum to the Commission of Government, 16 June 1941, GN 38, box S5-5-1, file 5, Rooms.

18 Ibid.

19 Ibid.

20 SSDA to Walwyn, 15 July 1941, ibid.

21 Governor to SSDA, 11 and 16 July 1941, GN 38, box S5-5-2, file 2, Rooms.

22 S.L. de Carteret to MAP, 22 July 1941, file S19-55-1, vol. 1, LAC.

23 Christie, *Ocean Bridge*, pp. 93–4.

24 Wilcockson, "Report Covering," subsection "Construction Programme and Facilities at Gander and Dorval," p. 1, TNA. Construction estimates for Beaver Centre, the marine base, and the Eastbound and Gander Inns came in at 1.9 million dollars. See Hildred, Air 20/6154, TNA.

25 Bowhill to de Carteret, 18 September 1941, file S19-55-1, vol. 1, LAC.

26 De Carteret to Bowhill, 18 September 1941, ibid.

27 Wilcockson, "Report Covering," subsection "Construction Programme and Facilities at Gander and Dorval," p. 1, TNA.

28 "RAFTC," *The Propagander*, Fall 1944, p. 25. Initially, spouses and children of US personnel were permitted to live on base, but after Pearl Harbour the War Department ordered them to return home. See John N. Cardoulis, *A Friendly Invasion II: A Personal Touch* (St. John's: Creative Publishers, 1993), p. 84.

29 Gloria Lindsay, "Gander Airport, 1944–46." *Bob's Gander History*. Retrieved 1 December 2018, from http://bobsganderhistory.com/mog.html; and RAFFC Gander ORB daily diary and Appendices (hereafter RAFFC Gander), routine orders, 19 April, 23 June, 5 July, 15 August, and 5

Notes to pages 53–7

November 1942, and 8 January and 20 May 1944, AIR 29/467, TNA. When the unit closed down, Joseph Smallwood bought all the books in Beaver Centre library and donated them to his birthplace, Gambo. See Joseph R. Smallwood, *I Chose Canada: The Memoirs of the Honourable Joseph R. "Joey" Smallwood* (Toronto: The Macmillan Company of Canada Ltd., 1973), p. 221.

30 As per multiple entries in RAFFC Gander daily diary, TNA.

31 RAFFC Gander, daily diary, 4 February 1944, TNA; "RAFTC," *The Propagander*, p. 25; and Transport Canada, map of RAF side (copy courtesy of the Gander Airport Historical Society).

32 RAFFC Gander, routine orders, 9 September 1943, TNA.

33 Carol Walsh, "Remembering …… with Phyllis Locke." *Gander Airport Historical Society*. Retrieved 9 January 2019, from http://www.ganderairport historicalsociety.org/_html_war/phyllis_locke.htm.

34 James Reid, email message to author, 1 June 2010.

35 Robert Pelley, "A Radio Operator in Gander – Roland Masse's Story." *Bob's Gander History*. Retrieved 30 November 2018, from http://bobsganderhistory.com/Rollie.pdf.

36 RAFFC Gander, daily diary, 4 February and 21 June 1944, routine orders, 20 January 1943, 24 March, 10 April, and 17 July 1944, and 14 June 1945, TNA.

37 Murphy, email message to author, 18 May 2010.

38 Smallwood, *I Chose*, p. 222.

39 G/C R.E. McBurney to W/C Maxwell Muller, 18 November 1941, AIR 38/8, TNA.

40 W/C G.C. Cunningham to G/C G.H. Randle, 10 May 1943, ibid.

41 T.M. McGrath, *History of Canadian Airports* (Lugus Publications, 1992), pp. 106–7.

42 Governor to UK High Commissioner in Ottawa, 30 July and 9 December 1941, GN 38, box S5-5-1, file 5, Rooms.

43 Emerson to Commission, 30 January 1942, GN 38, box S5-5-2, file 1, Rooms.

44 "PJBD, Journal of Discussions and Decisions," 29 July 1941, Bridle, *Documents*; Pudney, *Atlantic Bridge*, pp. 28–9; and Christie, *Ocean Bridge*, pp. 128–9.

45 Henri-Paul Boudreau, email message to author, 10 August 2001. These details were confirmed in Gendron's logbook, which was in Boudreau's possession at the time of our correspondence. In 1939, Gendron took Boudreau on his first flight, inspiring him to become a pilot. The night before landing at Goose Bay on 3 December 1941, Gendron and Graham boarded at the Boudreau residence at Seven Islands.

Notes to pages 57–63

[46] W/C W.J. McFarlane, "Report on the Establishment of the R.C.A.F. Detachment at Goose Bay, Labrador, From September, 1941, to March, 1942," p. 3, C-12188, LAC.

[47] Henri-Paul Boudreau, email message to author, 10 August 2001.

[48] Dziuban, *Military Relations*, pp. 182–4.

[49] Guy Warner, "From IRA to MBE: John Joseph Gilmore," *Canadian Aviation Historical Society Journal* 51, no. 2 (Summer 2013): pp. 75–6; Robert Pelley, "John Joseph Gilmore, MBE." *Bob's Gander History*. Retrieved 4 December 2018, from http://bobsganderhistory.com/joegilmore.pdf; and Frank Tibbo, "Gilmore Honoured Again," *Beacon* (Gander), 19 November 2009, p. A7.

[50] Pelley, "John Joseph Gilmore, MBE."

Chapter Four | Working Towards a Common Cause

[1] Early History of the 1387th Army Air Forces Base Unit (AAFBU), vol. 1, May 1941–June 1944, Gander, pp. 19 and 48, A0163, Air Force Historical Research Agency (AFHRA), Maxwell AFB, Alabama.

[2] Bowhill, operational activities for January and June 1942, AIR 24/506, TNA; and list of persons employed by RAF Ferry Command at Gander, 30 March 1942, GN 13/1/B, Justice and Defence, box 457, file "Gander RAFFC," Rooms.

[3] W/C Wicks to Hildred, 16 August 1941, AIR 38/8, TNA.

[4] Warren, *Life at the Crossroads*, p. 37.

[5] Tom McGrath, "The RAF in Newfoundland," *Off Duty, or Out of Control, The Unofficial Journal of the RAF* 1, no. 1 (13 May 1946), Thomas M. McGrath fonds, MG 31, A 23, vol. 15, file 5, LAC. McGrath identified O'Bryen as the first RAF officer posted to the Gander unit. Having served at Gander throughout the war, first as airport operations officer and then as flying control officer with Ferry Command, McGrath presumably had knowledge of such matters. A review of the Dorval ORB dairy diary from July 1941 when the RAF took over from ATFERO to year's end, reveals many postings of officers to Ferry Command headquarters as Bowhill assembled his cadre of staff, but does not refer specifically to RAF personnel at Gander until early in 1942.

[6] Woods, memo for the Commission of Government, 6 August 1943, GN 38, box S5-5-2, file 1, Rooms.

[7] McGrath, employment card, DHH 84/44.

[8] RAFFC Gander, McGrath to G/C Anderson, 22 October 1942, and McGrath to Anderson, 17 October 1942, with attached report on his visit to Prestwick Transatlantic Air Control and associated units in the UK,

Notes to pages 64–8

appendix "A", pp. 1–3, TNA. Unlike McGrath, another visiting unit member, Pilot Officer Robert Simpson, saw little value in duplicating Prestwick's plotting system "as it is impossible to get a radio fix on an aircraft at Gander owing to existing [late 1942] radio conditions." He agreed, however, that the installation of a weather board should proceed as soon as possible, and recommended that the duty signals officer be present in the control room when aircraft were in flight. At that time, Dorval handled the main briefings for Atlantic crossings, but weather and mechanical problems often delayed crews at Gander for extended periods. Simpson therefore suggested that Gander provide such briefings, with those at Dorval "limited navigationally to the first stages of the route." See RAFFC Gander, Simpson to Anderson, 30 November 1942.

9 Christie, *Ocean Bridge*, p. 131.

10 RAFFC Gander, G/C Anderson to headquarters, 24 October 1942, TNA.

11 Early History of the 1387th AAFBU, Gander, pp. 66–8, AFHRA.

12 Lt. Colonel Arthur Fickel, Commanding US Army Air Base Gander, to commanding general, Newfoundland Base Command (Fort Pepperrell), 26 August 1942, 1387th AAFBU, Gander, AFHRA.

13 Early History of the 1387th AAFBU, Gander, p. 96, AFHRA.

14 Fickel to commanding general, 26 August 1942, AFHRA.

15 Bowhill, operational activities for October 1942, AIR 24/506, TNA.

16 G/C G.H. Randle to Lt.-Col. Pillett, 11 September 1942, Pillett to Randle, 17 September 1942, and Chief Signals Officer to Director of Signals, 7 October 1942, AIR 38/14, TNA.

17 Fickel to commanding general, 26 August 1942, AFHRA.

18 Early History of the 1387th AAFBU, Gander, p. 83, AFHRA.

19 Samuel Milner, "Establishing the Bolero Ferry Route," *Military Affairs* 11, no. 4 (Winter 1947): pp. 213 and 222. To ferry short-range single-engine fighter aircraft from the factories in North America to the UK via Goose Bay, a series of airfields was needed in northern Canada. Starting early in 1942, Ferry Command had Canadian bush pilot Louis Bisson head up exploratory work in the Canadian Arctic. Airfield construction on this northern or Crimson Route as it became known, began that same year, financed by the United States. See Christie, *Ocean Bridge*, pp. 132–4.

20 Early History of the 1387th AAFBU, Gander, pp. 81–4, AFHRA.

21 Guthrie to AOC, EAC, 10 February 1943, Bridle, *Documents*, pp. 392–3.

22 Bowhill, operational activities for December 1942, AIR 24/506, TNA.

23 RAFFC Gander, daily diary, 18 December 1942, TNA.

24 Bowhill, operational activities for December 1942, AIR 24/506, TNA.

25 "Report No. 1 of the Joint USAAF-RAFFC Board for Establishment of Joint Operational Units on the North Atlantic Air Routes," pp. 2–3, ibid.

Notes to pages 68–75

[26] RAFFC Gander, daily diary, 21 December 1942; and McGrath, pocket diary, 21 December 1942, vol. 1, file 17, LAC.

[27] Proceedings of Joint USAAF/RAFTC Transatlantic Control (Signals Aspect), AIR 38/70, TNA.

[28] Guthrie to AOC, 10 February 1943, Bridle, *Documents*, pp. 392–3.

[29] Bowhill, operational activities for January, February, and March 1943, AIR 24/506, TNA.

[30] McGrath, *History of Canadian*, p. 107; and RAFFC Gander, daily diary, 13 May 1943 and 11 February 1944, TNA.

[31] Proceedings of Joint USAAF-RAFTC Control, AIR 38/170, TNA.

[32] "RAFTC," *The Propagander*, p. 23.

[33] "Questions concerning Air Control of Trans-Atlantic Air Traffic," 44 Group Air Staff Instructions, Part 2, Aircraft Control, Transatlantic Route, 26 November 1941, pp. 3 and 9, AIR 2/8151, TNA.

[34] G/C G.J. Powell to AOC-in-C, 3 March 1943, AIR 38/8, TNA; and McGrath, "The RAF in Newfoundland," LAC.

[35] Pelley, "A Radio Operator in Gander."

[36] List of persons employed by RAF Ferry Command at Gander, 30 March 1942, Rooms. The radio supervisors lived on Chestnut Street in the original airport town site and continued living there after Ferry Command absorbed the signals section and Beaver Centre opened. Although formally named Chestnut Road, residents often referred to it as Chestnut Street. After the RCAF arrived and began building up infrastructure around the town site, the area became known colloquially as the Canadian side.

[37] Lost were Newfoundlanders William B. Collins and Cyril H. Small, and Nova Scotian John J. MacDonald. Harry T. Moores of Blackhead, Conception Bay, Newfoundland, was killed when Catalina FP151 crashed at Cape Charles, Virginia, in August 1942. Francis W. Coughlan of St. John's, veteran of sixteen crossings via Gander, was the only survivor among the five radio operator enlistees. See Tom McGrath, "Gander Radio (VOAC) and Ferry Command," unpublished document, pp. 2–4. Copy on file at Centre for Newfoundland Studies, Memorial University of Newfoundland; and Christie, *Ocean Bridge*, p. 313.

[38] RAFFC Dorval, 28 March 1942, TNA.

[39] Early History of the 1387th AAFBU, Gander, p. 99, AFHRA.

[40] Pelley, "A Radio Operator in Gander." In January 1947, new traffic laws required motorists to switch from the left to the right side of the road.

[41] Ibid.

[42] Ibid.

[43] Ibid.

[44] Lindsay, "Gander Airport," and Hazel B. Fausak, "My History With the

Notes to pages 75–81

Royal Air Force Ferry Command/Royal Air Force Transport Command." *Bob's Gander History*. Retrieved 1 December 2018, from http://bobsgander history.com/moh1.pdf.

45 Murphy, email message to author, 18 May 2010; and Captain I.G. Ross, letter to heads of departments, 31 March 1942, John Murphy private collection.

46 Murphy, email message to author, 21 May 2010.

47 RAFFC Gander, routine orders, 12 April 1942, TNA; "Sidney Joseph Cottle." *The Aerodrome*. Retrieved 5 December 2018, from http://www.theaerodrome.com/aces/england/cottle.php; and *Second Supplement to the London Gazette*, no. 30989, 2 November 1918, p. 12963.

48 Captain I.G. Ross, letter to heads of departments, John Murphy private collection.

49 Murphy, email message to author, 21 May 2010.

50 Billy Gottwald, "RAF Sends Captain Anderson to VMI for Discussion of Allied War Effort in Last Half of War's Third Year," *VMI Cadet* (Lexington, Va.), 23 February 1942, p. 1.

51 *RAF Commands*. Information courtesy Hugh Halliday. Retrieved 12 May 2010, from http://www.rafcommands.com/forum/showthread.php?8346 -G-C-D-F-Anderson-(Ferry-Command).

52 Murphy, email message to author, 18 May 2010.

53 John Warwick Narburgh, "Keep 'Em Crossed: Memories and Letters From World War Two," unpublished manuscript, no date, p. 136.

54 J.R. Smallwood, "Gander – And Newfoundland Aviation History," *Western Star* (Corner Brook), 20 January 1945, p. 2.

55 Sean Gilmore, email message to author, 21 February 2018.

56 Smallwood, "Gander – And Newfoundland," p. 2.

57 Murphy, email message to author, 24 May 2010.

58 Reid, email message to author, 1 June 2010; and Frank Tibbo, "Gander and Ferry Command," *Ferry Command Commemoration*, North Atlantic Aviation Museum, 2000, p. 8.

Chapter Five | Mishaps and Salvage Sagas

1 RAFFC Dorval, 9 and 24 January 1942, TNA; RCAF Gander, 9, 22, and 26 January 1942, LAC; McGrath, professional diary, 8–9, 23, and 26 January 1942, vol. 1, file 16, LAC; and Christie, *Ocean Bridge*, pp. 311–12.

2 McGrath, professional diary, 16–17 March 1942, vol. 1, file 16, LAC. A photograph of the crew taken at Codroy identifies each airman by name. See Newfoundland Ranger Force Association fonds, photograph albums, MG 621, Rooms.

Notes to pages 81–9

[3] Brodie Thomas, "The Spirit of Codroy," *Gulf News* (Port aux Basques), 4 April 2011.
[4] Gilmore notes on salvage of FH235, Gilmore family private collection, courtesy Pat Gilmore; and Murphy, email message to author, 24 May 2010.
[5] Gilmore salvage notes.
[6] Bowhill to Emerson, 15 April 1942, Newfoundland Ranger Force Association fonds, MG 621, box 4, file 64, Rooms.
[7] Bowhill to Emerson, 15 April 1942, GN 13/1/B, box 364, file "Planes," Rooms.
[8] Accident to FH235, C-5037, LAC.
[9] Reid, email message to author, 11 and 20 May 2010.
[10] Ibid., 18 May 2010.
[11] Bowhill, operational activities for April 1942, AIR 24/506, TNA; RAFFC Dorval, 7 and 25 April 1942, TNA; and Christie, *Ocean Bridge*, p. 312.
[12] RAFFC Dorval, 3 May 1942, TNA; RCAF Gander, 4 and 6–7 May 1942, LAC; and Christie, *Ocean Bridge*, p. 312.
[13] Pattison to Newfoundland secretary for PW, 10 February 1944, GN 38, box S5-1-3, file 21, Rooms.
[14] Bowhill, operational activities for May 1942, AIR 24/506, TNA; RCAF Gander, 9–10 May 1942, LAC; RAFFC Dorval, 10 May 1942, TNA; and Christie, *Ocean Bridge*, p. 312.
[15] RCAF Station Goose Bay ORB daily diary, 23 May 1942, C-12188, LAC; Eastern Air Command ORB daily diary, 23 May 1942, LAC; and RCAF Gander, 26 May 1942, LAC.
[16] Harold Chubbs and Wade Kearley, *Facing the Sea: Lightkeepers and Their Families* (St. John's: Flanker Press Ltd., 2013), p. 81.
[17] Early History of the 1387th AAFBU, Gander, pp. 78–9, AFHRA.
[18] Chubbs and Kearley, *Facing the Sea*, pp. 81–2.
[19] RAFFC Dorval, 30 May 1942, TNA; and Christie, *Ocean Bridge*, p. 313.
[20] Frank Tibbo, *The Best of Aviation: 101 Tales of Fliers and Flying as Published in The Gander Beacon* (St. John's: Creative Book Publishing, 1997), pp. 125–6; and Stackhouse and Pearson, crew assignment cards, DHH 84/44.
[21] RAFFC Dorval, 12 July 1942, TNA; and Christie, *Ocean Bridge*, p. 313.
[22] Bowhill, operational activities for August 1942, AIR 24/506, TNA; McGrath, pocket diary, 28 August 1942, vol. 1, file 17, LAC; RAFFC Dorval, 27 August 1942, TNA; and Christie, *Ocean Bridge*, p. 314.
[23] Nathan Miller, *War at Sea: A Naval History of World War II* (New York: Oxford University Press, 1995), pp. 295 and 302.
[24] Jock Manson, *United in Effort: The Story of No. 53 Squadron, Royal Air Force, 1916–1976* (Tunbridge Wells, Kent, UK: Air-Britain, 1997), p. 43; RAFFC

Notes to pages 89–98

Gander, daily diary, 19 April 1943, TNA; and Jock Manson, email message to author, 9 October 2010.

25 RAFFC Gander, daily diary, 19 April 1943, TNA.

26 Ibid., 16 September 1942; and Schaffer, crew assignment card, DHH 84/44.

27 RAFFC Gander, daily diary, 27 September and 5 October 1942, and 19 April 1943, TNA.

28 Kathleen Tucker, researcher, "North Boat Harbour," St. Anthony Basin Resources Inc., Oral History Project 2009, pp. 2–3; Smith, crew assignment card, DHH 84/44; and RAFFC Gander, daily diary, 30 September 1942 and 2, 4, 9–11, and 18 October 1942, TNA. Schiller was killed in March 1943 when the Catalina he was piloting crashed near Bermuda. Also lost with Schiller was former Gander radio operator William B. Collins of St. John's, Newfoundland.

29 Tucker, "North Boat Harbour," p. 3.

30 RAFFC Gander, daily diary, 19 April 1943, TNA.

31 Ibid., 8, 13–14, 20, and 25 October 1942; RAFFC Dorval, 8 and 15 October 1942, TNA; and Christie, *Ocean Bridge*, p. 314.

32 RAFFC Dorval, 25 October 1942, TNA; and Christie, *Ocean Bridge*, p. 314.

33 RAFFC Gander, daily diary, 10, 12, 17, and 26 November 1942, and routine orders, January 1943, TNA.

34 Flying Officer Albert Nash to Abner Knee, 21 June 1943. Courtesy Richard Goodlet. Copy posted at http://my.kwic.com/~pagodavista/knee2.htm.

35 Scouten biographical information, courtesy Verne Scouten.

36 Scouten, crew assignment card, DHH 84/44.

37 Don McVicar, *Ferry Command* (Shrewsbury, England: Airlife Publishing Ltd., 1981), p. 169.

38 Scouten, crew assignment card, DHH 84/44.

39 Bowhill, operational activities for November 1942, AIR 24/506, TNA.

40 RAFFC Gander, daily diary, 18–19 November 1942, TNA.

41 Ibid., 25 November 1942.

42 Ibid., 22–3 and 28 December 1942, and 11 January 1943.

43 Ibid., 12 January 1943; and 127 (Fighter) Squadron, RCAF, ORB daily diary, 12 January 1943, C-12320, LAC.

44 "Daily Climatological Data, Gander International Airport, Newfoundland, January 1937 – December 1970," Environment Canada, Toronto, 1972.

45 RAFFC Gander, daily diary, 15 January 1943, TNA.

46 Reid, email message to author, 11 and 20 May 2010. The Gander Ferry Command diary for July 1943 records numerous communication flights to the site by ferry pilot Captain Thomas M. Bante in Fox Moth 4810.

Notes to pages 98–105

47 RAFFC Gander, daily diary, 26 January and 13 February 1944, TNA.
48 Ibid., 28 November 1942.
49 *RCAF Honours and Awards* database. Retrieved 1 December 2018, from http://rcafassociation.ca/heritage/search-awards/.
50 Morrow to town of Conche, no date, ca. 1980. Copy courtesy David Fitzpatrick.
51 Morrow to G/C Anderson, memorandum on accident to BZ277, 5 December 1942. Copy courtesy Glenn Keough.
52 Ibid.
53 Allan Bock, "1942 Plane Crash at Conche Recalled," *Northern Pen* (St. Anthony), 4 November 1987, p. 6.
54 Frank Tibbo, "The Conche Crash," *Beacon*, 7 January 2010, p. 10A.
55 Morrow letter to town.
56 Tibbo, "The Conche Crash."
57 Morrow letter to town.
58 RAFFC Gander, daily diary, 1 December 1942, TNA.
59 Morrow to Anderson, 5 December 1942.
60 Quoted in Tibbo, "The Conche Crash."
61 Morrow letter to town.
62 Morrow to Anderson, 5 December 1942.
63 "Legs Useless, Robt. Morrow Swam Ashore," *Globe and Mail*, 27 May 1943.
64 Michael Seamark, "A Whole Life Spent Reaching for the Sky," *Daily Mail* (London), 11 February 1998.
65 Allan Bock, "1942 Plane."
66 "1942 Plane Crash Municipal Heritage Site." *Canada's Historic Places*. Retrieved 5 December 2018, from https://www.historicplaces.ca/en/rep-reg/place-lieu.aspx?id=11949&pid=0.
67 Bowhill, operational activities for November 1942, AIR 24/506, TNA.
68 Ibid., December 1942.
69 RAFFC Gander, daily diary, 5 and 7 December 1942, TNA.
70 Moorehouse to Air Board, Melbourne, 14 December 1942, A705, 163/24/355, National Archives of Australia. My thanks to Dr. Lisa Daly for bringing this document to my attention.
71 RAFFC Gander, daily diary, 8 December 1942, TNA.
72 Ibid., 8 December 1942; RAFFC Dorval, 8 December 1942, TNA; Christie, *Ocean Bridge*, p. 316; and Steel, crew assignment card, DHH 84/44. The Dorval entry suggests that Boston BZ222 crash-landed, leaving the pilot slightly injured. It may be that the RCAF radio operator and navigator, Loring and McLean, were the only crewmembers to bail out.
73 RAFFC Gander, daily diary, 8 and 12 December 1942, TNA.
74 Douglas Gordon Chown, Record of Service Officers, military service file,

Notes to pages 105–14

LAC; Spencer Dunmore, *Wings For Victory* (Toronto: McClelland and Stewart Inc., 1994), pp. 33 and 78; and Chown, crew assignment card, DHH 84/44.

[75] Kenneth Herbert Wells, Record of Service Officers, military service file, LAC.

[76] RAFFC Gander, daily diary, 8–9 December 1942, TNA.

[77] Ibid., 10–11 December 1942.

[78] Ibid., 12 December 1942.

[79] Ibid.

[80] Ibid., 19, 21, and 23 December 1942, and 8–9 and 14 August 1944.

[81] Bowhill, operational activities for December 1942, AIR 24/506, TNA. De-icing equipment on these aircraft was presumably limited to mechanical or inflatable rubber de-icing boots, installed on the leading edge of the wings and control surfaces and used to splinter and remove ice build-up.

[82] RAFFC Gander, daily diary, 9–12, 15–17, 20, 24–5, and 31 December 1942.

[83] Bruce West, *The Man Who Flew Churchill* (Toronto: McGraw-Hill Ryerson Ltd., 1975), p. 83.

[84] Powell, *Ferryman*, pp. 91–3.

[85] Christie, *Ocean Bridge*, p. 201.

[86] Berry, "Trans-Atlantic Air Deliveries"; Bowhill, operational activity reports for January–December 1942, AIR 24/506, TNA; RAFFC Gander, daily diary, October–December 1942, TNA; and Christie, *Ocean Bridge*, p. 140.

Chapter Six | Search and Rescue, Salvage and Swine

[1] RAFFC Gander, daily diary, 24 December 1942, 3 and 18 January, and 19 April 1943, TNA.

[2] Don McVicar, *North Atlantic Cat* (Shrewsbury, England: Airlife Publishing Ltd., 1983), p. 135.

[3] RAFFC Gander, daily diary, 19 April 1943, TNA.

[4] Ibid., 7–8 and 31 January 1943.

[5] Schaffer, crew assignment card, DHH 84/44.

[6] RAFFC Gander, daily diary, 8 January 1943, TNA.

[7] Ibid., 10–13 January 1943.

[8] Ibid., 6 February 1943; and Walmsley, crew assignment card, DHH 84/44.

[9] RAFFC Gander, daily diary, 8 and 10–13 January 1943, 8 and 10 February 1943, and 25 March 1943, TNA. The aircraft sat in the hangar for almost a year as maintenance did repairs and awaited parts. It was finally test flown on 12 March 1944 by Captain McNaughton. See diary entry for 12 March 1944.

Notes to pages 114–18

[10] Christie, *Ocean Bridge*, pp. 310–11.
[11] McGrath, "Gander Radio (VOAC)," p. 4.
[12] Ian Davies, "Crash of BOAC Return Ferry Service Liberator AL591, Gander, 9 February 1943," unpublished manuscript, pp. 7–9. Copy on file at LAC; and RAF Watch Log, vol. 2, DHH.
[13] Hildred to chief secretary, BOAC, 19 April 1943, file 1758, British Airways Museum.
[14] RAFFC Gander, daily diary, 9 February 1943, TNA.
[15] McVicar, *North Atlantic Cat*, pp. 110–11.
[16] RAFFC Gander, daily diary, 9 February 1943, TNA.
[17] Eastern Air Command, RCAF, monthly report for Gander, February 1943, p. 5, LAC.
[18] Walter Vivian, interviewed by Michael Henry, CBC Radio, date unknown. Recording courtesy Larry O'Brien.
[19] G/C F.S. Wilkins, Chief Inspector of Accidents, RCAF, to RCAF headquarters, 15 February 1943, RG24 1983-84/GAD, file 235-5-3, part 1, LAC.
[20] Davies, "Crash of BOAC," p. 11.
[21] RAFFC Gander, daily diary, 10–11 February 1943, TNA.
[22] 127 Squadron, ORB daily diary and operations record entries, 11 February 1943, LAC.
[23] Philip Vickers, *Surviving Victory: World War II Pilot, Actor, Sculptor, Writer* (Sedona, Arizona: Vibrant Books, 2009), pp. 121–2.
[24] RAFFC Gander, daily diary, 11 February 1943, TNA; and Parker and Abelson, crew assignment cards, DHH 84/44.
[25] Christie, *Ocean Bridge*, p. 256.
[26] RAFFC Gander, daily diary, 15–22 February 1943, TNA.
[27] Ibid., 18 and 20 March 1943. Salt, a former RCMP officer, handled administrative and security duties. He was suspicious of everyone, said John Murphy, and consequently unpopular with the staff. Indeed, when Salt was posted to Dorval in November 1944, everyone was relieved to see him go, wrote McGrath in his diary. Murphy, email message to author, 20 May 2010; and McGrath, personal diary, 9 November 1944, vol. 1, file 18, LAC.
[28] Vivian, CBC radio interview.
[29] RAFFC Gander, daily diary, 24 and 26–7 March 1943, TNA; and Powell, *Ferryman*, p. 71.
[30] Ibid., 29 March, 20 April, and 27 May 1943; and Vivian, CBC radio interview.
[31] RAFFC Gander, daily diary, 23 February 1943, TNA. Also lost on Mitchell FR148 with American civilian Annibal was Flying Officer Leslie E.

Notes to pages 118–25

Triplett, RCAF, navigator, and Canadian civilian Clifford D. Saugstad, radio operator. See Christie, *Ocean Bridge*, p. 318.

32 No. 83 Staging Post, RAF, Gander, list of files to be forwarded to the Air Ministry, 28 March 1946, AIR 38/62.

33 "Risked Death by Cold Stealing Ocean Ride to Join Her Husband," *Toronto Daily Star*, 8 March 1943. Another stowaway incident originated in Prestwick when British civilian Elizabeth Drewery boarded a Return Ferry Service Liberator and stood hiding in a narrow gap between the wheel-well and rear of the instrument panel. She remained hidden during the stopover at Gander but was spotted climbing from the aircraft after it was hangared at Dorval. See Christie, *Ocean Bridge*, p. 260.

34 "Gordon J. Darling, Flyer Long Lost, Presumed Dead," *Ottawa Citizen*, 8 December 1943, p. 20.

35 RAFFC Gander, daily diary, 16 February 1943, TNA.

36 Gavriloff, crew assignment card, DHH 84/44; RAFFC Gander, daily diary, 16 and 26 February 1943, and 9 March and 11 June 1943, TNA; and Gary Rideout, "A Piece of Community History," *Nor'wester* (Springdale), 22 April 2010.

37 RAFFC Gander, daily diary, 9 March and 17 June 1943, TNA; and Rideout, "A Piece."

38 Christie, *Ocean Bridge*, p. 318; and Walmsley, crew assignment card, DHH 84/44.

39 Letter initialled "JFON" (J.F. O'Neill), 1 March 1943, and secretary for PW to secretary for Public Health and Welfare, 8 March 1943, GN 4/5, box 3, file AG/59, Rooms; and RAFFC Gander, daily diary, 5 March 1943, TNA.

40 "Air Force Cross for F/O Westaway," *The Gander*, RCAF Station Gander publication, Yuletide 1944, p. 17.

41 RAFFC Gander, daily diary, 19 April 1943, TNA; and Murphy, email message to author, 27 May 2010.

42 RAFFC Gander, daily diary, 19 April 1943, TNA.

43 Ibid., 1, 3–4, 8, and 10 May 1943.

44 McVicar, *North Atlantic Cat*, pp. 176–82.

45 RAFFC Gander, daily diary, 28 April 1943, TNA; and Pudney, *Atlantic Bridge*, p. 50.

46 "The Glider Flight across the Atlantic," *Flight and the Aircraft Engineer*, 8 July 1943, p. 28; and Christie, *Ocean Bridge*, p. 214.

47 Christie, *Ocean Bridge*, pp. 195–6; and RAFFC Gander, order of the day, 21 July 1944, TNA.

48 Christie, *Ocean Bridge*, p. 195.

49 Ted Beaudoin, *Walking on Air* (Vernon, British Columbia: Paramount House Publishing Ltd., 1986), pp. 206–9.

Notes to pages 125–32

[50] RAFFC Gander, daily diary, 8–9 and 28 May 1943, TNA.

[51] Handwritten notes initialled "JFON," 11 May 1943, and Squadron Leader Turnbull to Pattison, 10 May 1943, GN 4/5, box 2, file AG/57/5, Rooms; and "Four Occupants of Plane Missing on Flight from Goose to Gander," *ET*, 25 May 1943, p. 3.

[52] RAFFC Gander, daily diary, 14 May and 1 June 1943, TNA.

[53] Ibid., 26 June 1943.

[54] "Ranger and Airman Missing since May 8 Are Safe and Well," *ET*, 28 June 1943, p. 3.

[55] RCAF Gander, 30 June 1943, LAC. The RCAF diary gave a different version of events, telling that an engine had caught fire and was subsequently extinguished, but not before the captain had ordered the passengers to don their parachutes. See entry for 8 May 1943.

[56] Ranger John Hogan, "Official report regarding his flight of 8 May 1943," Department of Natural Resource, Newfoundland Commission of Government, pp. 1–2. Copy on file at Centre for Newfoundland Studies.

[57] Darrin McGrath, Robert Smith, Rangers Ches Parsons and Norman Crane, *The Newfoundland Rangers* (St. John's: DRC Publishing, 2005), p. 175.

[58] Hogan, "Official report," pp. 2–3.

[59] Ibid., pp. 3–5.

[60] RAFFC Gander, daily diary, 4, 10, 12, and 16–18 July, and 2 and 4–5 August 1943, TNA.

[61] Harold Horwood, *A History of the Newfoundland Ranger Force* (St. John's: Breakwater Books, 1986), p. 116.

[62] Quoted in McGrath, et al, *The Newfoundland Rangers*, p. 171.

[63] RAFFC Gander, daily diary, 26 May 1943, TNA; and RCAF Station Botwood ORB daily diary, 26 May 1943, C-12177, LAC.

[64] RAFFC Gander, daily diary, 9 June 1942, TNA.

[65] Report of Aircraft Accident, B-17F, AAF No. 42-30041, "Description of Accident," and statements of 1st Lt. Kelmer Hall and Flight Officer Bradley Summers, 12 June 1943, AFHRA.

[66] "Georgian Crew Rescues Fliers from Icefloes," *Globe and Mail*, 20 October 1943.

[67] RAFFC Gander, daily diary, 10 June 1942, TNA.

[68] Ibid., 6 and 11 July 1943; and Gander Airport, Record of External Flights, May 1943–December 1944, GN 166.9, box 1, Rooms.

[69] Thompson, crew assignment card, DHH 84/44.

[70] RAFFC Gander, daily diary, 5, 8–10, and 26–7 October 1943, TNA; Gander Airport, Record of External Flights, GN 166.9, box 1, Rooms; and Christie, *Ocean Bridge*, footnote 66, pp. 379–80. Catalina JV935 was damaged on landing at Gander Lake at the hands of Captain Singleton. The

Notes to pages 132–8

Gander Ferry Command internal flight log indicates that a Captain Baird flew the Catalina back to Dartmouth, Nova Scotia, on 30 October 1943. Opal Anderson's crew assignment card suggests that she was aboard on the flight to Dartmouth, although there are no entries after her departure from Gander. This appears to be Anderson's only flight attempt as a supernumerary crewmember with Ferry Command. See RAFFC Gander, daily diary, 26 October 1943, TNA; Gander Airport, Record of Internal Flights, May 1943–December 1945, GN 166.10, box 1, Rooms; and Anderson, crew assignment card, DHH 84/44.

71 RAFFC Gander, daily diary, 27 and 30 December 1943, TNA.

72 Pattison to secretary for PW, 14 December 1942, GN 4/5, box 9, file NA/50, Rooms.

73 RAFFC Gander, daily diary, 30 April and 9–10 November 1943, TNA.

74 Sergeant Neale Reinitz, "Newfoundland 'Barrelman' Raises Pigs," *The Propagander*, Fall 1944, p. 7; and Richard Gwyn, *Smallwood: The Unlikely Revolutionary* (Toronto: McClelland and Stewart Ltd., 1972), p. 56.

75 Murphy, email message to author, 9 June 2011.

76 Pattison to secretary for PW, 20 January 1944, GN 4/5, box 9, file NA/50, Rooms.

77 Smallwood, *I Chose*, p. 217.

78 Pattison to Woods, 24 May 1944, GN 4/5, box 9, file NA/50, Rooms.

79 Pattison to secretary for PW, 20 January 1944, ibid.

80 Woods to P.A. Clutterbuck, 29 January 1944, ibid.

81 Clutterbuck to Woods, 27 April 1944, ibid.

82 RAFFC Gander, daily diary, 25 February 1944, TNA.

83 Smallwood, *I Chose*, p. 219.

84 Pattison to secretary for PW, 20 January 1944, GN 4/5, box 9, file NA/50, Rooms.

85 McGrath, pocket diary, 15 October 1943, vol. 1, file 17, LAC.

86 RAFFC Gander, daily diary, 7 December 1943, TNA.

87 Berry, "Trans-Atlantic Air Deliveries"; Bowhill, operational activity reports for January–March 1943, AIR 24/506, TNA; RAFFC Gander, daily diary, April–May 1943, TNA; and Gander Airport, Record of External Flights, GN 166.9, box 1, Rooms.

Chapter Seven | The Commanding Officer Has Gone Missing

1 RAFFC Gander, daily diary, 11–12 January 1944, TNA; and Dickens, crew assignment card, DHH 84/44.

2 Ibid., 14 January 1944.

Notes to pages 138–47

[3] Gary Saunders, *Rattles and Steadies: Memoirs of a Gander River Man* (St. John's: Breakwater Books, 1986), pp. 197–8.
[4] RAFFC Gander, daily diary, 14–18, 21, 23, and 25 January 1944, TNA.
[5] Saunders, *Rattles and Steadies*, pp. 199 and 174–5.
[6] Ibid., p. 199.
[7] Ibid., pp. 199–200.
[8] Ibid., pp. 200–1; and RAFFC Gander, daily diary, 22 and 25 February, 1, 9, 16, and 24 March, and 10 May 1944, TNA.
[9] RAFFC Gander, daily diary, 20–3 May 1944, and Flying Control Report for Month Ending 31 May 1944, p. 2, TNA; and Adkison, crew assignment card, DHH 84/44.
[10] Hogan to Chief Ranger, 30 May 1944, GN 13/1/B, box 324, file 19, Rooms. The few recovered remains of the crew were brought to Deer Lake, certificated by the local doctor as human and buried there. The British had recently discontinued using Gander cemetery, instead choosing the Joint Services Cemetery in St. John's for future burials. It is unclear why these remains were not sent to St. John's. A civilian grave marker for Adkison is presently located at the Deer Lake Anglican cemetery. The author could find no such marker for Zyvitski.
[11] RAFFC Gander, daily diary, 17 and 24 May 1944, and Flying Control Report for Month Ending 31 May 1944, pp. 1–2, TNA; and Christie, *Ocean Bridge*, p. 324.
[12] Reid, email message to author, 18 May 2010; and RAFFC Gander, daily diary, 3 and 5 June 1944, TNA.
[13] Pattison to Newfoundland secretary for PW, 10 February 1944, GN 38, box S5-1-3, file 21, Rooms.
[14] Reid, email message to author, 18 May 2010.
[15] RAFFC Gander, daily diary, 9 June 1944, and unit activity notes for June 1944, TNA.
[16] Narburgh, "Keep 'Em Crossed," p. 119; and Powell, *Ferryman*, p. 106.
[17] Robert Pelley, " 'Mosla' and 'Benzin' – Russian PBN Flying Boats in Gander." *Bob's Gander History*. Retrieved 5 December 2019, from http://bobsganderhistory.com/PBN.pdf.
[18] RAFFC Gander, unit activity notes for June 1944, TNA.
[19] Ibid., unit activity notes for July 1944.
[20] Narburgh, "Keep 'Em Crossed," pp. 119–20.
[21] Powell, *Ferryman*, p. 107.
[22] RAFFC Gander, daily diary, 4 and 7 July 1944, and unit activity notes for July 1944; and Perlick, crew assignment card, DHH 84/44.
[23] Kabin, crew assignment card, DHH 84/44; "Leading Ukrainian Canadian Flier Killed in Crash," *Ukrainian Weekly* (New York and New Jersey),

Notes to pages 147–52

9 September 1944, p. 1; "Atlantic Flight Leaves Mourning in Home City," *Toronto Evening Telegram*, 1 September 1944; and Gander Airport, Record of External Flights, GN 166.9, box 1, Rooms.

24 Flood and Sheldrick, crew assignment cards, DHH 84/44.

25 Personal communication with Douglas Pelley.

26 Gander Airport, Record of External Flights, GN 166.9, box 1, Rooms; and Accident Card, Mitchell KJ584, Royal Air Force Museum.

27 "Atlantic Flight Leaves"; and No. 1 Group, RCAF, ORB daily diary, 1 September 1944, LAC.

28 RAFFC Gander, daily diary, 3 and 24 September 1944, and unit activity notes for September, TNA.

29 Ibid., commanding officer, 83 Staging Post, to SASO, 45 Group, Dorval, 1 October 1944, and unit activity notes for September 1944.

30 Ibid., daily diary, 22 and 24 October 1944, Gander notes, October 1944, and Message Form, 83 Staging Post to 45 Group, Dorval, 2 November 1944.

31 Senior Flying Control Officer (SFCO) office diary, 12–15 November 1944, GN 166.13, box 2, and Gander Airport, Record of External Flights, GN 166.9, box 1, Rooms; and Teas, crew assignment card, DHH 84/44.

32 SFCO office diary, 30 November 1944, GN 166.13, box 2; and Christie, *Ocean Bridge*, p. 226.

33 RAFFC Gander, Message Form, 83 Staging Post to 45 Group, 1–2 December 1944, TNA.

34 Reid, email message to author, 1 June 2010.

35 SFCO office diary, 4 November 1944, GN 166.13, box 2, Rooms; and Acheson, crew assignment card, DHH 84/44.

36 Kemp to chief of police, Newfoundland Constabulary, 16 December 1944, GN 13/1/B, box 363, file 1, Rooms.

37 Constable Whittey to L. Strange, Assistant Chief of Police, 27 December 1944, ibid.

38 Gander Airport, Record of External Flights, GN 166.9, box 1, Rooms.

39 Acheson, crew assignment card, DHH 84/44.

40 "Cecil Edison – He First Saw Gander as Camp 34," *Beacon*, 27 July 1977. Reproduced and posted at *Gander Airport Historical Society*. Retrieved 5 December 2018, from http://www.ganderairporthistoricalsociety.org/_html_thirtys/cecil_edison.htm.

41 Christie, *Ocean Bridge*, appendix B. From the start of ferrying operations to the date of the cork incident, roughly eight Mitchells were lost on the North Atlantic route. By war's end, Ferry Command had lost a similar number of Mosquitos and a slightly lesser number of Venturas and Bostons along the same route. Hudson losses ranked among the highest, but

Notes to pages 152–8

delivery numbers of this aircraft type were among the highest. Total losses as a percentage of type delivered might bring matters into sharper view.

[42] "Cecil Edison – He First."

[43] RAFFC Gander, daily diary, 9 July 1943, and routine orders, 12 April 1942, TNA; and Ian Ross to Chief of Police P.J. O'Neill, 16 January 1942, GN 13/1/B, box 457, file "Gander RAFFC," Rooms.

[44] Ross to O'Neill, 16 January 1942, Rooms; and "RAFTC," *The Propagander*, p. 25.

[45] RAFFC Gander, routine orders, 19 April 1942 and 16 May 1942, TNA.

[46] SFCO office diary, 11 December 1944, GN 166.13, box 2, Rooms.

[47] RAFFC Gander, routine orders, 25 May 1944, TNA.

[48] Fausak, "My History With."

[49] RAFFC Gander, routine orders, 16 and 25 May 1942, and 24 May 1944, TNA.

[50] Christie, *Ocean Bridge*, p. 290.

[51] Gander Airport, Record of External Flights, GN 166.9, and Record of External Flights, December 1944–December 1945, GN 166.11, box 1, Rooms.

[52] Narburgh, Hutchings, and Caddick, crew assignment cards, DHH 84/44; and Narburgh, "Keep 'Em Crossed," p. 126.

[53] Narburgh, "Keep 'Em Crossed," pp. 131, 133–5, and 152.

[54] Ibid., p. 142.

[55] SFCO office diary, 21–2 December 1944, GN 166.13, box 2, Rooms. An entry in the Gander Ferry Command diary on 10 December 1942 notes the arrival of Mrs. Parry, civilian cypher officer, on an eastbound ferry flight. This, presumably, is the lady in question.

[56] Narburgh, "Keep 'Em Crossed," pp. 143–5; and No. 1 Group, RCAF, ORB daily diary, 23 December 1944, LAC. An entry on 23 December 1944 in the unit's logbook of local flights suggests that the aircraft landed at Rockland, Maine, and not Bangor. See Gander Airport, Record of Internal Flights, GN 166.10, box 1, Rooms.

[57] Narburgh, "Keep 'Em Crossed," p. 145.

[58] Attack data cited at *Number 59 Squadron* website. Retrieved 26 January 2018, from http://number59squadron.com/uboats/01.08.43.html.

[59] Hutchings, crew assignment card, DHH 84/44.

[60] Phyllise Stickel, email message to author, 7 May 2011.

[61] Narburgh, "Keep 'Em Crossed," p. 144.

[62] Stickel, email message to author, 5 May 2011.

[63] Georgie Narburgh, "Three Nights in the Snow," unpublished short story, no date.

Notes to pages 158–66

64 Narburgh, "Three Nights"; Narburgh, "Keep 'Em Crossed," p. 146; and Stickel, email message to author, 5 May 2011.

65 Narburgh, "Three Nights"; and Narburgh, "Keep 'Em Crossed," p. 146.

66 SFCO office diary, 23 December 1944, GN 166.13, box 2, Rooms; "Keep 'Em Crossed," pp. 143 and 146; RCAF Gander, 24 December 1944, LAC; and RAFFC Gander, daily diary, 23 December 1944, TNA.

67 SFCO office diary, 24 December 1944, GN 166.13, box 2, Rooms; and RAFFC Gander, daily diary, 24 December 1944, TNA. McGrath was in St. John's on leave during this incident. In his absence, Newfoundlander F/L Frank Stirling took over as acting SFCO, updated the office diary, and apprised McGrath by telephone of developments.

68 Narburgh, "Keep 'Em Crossed," pp. 146–7.

69 Narburgh, "Three Nights."

70 SFCO office diary, 25–8 and 30–1 December 1944, GN 166.13, box 2, Rooms; RAFFC Gander, daily diary, 28 December 1944, TNA; and "Keep 'Em Crossed," p. 144. Narburgh says that the USAAF C-47 carried sled dogs and drivers and was prepared to drop them by parachute.

71 Narburgh, "Keep 'Em Crossed," p. 144; and Narburgh, "Three Nights."

72 Stickel, email message to author, 8 May 2011.

73 Gander Airport, Record of External Flights, GN 166.9 and GN 166.11, box 1, Rooms.

Chapter Eight | A Sad Day for Gander

1 Powell, *Ferryman*, p. 119.

2 SFCO office diary, 4 January 1945, GN 166.13, box 2, Rooms; and RAFFC Gander, daily diary, 4 and 27 January 1945, and G/C Anderson, "Special Order of the Day," 4 January 1945, TNA.

3 Narburgh, "Keep 'Em Crossed," pp. 152–3. The group captain, says Narburgh, enjoyed his drink on occasion, and for this reason too, he refused to turn over the controls.

4 Smallwood, *I Chose*, p. 224. Ramsay also worked at the unit, first as a cleaner with aircraft maintenance, and then as a mechanics helper.

5 SFCO office diary, 6 January and 17 February 1945, GN 166.14, box 2, Rooms.

6 Gander Airport, Record of Internal Flights, GN 166.10, box 1, Rooms.

7 Narburgh, "Keep 'Em Crossed," letter to parents, 10 March 1945, p. 151.

8 Gander Airport, Record of External Flights, GN 166.11, box 1, Rooms.

9 RAFFC Gander, daily diary, 6 March 1945, TNA; and Christie, *Ocean Bridge*, p. 327.

10 Narburgh, "Keep 'Em Crossed," letter to parents, 10 March 1945, p. 151.

Notes to pages 166–70

[11] SFCO office diary, 7–9 March 1945, GN 166.14, box 2, Rooms.

[12] RAFFC Gander, routine orders, 12 March 1945, TNA.

[13] SFCO office diary, 16 April 1945, GN 166.15, box 2, and Gander Airport, Record of External Flights, GN 166.11, box 1, Rooms.

[14] McGrath, personal diary, 28–9 March 1945, vol. 1, file 19, LAC.

[15] Smallwood, "Gander – And Newfoundland," p. 2.

[16] Reid, email message to author, 18 May 2010.

[17] Tibbo, "Reminiscing"; and Smallwood, "Gander – And Newfoundland," p. 2.

[18] RAFFC Gander, daily diary, 30 April 1945, TNA; Narburgh, "Keep 'Em Crossed," p. 150; and "Gander Station Shocked on Fliers' Tragic Death," *ET*, 7 May 1945, p. 3.

[19] SFCO office diary, 3 May 1945, GN 166.15, box 2, Rooms; and McGrath, personal diary, 4 May 1945, vol. 1, file 19, LAC.

[20] "Gander Station," p. 3.

[21] Narburgh, "Keep 'Em Crossed," p. 150.

[22] McGrath, personal diary, 7–8 May 1945, vol. 1, file 19, LAC. Germany signed an unconditional surrender document at the Allied headquarters in Reims, France, on 7 May 1945, to take effect on 8 May. Victory in Europe Day (V-E Day) on 8 May celebrated the formal acceptance of Germany's surrender.

[23] RAFFC Gander, daily diary, 8 May 1945, and routine orders, 7 May and 4 June 1945, TNA.

[24] Captain Clement Maloney, post historian, 1387th AAFBU, Gander, post history for April 1945, p. 16, AFHRA.

[25] This is a cumulative total for the period May 1943 when the centre opened, to May 1945 when joint operations ended. The main sources consulted to arrive at this figure of 7,500 were the Gander Airport Record of External Flights, Rooms; Early History of the 1387th AAFBU, Gander, vol. 1, May 1941–June 1944, AFHRA; and the monthly historical data reports of the 1387th AAFBU, Gander, AFHRA.

[26] SFCO office diary, 9 June 1945, GN 166.16, box 2, and Gander Airport, Record of External Flights, GN 166.11, box 1, Rooms. Not all the returned 164 Lancasters landed at Gander. Weather forced about a dozen to divert to stations in the Canadian Maritimes and two to land at the US Naval Air Station at Argentia, Newfoundland, where they remained overnight before proceeding to Gander. Another landed at Argentia but from there flew direct to Scoudouc, New Brunswick. See SFCO diary, 15 and 25–6 June 1945.

[27] Historical Section of the RCAF, *The RCAF Overseas: The Sixth Year* (Toronto: Oxford University Press, 1949), p. 6.

Notes to pages 171–9

[28] Christie, *Ocean Bridge*, p. 259; SFCO office diary, 4, 7, and 11 July 1945, GN 166.16, box 2, Rooms; and *RCAF Honours and Awards* database. Retrieved 1 December 2018, from http://rcafassociation.ca/heritage/search-awards/.

[29] Robert Pelley, "Ground Controlled Approach in Early Gander – A Very Serious Game of Hide-and-go-Seek." *Bob's Gander History*. Retrieved 30 November 2018, from http://bobsganderhistory.com/gcap1.pdf; and Captain Clement Maloney, post historian, 1387th AAFBU, Gander, post history for July 1945, p. 28, AFHRA.

[30] SFCO office diary, 18, 24, and 29 July 1945, GN 166.16, box 2, Rooms.

[31] "Gala Celebration at Gander, Parade & Fire Crackers," *The Prop*, Gander, 17 August 1945, p. 1, A0164, AFHRA.

[32] RAFFC Gander, daily diary, 16 and 21 August 1945, TNA.

[33] Gilmore, email message to author, 9 March 2019.

[34] Gander Airport, Record of External Flights, GN 166.11, box 1, Rooms.

[35] Christie, *Ocean Bridge*, pp. 303–4.

[36] Gander Airport, Record of External Flights, GN 166.11, box 1, Rooms.

[37] *RCAF Honours and Awards* database. Retrieved 1 December 2018, from http://rcafassociation.ca/heritage/search-awards/.

[38] "St. John's Airman Has Narrow Escape When Mercy Plane Sinks," *ET*, 8 October 1945, p. 6; Buxton, crew assignment card, DHH 84/44; and Gander Airport, Record of Internal Flights, GN 166.10, box 1, Rooms.

[39] "Belle Isle Rescue," *Them Days*, July 1990, pp. 23–5.

[40] RAFFC Gander, daily diary, 2, 4–6, and 16 October 1945, TNA.

[41] Ibid., 21–2 and 29 October 1945, and routine orders 17 August and 2 November 1945.

Chapter Nine | Crossroads: A New Beginning

[1] "Pan-American to Use High Speed Land Planes on Atlantic Service," *Daily News* (St. John's), 19 September 1945, p. 3; and 1st Lt. Edward Carlin, post historian, 1387th AAFBU, Gander, post history for September 1945, p. 3, AFHRA.

[2] Neary, *Newfoundland*, pp. 261 and 272.

[3] "Permit Granted Airlines," *Daily News*, 24 October 1945, p. 3.

[4] Neary, *Newfoundland*, pp. 272–3.

[5] Pattison, memorandum on commercial air operations by US companies, 15 September 1945, p. 2, GN 38, box S5-5-3, file 4, Rooms.

[6] Rupert Jackson, "Growing Gander," *Collier's*, 3 May 1947, p. 92.

[7] Pattison, memorandum on commercial air operations, pp. 3–4.

[8] H.H. Elliott, station report, Gander, PAA, Atlantic Division, 28 November

Notes to pages 180–4

1945, p. 2, Pan American World Airways Inc., Coll. 0341, box 1-606, folder 23, University of Miami Libraries, Special Collections.

9 Pattison, memorandum on commercial air operations, p. 4, and F.G. Smallwood, "Report by Auditor Regarding Gander Airport Accounts," 6 February 1947, pp. 7–8, 11, and 18, GN 4/5, box 8, file NA/24/2, Rooms.

10 "Gander Airport Has Not Reverted to Nfld.," *Daily News*, 23 November 1945, p. 3.

11 G.E. London, Commissioner for PU and Supply, Memorandum for the Commission of Government, 4 October 1945, GN 38, box S5-5-3, file 10, Rooms.

12 "Gander Airport Has Not," p. 3.

13 Memorandum by Special Assistant to Under-Secretary of State for External Affairs, 2 January 1946, Bridle, *Documents*, p. 1001.

14 "Gander Airport Is Becoming a Very Busy Place," *Daily News*, 1 December 1945, p. 3.

15 H.H. Elliott, station report, Gander, PAA, Atlantic Division, 28 November 1945, p. 8, Coll. 0341, box 1-606, folder 23, University of Miami. On 2 November 1945, Gander welcomed the first SILA B-17s, registration SE-BAO and SE-BAK. See RCAF Gander, 2 November 1945, LAC.

16 Report of Canadian Delegation on a Meeting Held in St. John's to Discuss the Disposition of Air Bases and Problems of Post-War Defence, February 1946, Bridle, *Documents*, pp. 1011–12.

17 Neary, *Newfoundland*, p. 271.

18 Handover of Gander to Newfoundland Government, 45 Group to 83 Staging Post, 18 February 1946, and notes on meeting regarding handover 83 Staging Post to Newfoundland government, 19 February 1946, AIR 38/62, TNA.

19 Botting to Sir John Puddester, Commissioner for Public Health and Welfare, 19 February 1946, enclosure "Plan for Gander Airport," GN 38, box S5-5-4, file 4, Rooms.

20 Gander Airport, Record of External Flights, December 1945–July 1946, GN 166.12, box 2, Rooms.

21 Handover, Air Ministry meeting to discuss 45 Group contraction programme, 30 January 1946, AIR 38/62, TNA.

22 RAFFC Gander, daily diary, 16, 22, and 25 January 1946, TNA. The extent of dismantling to VO-ADE is unclear. Eventually, the unit was to return the aircraft to Newfoundland, so it may be that maintenance removed only those components owned and installed by the RCAF and RAF. The Fox Moth was intact during the immediate postwar years and reportedly destroyed when snow fell from the roof of Hangar 20.

23 83 Staging Post to Dorval, 30 March 1946, AIR 38/62, TNA.

Notes to pages 184–92

[24] RCAF Gander, 31 March 1946, LAC.

[25] Handover, Dorval to 83 Staging Post, 21 March 1946, and 83 Staging Post to Dorval, 5 April 1946, AIR 38/62, TNA.

[26] Gander Tower, Flying Control Officer daily log, February–August 1946, Gander Airport, GN 166.1, box 1, Rooms.

[27] Neill, Memorandum for the Commission of Government, 19 February 1946, pp. 4–5, GN 38, box S5-5-4, file 1, Rooms.

[28] Neill, Memorandum for the Commission of Government, 1 April 1946, pp. 3, 7–8, and 14, ibid.

[29] Report on joint airline meeting at Gander, 20–7 March 1946, memorandum to Vice Presidents Bixby and Ingalls, Coll. 0341, box 2-873, folder 8, University of Miami.

[30] Smallwood, "Report by Auditor," pp. 5–6. The amount contributed by each airline was based on usage, with those contemplating daily landings, specifically AOA, PAA, TCA, BOAC, and TWA, advancing $11,000 each, while Air France, KLM and SILA advanced $5,500 each. See Paul M. Strieffler, PAA, agreement and lease with Newfoundland government, 7 June 1946, Coll. 0341, box 2-873, folder 8, University of Miami.

[31] Ibid., pp. 3–4; and Strieffler, agreement and lease with Newfoundland, University of Miami.

[32] "3rd, 4th Freedoms Are Now in Effect at Gander Airport," *Daily News*, 4 July 1946, p. 3.

[33] Neill to Eaton, 4 July 1946, GN 4/5, box 10, file NA/92, Rooms.

[34] "Many Passengers Are Stranded at Gander Airport," *Daily News*, 13 July 1946, p. 3.

[35] Pattison to secretary for PW, 22 July 1946, and Eaton to Pattison, 23 July 1946, GN 4/5, box 10, file NA/92, Rooms.

[36] Winsor to secretary for PW, 21 August 1946, ibid.

[37] Smallwood, "Report by Auditor," pp. 1–2; and *Starliner* (weekly publication for TWA employees), vol. 1, no. 32, 21 November 1946, pp. 4–5. In correspondence from September 1946, James Eaton referred to the stewardesses' lounge and sleeping quarters building as Diana. It may be that this was tentative and Venus the final chosen name. See Eaton to Augustinus and George, 26 September 1946, GN 4/5, box 10, file NA/92, Rooms.

[38] Neill's address, 14 September 1946, pp. 2–4, GN 4/5, box 10, file NA/92, Rooms.

Chapter Ten | Gander's Helping Hands

[1] J.S. Neil, Memorandum for the Commission of Government, 29 July 1946, GN 38, box S5-5-3, file 10, Rooms.

Notes to pages 192–9

2 Ibid., Middleton résumé.

3 Gwyn, *Smallwood*, p. 56.

4 1st Lt. Leo A. Beaupre, intelligence and security officer, 1387th AAFBU, Gander, weekly activity report, period ending 21 January 1945, p. 7, A0164, AFHRA.

5 Murphy, email message to author, 25 May 2010.

6 Unknown author to Eaton, 20 August 1946, Coll. 0341, box 2-873, folder 8, University of Miami; and Neary, *Newfoundland*, p. 270.

7 Gwyn, *Smallwood*, p. 57.

8 Warren, *Life at the Crossroads*, pp. 159–60.

9 Pattison to secretary for PW, 24 March 1947, GN 4/5, box 9, file NA/50, Rooms.

10 Neill, Memorandum for the Commission of Government, 31 March 1947, and secretary for PW to Smallwood, 14 April 1947, ibid.

11 Civil Aviation Division to secretary for PW, 1 May 1948, ibid.

12 Robert Pelley, " 'Farming' in Old Gander." *Bob's Gander History*. Retrieved 18 October 2020, from http://bobsganderhistory.com/FARMING.pdf.

13 Murphy, email message to author, 25 May 2010.

14 Botting to Neill, 20 June 1946, GN 4/5, box 9, file NA/48, Rooms.

15 Pattison to Neill, 13 July 1946, ibid.

16 Pattison to secretary for PU, 24 August 1946, and secretary PU to Pattison, 3 September 1946, ibid.

17 Pattison, Department of Transport inter-departmental correspondence, 10 February 1951, ibid.

18 Assistant deputy minister, PU, to Pattison, 9 March 1951, ibid.

19 Winsor to J.F. O'Neill, Assistant Deputy Minister, PU, 7 June 1951, ibid.

20 O'Neill to Winsor, 15 June 1951, ibid.

21 Winsor to O'Neill, 9 July 1951, ibid.

22 Manning to Winsor, 4 August 1951, ibid.

23 Reid, email message to author, 1 June 2010.

24 "Jim and Beryl Reid: Quality Involvement," *Decks Awash*, Mar–Apr 1990, p. 32.

25 "Surprise reunion for Ferry Command radio operators in Gander." *CBC*, 12 November 2015. Retrieved 31 October 2020, from https://www.cbc.ca/news/canada/newfoundland-labrador/surprise-reunion-for-ferry-command-radio-operators-in-gander-1.3315763.

26 Biography included with McGrath fonds description at LAC. Retrieved 26 March 2019, from http://www.bac-lac.gc.ca/eng/Pages/home.aspx.

27 Gilmore, email message to author, 26 March 2018.

28 Frank Tibbo, "Joe Gilmore, MBE." *Gander Airport Historical Society*. Retrieved 9 December 2018, from http://www.ganderairporthistoricalsociety.org/_html_war/Joe%20Gilmore.htm.

Notes to pages 203–11

Chapter Eleven | Mission Accomplished

[1] Darrell Hillier, "Stars, Stripes, and Sacrifice: A Wartime Familial Experience of Hope, Loss, and Grief, and the Journey Home of an American Bomber Crew," MA thesis, Memorial University of Newfoundland, May 2017, pp. 107, 111–12, and 114.

[2] Report of Aircraft Accident, B-24D Liberator BZ935, Department of the Air Force, Headquarters Air Force Inspection and Safety Center, Norton Air Force Base, California.

Postscript: From A Child's Perspective

[1] Eileen Elms, email message to author, 16 January 2018.

[2] Gilmore, email message to author, 21 February 2018.

[3] Corinne Flynn, compiled by, *I Remember When … Stories of Early Gander* (Gander: North Atlantic Aviation Museum, 1999), pp. 18–20.

[4] Peter Blackie, email message to author, 31 March, and 3 and 5 April 2021. Charles Blackie was one of Gander's original radio operators and arrived from Botwood in the summer of 1938.

[5] Gilmore, email message to author, 3 January 2019.

[6] "RAFTC," *The Propagander*, p. 25.

[7] Gilmore, email message to author, 3 January 2019.

[8] Ibid., 21 February 2018.

BIBLIOGRAPHY

MANUSCRIPT SOURCES

Air Force Historical Research Agency, Maxwell AFB, Alabama
1387th Army Air Forces Base Unit History, Gander, microfilm A0163.
Report of Major Aircraft Accident, B-17F, AAF No. 42-30041.

British Airways Museum Collection
Hildred to chief secretary, BOAC, 19 April 1943, file 1758.

Department of the Air Force, Headquarters Air Force Inspection and Safety Center, Norton Air Force Base, California
Report of Aircraft Accident, B-24D Liberator, BZ935.

Department of National Defence, Directorate of History and Heritage, Ottawa
"Address by Dr. P.D. McTaggart-Cowan on Early Trans-Atlantic Aviation in Newfoundland," 18 November 1975, 80/350.
Crew Assignment and Employment Cards, 84/44.
Excerpts from Thomas McGrath diaries concerning operations at Gander and Botwood, 1939–1945, 74/635.
Newfoundland Airport Landing Register, 79/1, Vol. 1.
RAF Watch Log, Newfoundland Airport, 79/1, Vols. 2 and 3.

Library and Archives Canada
Department of External Affairs, RG25.
Department of National Defence, RG24.
Eastern Air Command, RCAF, ORB daily diary.

No. 1 Group, RCAF, ORB daily diary.
No. 10 (Bomber Reconnaissance) Squadron, RCAF, ORB daily diary.
No. 127 (Fighter) Squadron, RCAF, ORB daily diary.
RCAF Station Botwood, ORB daily diary.
RCAF Station Gander, ORB daily diary.
RCAF Station Goose Bay, ORB daily diary.
Second World War service files.
The Royal Rifles of Canada war diary.
Thomas M. McGrath fonds, MG 31, A 23.

National Archives of Australia
Royal Australian Air Force, Casualty Section, F/O R.G.S. Burrows, A705, 163/24/355.

Royal Air Force Museum, London
Air Ministry Form 1180, Accident Cards.

The National Archives of the UK and Northern Ireland
ATFERO, Report by Mr. W.P. Hildred, July 1941, AIR 20/6154.
Capt. A.S. Wilcockson, Report Covering Return Ferry Service, 22 September 1941, AIR 38/2.
Dorval, RAF Ferry Command, ORB daily diary, July 1940–March 1943, AIR 24/505.
Gander Airport, General Agreement, Signals, April 1941–May 1943, AIR 38/8.
Gander, General Policy of Handover to Newfoundland Government, January–April 1946, AIR 38/62.
Gander, RAF Ferry Command, ORB daily diary and appendices, April 1942–March 1946, AIR 29/467.
Proceedings of Joint USAAF-RAFTC Transatlantic Control, March–September 1943, AIR 38/170.
Survey of Newfoundland for Suitable Air Base for Transatlantic Service, 1935–1945, AVIA 2/1943.
Transatlantic Air Service, Correspondence Concerning Newfoundland, 1935–1936, AVIA 2/1946.
Transatlantic Air Service, Discussions in Ottawa and Washington, 1935–1936, AVIA 2/1957.
Transatlantic Air Service, Ground Organization, March 1936–September 1937, T 161/1031/2.

The Rooms Provincial Archives of Newfoundland and Labrador
Department of Justice and Defence, GN 13/1/B.
Department of Public Works and Services, Civil Aviation, GN 4/5.
Gander Airport fonds, GN 166.
Newfoundland Ranger Force Association fonds, MG 621.
Secretary of the Commission of Government, Public Utilities, GN 38, Box Series S5.

University of Miami Libraries, Special Collections
Pan American World Airways, Inc., Coll. 0341.

University of Toronto, Thomas Fisher Rare Book Library
F.G. Banting Papers, Manuscript Coll. 76, 1908–1998.

GOVERNMENT DOCUMENTS

"Newfoundland Royal Commission, 1933, Report. Presented by the Secretary of State for Dominion Affairs to Parliament by Command of His Majesty, November 1933," London: His Majesty's Stationery Office, 1934.

Ranger John Hogan, "Official report regarding his flight of 8 May 1943," Department of Natural Resource, Newfoundland Commission of Government.

NEWSPAPERS AND NEWSLETTERS

Air Corps News Letter
Beacon, Gander
Daily Mail, London
Daily News, St. John's
Evening Telegram, St. John's
Gazette, Montréal
Globe and Mail, Toronto
Gulf News, Port aux Basques
Hamilton Spectator
Lethbridge Herald
London Gazette
Northern Pen, St. Anthony
Nor'wester, Springdale
Ottawa Citizen
Packet, Clarenville
Toronto Daily Star Weekly
Toronto Evening Telegram
Toronto Star
Ukrainian Weekly
VMI Cadet, Lexington, Va.
Western Star, Corner Brook

BOOKS, ARTICLES, AND THESES

"Air Force Cross for F/O Westaway." *The Gander*, Yuletide 1944.

Allport, Floyd H. and Milton Lepkin. "Wartime Rumors of Waste and Special Privilege: Why Some People Believe Them." *The Journal of Abnormal and Social Psychology* 40, no. 1 (January 1945): pp. 3–36.

Baker, Melvin, and Peter Neary. "Governor Sir Humphrey Walwyn's Account of His Meetings with Churchill and Roosevelt, Placentia Bay, Newfoundland, August 1941." *Newfoundland and Labrador Studies* 31, no. 1 (2016): pp. 165–180.

Beaudoin, Ted. *Walking on Air*. Vernon, British Columbia: Paramount House Publishing Ltd., 1986.

"Belle Isle Rescue." *Them Days*, July 1990.

Bennett, Air Vice-Marshal D.T.C. *Pathfinder: A War Autobiography*. London and St. Albans: Goodall Publications Ltd., 1988.

Bliss, Michael. *Banting: A Biography*. Toronto: McClelland and Stewart Ltd., 1985.

Bobbitt, Staff Sergeant Vernon. "A Brief History of an Airport in Newfoundland." *The Propagander*, Fall 1944.

Bray, Winston. *The History of BOAC*. Surrey: The Wessex Press, 1975.

Bridle, Paul, editor. *Documents on Relations Between Canada and Newfoundland*, Vol. 1, 1935–1949, Defence, Civil Aviation and Economic Affairs. Ottawa: Department of External Affairs, 1974.

Cardoulis, John N. *A Friendly Invasion II: A Personal Touch*. St. John's: Creative Publishers, 1993.

Christie, Carl. *Ocean Bridge: The History of RAF Ferry Command*. Toronto: University of Toronto Press, 1995.

Chubbs, Harold, and Wade Kearley. *Facing the Sea: Lightkeepers and Their Families*. St. John's: Flanker Press Ltd., 2013.

Dawydoff, Alex. "How Atlantic Aviation Serves Business Flying." *Flying*, October 1959.

Douglas, W.A.B. *The Creation of a National Air Force: The Official History of the Royal Canadian Air Force,* Vol. II. University of Toronto Press, 1986.

Dunmore, Spencer. *Wings For Victory*. Toronto: McClelland and Stewart Inc., 1994.

Dziuban, Colonel Stanley W. *Military Relations Between the United States and Canada, 1939–1945*. Washington: Office of the Chief of Military History, Department of the Army, 1959.

Flory, Henry. *Rich Mixture, Fine Pitch*. Southern Pines, NC: Bluegreen Publishing, 1995.

Flynn, Corinne. *I Remember When … Stories of Early Gander*. Gander: North Atlantic Aviation Museum, 1999.

Goff, Roderick B. *Crossroads of the World: Recollections from an Airport Town*. St. John's: Flanker Press Ltd., 2005.

Gwyn, Richard. *Smallwood: The Unlikely Revolutionary*. Toronto: McClelland and Stewart Ltd., 1972.

Hillier, Darrell. "Stars, Stripes, and Sacrifice: A Wartime Familial Experience of Hope, Loss, and Grief, and the Journey Home of an American Bomber Crew." MA thesis, Memorial University of Newfoundland, May 2017.

Historical Section of the RCAF. *The RCAF Overseas: The Sixth Year*. Toronto: Oxford University Press, 1949.

Horwood, Harold. *A History of the Newfoundland Ranger Force*. St. John's: Breakwater Books, 1986.

Jackson, Rupert. "Growing Gander." *Collier's*, 3 May 1947.

Jamieson, Don. *No Place for Fools: The Political Memoirs of Don Jamieson*. St. John's: Breakwater Books, 1989.

"Jim and Beryl Reid: Quality Involvement." *Decks Awash*, March–April 1990.

Knapp, Robert H. "A Psychology of Rumor." *The Public Opinion Quarterly* 8, no. 1 (March 1944): pp. 22–37.

Long, Gene. *Suspended State: Newfoundland Before Canada*. St. John's: Breakwater Books Ltd., 1999.

McGrath, Darrin, Robert Smith, Rangers Ches Parsons and Norman Crane. *The Newfoundland Rangers*. St. John's: DRC Publishing, 2005.

McGrath, T.M. *History of Canadian Airports*. Lugus Publications, 1992.

McTaggart-Cowan, P.D. "Transatlantic Aviation and Meteorology." *The Journal of the Royal Astronomical Society of Canada* XXXII, no. 5 (May–June 1938): pp. 217–31.

McVicar, Don. *Ferry Command*. Shrewsbury, England: Airlife Publishing Ltd., 1981.

———. *North Atlantic Cat*. Shrewsbury, England: Airlife Publishing Ltd., 1983.

Manson, Jock. *United in Effort: The Story of No. 53 Squadron, Royal Air Force, 1916–1976*. Tunbridge Well, Kent, UK: Air-Britain, 1997.

Miller, Nathan. *War at Sea: A Naval History of World War II*. New York: Oxford University Press, 1995.

Neary, Peter. *Newfoundland in the North Atlantic World, 1929–1949.* Kingston and Montreal: McGill-Queens University Press, 1988.

Nicklin, Sean. "Hopping the Pond: The Normalization of North Atlantic Civil Aviation from its Origins to the Rise of the Jumbo Jet, 1919–1970." Ph.D. dissertation, University of Ottawa, 2016.

Powell, Air Commodore Griffith. *Ferryman: From Ferry Command to Silver City*. Shrewsbury, England: Airlife Publishing Ltd., 1982.

Princeton Alumni Weekly, 4 November 1938.

Pudney, John. *Atlantic Bridge: The Official Account of R.A.F. Transport Command's Ocean Ferry*. London: His Majesty's Stationery Office, 1945.

"RAFTC." *The Propagander*, Fall 1944.

Reinitz, Sergeant Neale. "Newfoundland 'Barrelman' Raises Pigs." *The Propagander*, Fall 1944.

Saunders, Gary. *Rattles and Steadies: Memoirs of a Gander River Man*. St. John's: Breakwater Books, 1986.

Smallwood, Joseph R. *I Chose Canada: The Memoirs of the Honourable Joseph R. "Joey" Smallwood*. Toronto: The Macmillan Company of Canada Ltd., 1973.

"The Glider Flight across the Atlantic." *Flight and the Aircraft Engineer*, 8 July 1943.

Tibbo, Frank. *The Best of Aviation: 101 Tales of Fliers and Flying as Published in The Gander Beacon*. St. John's: Creative Book Publishing, 1997.

Tucker, Kathleen, researcher. "North Boat Harbour." St. Anthony Basin Resources Inc., Oral History Project 2009.

Vickers, Philip. *Surviving Victory: World War II Pilot, Actor, Sculptor, Writer*. Sedona, Arizona: Vibrant Books, 2009.

Walker, Robyn. *Sergeant Gander: A Canadian Hero*. Toronto: Natural Heritage Books, 2009.

Warner, Guy. "From IRA to MBE: John Joseph Gilmore." *Canadian Aviation Historical Society Journal* 51, no. 2 (Summer 2013): pp. 74–8.

Warren, C.F., editor. *Life at the Crossroads of the World: A History of Gander, Newfoundland, 1936–1988*. Gander, Newfoundland: Gander Seniors Club, 1988.

Watt, Sholto. *I'll Take the High Road: A History of the Beginning of the Atlantic Air Ferry in Wartime*. Fredericton: Brunswick Press, 1960.

West, Bruce. *The Man Who Flew Churchill*. Toronto: McGraw-Hill Ryerson Ltd., 1975.

Wynn, Captain Edgar J. *Bombers Across*. New York: E.P. Dutton and Co., Inc., 1944.

UNPUBLISHED MATERIAL

Abbott, Roland W. "The Story of the Banting Plane Crash." No date.

Berry, Peter. "Trans-Atlantic Air Deliveries, 1940–1946." No date.

Davies, Ian. "Crash of BOAC Return Ferry Service Liberator AL591, Gander, 9 February 1943," November 2002.

McGrath, Tom. "Gander Radio (VOAC) and Ferry Command." Centre for Newfoundland Studies, Memorial University of Newfoundland. No date.

Narburgh, Georgie. "Three Nights in the Snow." Narburgh family collection. No date.

Narburgh, John Warwick. "Keep 'Em Crossed: Memories and Letters From World War Two." Narburgh family collection. No date.

AUDIO

McTaggart-Cowan, Dr. Patrick D., interviewed by David W. Phillips, Bracebridge, Ontario, 5 October 1983. Transcript and recording at: https://opensky.ucar.edu/islandora/object/archives%3A8239.

Vivian, Walter, interviewed by Michael Henry, CBC radio, date unknown.

WEBSITES

Beaudoin, Ted. "Earth Angels Rising Chapter Four." *RAF Ferry Command.* http://www.ganderairporthistoricalsociety.org/_html_war/Lockheed.Vega/Earth%20Angels%20Rising%20Chapter%204%20%C2%BB%20RAF%20Ferry%20Command.htm.

Bernard, Lieutenant-Colonel William T. "The Queen's Own Rifles of Canada, 1860–1960, One Hundred Years of Canada." *The Queen's Own Rifles of Canada Regimental Museum and Archive.* https://qormuseum.org/history/timeline-1925-1949/the-second-world-war/newfoundland-and-new-brunswick-1940-1941/.

"Cecil Edison." *Gander Airport Historical Society.* http://www.ganderairporthistoricalsociety.org/_html_thirtys/cecil_edison.htm.

Fausak, Hazel B. "My History With the Royal Air Force Ferry Command/Royal Air Force Transport Command." *Bob's Gander History.* http://bobsganderhistory.com/moh1.pdf.

Hillier, Darrell. "The 'Spirit of Lockheed-Vega Employees':

A Counterargument." *Gander Airport Historical Society*. http://www.ganderairporthistoricalsociety.org/_html_war/Hudson_vega.part2.htm.

Hong Kong Veterans Commemorative Association. https://www.hkvca.ca/index.php.

Lindsay, Gloria. "Gander Airport, 1944–46." *Bob's Gander History*. http://bobsganderhistory.com/mog.html.

Number 59 Squadron. http://number59squadron.com/uboats/01.08.43.html.

Parks Canada. "1942 Plane Crash Municipal Heritage Site." *Canada's Historic Places*. https://www.historicplaces.ca/en/rep-reg/place-lieu.aspx?id=11949&pid=0.

Pelley, Robert. "Ground Controlled Approach in Early Gander – A Very Serious Game of Hide-and-go-Seek." *Bob's Gander History*. http://bobsganderhistory.com/gcap1.pdf.

———. "A Radio Operator in Gander – Roland Masse's Story." *Bob's Gander History*. http://bobsganderhistory.com/Rollie.pdf.

———. " 'Farming' in Old Gander." *Bob's Gander History*. http://bobsganderhistory.com/FARMING.pdf.

———. "John Joseph Gilmore, MBE." *Bob's Gander History*. http://bobsganderhistory.com/joegilmore.pdf.

———. " 'Mosla' and 'Benzin' – Russian PBN Flying Boats in Gander." *Bob's Gander History*. http://bobsganderhistory.com/PBN.pdf.

"RAF Australians – Wing Commander Norman George Mulholland (DFC)." *Militarian: Military History Forum*. http://www.militarian.com/threads/raf-australians-wing-commander-norman-george-mulholland-dfc.5835/.

RAF Commands (forum). http://www.rafcommands.com/forum/showthread.php?8346 -G-C-D-F-Anderson-(Ferry-Command).

RCAF Association, *RCAF Honours and Awards*. https://rcafassociation.ca/heritage/search-awards/.

"Sidney Joseph Cottle." *The Aerodrome*. http://www.theaerodrome.com/aces/england/cottle.php.

Tibbo, Frank. "Joe Gilmore, MBE." *Gander Airport Historical Society*. http://www.ganderairporthistoricalsociety.org/_html_war/Joe%20 Gilmore.htm.

———. "Reminiscing With John Murphy." *Gander Airport Historical Society*. http://www. ganderairporthistoricalsociety.org/_html_4658/JMreminiscing.htm.

Walsh, Carol. "Remembering …… with Phyllis Locke." *Gander Airport Historical Society*. http://www.ganderairporthistoricalsociety.org/_html_war/phyllis_locke.htm.

PERSONAL CORRESPONDENTS AND INFORMANTS

Bob Banting
Dr. Peter Blackie
Dennis Burke
Dr. Lisa Daly
Dr. Michael Deal
Eileen Elms
Patrick Gilmore
Sean Gilmore
Richard Goodlet
Hugh Halliday
David Hanson
David Hebbard
Gary Hebbard
Effie Hillier
Glenn Keough
Walter Longley
Jock Manson
Errol Martyn
David Moore
John Murphy
Beverley Narburgh
Dr. Sean Nicklin
Marilyn Pasternak
Douglas Pelley
Robert Pelley
Paddy Penney
Jack Pinsent
Rev. James Reid
Gary Rideout
Robert Schamper
Verne Scouten
Nelson Sherren
Heather Stemp
Phyllise Stickel
Robert Stitt
Robert Teteruck
Frank Tibbo
Diana Trafford
Guy Warner

INDEX

ABOUT THE AUTHOR

Darrell Hillier holds undergraduate and graduate degrees from Memorial University of Newfoundland. His aviation articles have appeared in the *Newfoundland Quarterly*, the *Canadian Aviation Historical Society Journal*, and the *American Aviation Historical Society Journal*. This is his first book.

Printed in Great Britain
by Amazon